ENTERPRISE RESOURCE PLANNING PROJECT

By

Dr. Ganesh L.
M.Phil, PGDM, Ph.D.
Assistant Professor
Christ University
Institute of Management
Bangalore (Karnataka)
(INDIA)

&

Arpita Mehta
B.B.A., M.B.A., M.F.A.
PGDHRM & Lic
Christ University
Institute of Management
Bangalore (Karnataka)
(INDIA)

DISCOVERY PUBLISHING HOUSE PVT. LTD.
NEW DELHI-110 002

Published by:

Tilak Wasan

DISCOVERY PUBLISHING HOUSE PVT. LTD.

4383/4B, Ansari Road, Darya Ganj

New Delhi-110 002 (India)

Phone : +91-11-23279245, 43596064-65

Fax : +91-11-23253475

E-mail : parul.wasan@gmail.com

discoverypublishinghouse@gmail.com

web : www.discoverypublishinggroup.com

***First Edition:* 2012**

ISBN: 978-93-5056-080-8

Enterprise Resource Planning Project

Printed at:

Shree Balaji Art Press

Delhi

Dedicated
to
God and Our Parents

Preface

Over the past decade, it has become increasingly difficult for ERP consultants, academicians, professionals and Indian SMEs to receive timely implementation of ERP systems for Indian SMEs. In past, difficulties were arised because of various internal and external factors forces and strong opposition by various stakeholders who perceive that such ERP implementation pose threats to the Indian SMEs and themselves due to lack of awareness and information. If many people hold such views, it seems logical to expect that people would not choose to live with ERP implementation and that, as a consequence, the probability of successful ERP implementation at Indian SMEs would decline and economic growth of the Indian SMEs would may be adversely affected due to not acceptance of technical advancement and development because it is the demand of new LPG (Liberalization, Privatisation and Globalization) based Global economy. Information based on the survey of real time ERP consultants and experts would enable utilities for various interested ERP related agencies and stakeholders to make better-informed decisions. This study aims to supply most of this information.

This book will help to ERP consultants, ERP academicians, ERP professionals, ERP students, Indian SMEs, and all other stakeholders to understand:

- What is ERP?
- How it works?
- Why it is important?
- What are the advantages and disadvantages of ERP implementation?
- How to make successful ERP implementation?
- How to do the management of ERP project?
- How to avoid the failure of ERP implementation?
- How to conduct research in area of ERP?
- How to customized survey instruments (questionnaires) for ERP research?

- How to conduct the gap analysis for the successful ERP implementation at Indian SMEs?
- What is the future of ERP implementation?

No practically survey based sound research has been conducted to examine the factors for the successful ERP implementation in Indian SMEs. Accordingly, the objectives of this Book are:

- To provide a survey based guide book for the successful ERP implementation at Indian SMEs
- To indentify the critical success and failure factors for the ERP implementation at Indian SMEs.
- To help the ERP consultants, academicians, professionals, students and Indian SMEs in formulation of strategies for the successful ERP Implementation at Indian SMEs
- To provide a handbook for avoiding the failure of ERP implementation at Indian SMEs
- To provide through literature review in area of ERP implementation research
- To provide a survey based statistically proved checklist for the successful ERP implementation at Indian SMEs
- To provide the guidelines and recommendations for the successful ERP Implementation at Indian SMEs
- To provide detail list of source for the successful ERP implementation, research and awareness
- To help in understand the ground reality and missing gap between the ERP theories and practice for the successful ERP implementation at Indian SMEs
- To facilitate the process of successful ERP implementation at Indian SMEs in the standardized and simple manner

Acknowledgements

Our deepest sense of gratitude goes to the management of Christ University Bangalore for their faith in this book and their constant encouragement. Working under such supportive and motivated environment has been a stimulating and rewarding experience. We feel very fortunate to have been part of the Christ University Bangalore. We would like to thank all of them for their insightful comments and suggestions. Without their help, this book would have never been a reality. We were greatly benefited from all their advice and guidance in all aspects of our life.

We are grateful to the Honourable Vice Chancellor, Christ University, Dr. (Fr.) Thomas C. Mathew Pro-Vice Chancellor, Christ University, Dr. (Fr.) Abraham V.M. and to the Fr. Thomas T .V For giving us the opportunity and support to carry out this project. We remember with gratitude the efforts taken by the dynamic research centre of Christ University headed by Dr. S. Srikantaswamy to develop and sustain the research culture in the Christ University, Bangalore.

We are also grateful to all the faculty members (special thanks to Dr. Harold Patrick, Dr. Rajesh Kumar and Professor Rajshekhar) for their expert reviews, questions, valuable time and constructive critiques for this project. We thank to the management and all the staff members of the library (Christ University, Bangalore) for proving great literature and continuous support. We would also like to thank all the organizations and personnel who assisted us in distributing the survey. Without their help and support, this project could never be possibly done. We are also thankful to all the Indian ERP consultants those who have participated in this exploratory survey, as their valuable response had made this book possible. We also appreciate the support and sincere friendship of our fellow research scholars.

Many thanks to the all earlier researchers (our deepest sense of gratitude goes to Shanks, G., Parr, A., Hu, B., Corbitt, B., Thanasankit, T., Seddon, P. and Ifinedo, P.) for providing sound theoretical base for this book. Many thanks to the Discovery Publishing House Pvt. Ltd New Delhi and all editors for giving due credit to this project work by accepting it as a part of their publication. This book would not have been possible without all the love and steadfast support of our parents, brothers, family members and friends. Finally, we owe our greatest regards to the Almighty for the best owing upon us in the courage to face the complexities of life and helping us to complete this book successfully.

Authors

Abstract

"ERP (Enterprise Resource Planning) comprises of a commercial software package that promises the seamless integration of all the information flowing through the company – financial, accounting, human resources, supply chain and customer information" (Davenport, 1998). Much has been written on implementation of Enterprise Resource Planning (ERP) in organizations of various sizes. The literature is replete with many case studies of both successful and unsuccessful ERP implementations. Research on the implementation of ERP in certain European countries shows that, the job of implementing an ERP is a riskier business for Small and Medium-size Enterprises (SMEs) than for Large Enterprises (LEs), still SMEs have been receiving lesser focus from the software vendors and consultants than LEs (Shanks *et al.*, 2000). There have been very few empirical studies that attempt to delineate the critical success and failure factors that drive the success and failure of ERP implementation at Indian SMEs. Much of the time, ERP software vendors and consultants are the targets for blame when anticipated results do not materialize. Are the ERP vendors and consultants that sold the software the real culprits for the lack of business performance improvement? (Rao, 2000).The failure rates of ERP implementations have been publicized widely but, this has not distracted companies from investing large sums of money on ERP implementation. Many companies in developing countries have implemented ERP to capture its benefits still there is a lack of examining Critical Factors (CFs) that contribute in the success and failure of ERP implementation at Indian SMEs(Ranganathan and Kannabiran, 2004).

In this book, a framework has been adopted to cover both the national (Indian) and the organization size (SMEs) aspects to identify and rank the CFs that contribute in the success and failure of ERP implementation at Indian SMEs. Four models (ERP model, ERP Implementation Success Model, ERP Implementation Failure Model and ERP Gap (Strategic ERP) Model) were developed to explore and rank the thirty Critical Success Factors (CSFs) along with the twenty Critical Failure Factors (CFFs) that contribute in the success and failure of ERP implementation at Indian SMEs. Key Critical Success Factors

(KCSFs) and Key Critical Failure Factors (KCFFs) were identified by ranking of these CSFs and CFFs according to their importance to decide their priorities during the ERP implementation at Indian SMEs. Quantitative survey based method was used to explore "what are the possible critical success and failure factors" that contribute in the success and failure of ERP implementation at India SMEs. Three close ended questionnaire were used to collect the data from the 500 Indian ERP consultants those who are having experience of ERP implementation in India for almost all types of Indian industries including Indian SMEs. Sample was drawn from ten national and international well known IT (ERP) sector companies which are involve in world wide ERP implementation including Indian SMEs. The Indian ERP consultants have been selected for the data collection using non-probabilistic sampling method. The data collected were analyzed using statistical techniques such as descriptive statistics, reliability tests, validity tests, exploratory factor analysis and non-parametric tests. In order to explore thirty CSFs and twenty CFFs along with the KCSFs and KCFFs, three close ended questionnaires were customized with the help of literature reviews and expert's opinions. Later on it has been standardized for this book with the help of Cronbach's Alpha readability and validity test (Guilford's formula) supported by exploratory factor analysis. Based on the Indian ERP consultants perceptions, literature review, and secondary data review it was found that an ERP implementation at Indian SMEs is not exactly same from the ERP implementations found in the existing literature for the worldwide Large Enterprises (LEs). When discussing the CSFs and CFFs for an ERP implementation at Indian SMEs, it was found that although the factors are more or less same but the importance of factors in term of their priorities (importance) are defiantly different from the ERP implementation of the LEs.

Regarding the link between factors and ERP implementation phases, majority of the respondents were identified that all the factors start contribution from the early stages to the end of the ERP project at Indian SMEs. This book argues that ERP implementation at Indian SMEs should extend its scope beyond the configuration to the process, enterprise, technology, vendor, end-user, human resource, performance, quality, strategy, project and risk related issues by considering these thirty critical success factors along with the twenty critical failure factors for the successful ERP implementation at Indian SMEs, that may put Indian SMEs on the competitive position. Implementation of ERP at Indian SMEs is not just a technological challenge. It's a socio-technological endeavour, which mandates modifying existing applications and redesigning business processes to facilitate the successful ERP implementation at Indian SMEs. This book presents a framework in terms of fifty recommendations for managing this CFs that differs from existing models in that it has a broader and more holistic focus due to the coverage of thirty CSFs and twenty CFFs. This book attempt to build a consensus from the previous book and to derive unified models along with the guidelines so that these factors can be put into practice. Four ERP implementation related models simplifies the functionality of ERP implementation at Indian SMEs. The simplification of system makes easier to understand the ERP implementation requirements at Indian SMEs.

The implication of the book may help to the ERP consultants, ERP vendors, ERP students and Indian SMEs for the successful ERP implementation at Indian SMEs by promoting 30 CSFs and avoiding 20 CFFs during all the phases of ERP implementation at Indian SMEs. The efficient and effective management of these thirty CSFs along with the twenty CFFs based on the fifty recommendation and guidelines supported by four ERP related models may help in simplifying the process of ERP implementation at Indian SMEs. KCSFs and KCFFs may helps to ERP consultants, ERP vendors and Indian SMEs in determining the priorities of these factors according to their importance while implementing ERP system for an Indian SMEs. Indian SMEs address the gap by customizing the software, building extensions or buying specialized, best of-breed packages. These remedies limit flexibility as business needs evolve and increase implementation and integration costs for ERP implementation at Indian SMEs. Customization is compounded by an unwillingness of the Indian SMEs to change business processes. Alignment of business processes to ERP software, rather than modifying the software, may prove to be a success factor for the successful ERP implementations at Indian SMEs. Another implication is that ERP systems for any Indian SMEs must be designed in such a way that they become easy to use, simple to learn, and flexible to interact with ERP system that is easy to use is less threatening to the user. That is, perceived ease of use may have a positive influence on users' acceptance for the successful ERP implementation at Indian SMEs. This book also argues that ERP consultants, ERP vendors and Indian SMEs often fail in recognizing the technology, vendor, employee, performance, project, quality, strategy and enterprise related contribution to the ERP implementation, as a consequence for the evaluation of ERP package at Indian SMEs. Instead of choosing a system supporting specific business functions, it is a strategic decision that, mostly within ERP consultants, ERP vendors and Indian SMEs so it should be supported by in-depth evaluation.

Proper knowledge about the ERP products, proper budget planning and appropriate training to the staffs is needed to avoid the failure of ERP implementation at Indian SMEs. There is a need to learn from previous failure by considering these fifty factors into practice. The result of this book provides considerable insight into the ERP consultants' perception for thirty CSFs and twenty CFFs that contribute in the success and failure of ERP implementation at Indian SMEs. It is therefore important that ERP consultants, ERP vendors and Indian SMEs should not ignore all these factors while implementation ERP systems for an Indian SMEs.

ERP consultants, ERP vendors and Indian SMEs should consider the given guidelines and fifty recommendations; cross verified it with the given checklist while developing strategies for successful ERP implementation at Indian SMEs. Even if in some cases these models, guidelines and recommendation may not help (due to the limitation of this book as discusses in last the chapter) still there will be no harm to any involve party if they will manage these CSFs and CFFs efficiently and effectively during all the phases of ERP implementation at Indian SMEs. The focus of ERP consultants, ERP vendors and Indian SMEs should be to give more consideration to CSFs at the same time they should try to minimize the effects of CFFs as much as possible. Findings are discussed in detail along with the implications of this book for the future work. It is hoped that this book will help to bridge the current literature gap and provide practical advice for both ERP academicians and ERP practitioners for the successful ERP implementation at Indian SMEs.

This book consists of seven chapters. *Chapter 1* introduces background information by providing the general concept of ERP systems and motivation for the book in the area of ERP implementation at Indian SMEs. *Chapter 2* reviews the previous efforts and findings in related areas. It presents an overview of previous work on ERP implementation in information systems. *Chapter 3* has two main sections. In the first section, previous work, theories and fundamentals of project management in ERP implementation were presented to form the theoretical background of the ERP models. The second section provides the conceptual ERP models, describing factors and components along with their definitions and causal relationships. *Chapter 4* presents the research design, showing survey instruments and their descriptions. The results of the pilot survey were examined by reliability, validity test etc, to know that whether the survey instrument was developed properly or not. *Chapters 5* and *6* contain the analysis and interpretation of main research findings. *Chapter 7* summarizes the study and concludes by examining the contributions of the complete ERP models and presents the recommendations for further advance research in this area.

Key Findings:

- 30 Critical Success Factors(CSFs) for successful ERP implementation at Indian SMEs

- Key Critical Success Factors(KCSFs) for successful ERP implementation at Indian SMEs
- 20 Critical Failure Factors (CFFs) for the failure of ERP implementation at Indian SMEs
- Key Critical Failure Factors (KCFFs) for the failure of ERP implementation at Indian SMEs
- ERP Model, ERP Implementation Success Model and ERP Implementation Failure Model
- Gap Analysis to know why ERP implementation get fail
- How to make successful ERP implementation by Strategic ERP Model, Guidelines, Checklist, 50 Recommendations
- Theoretical Framework to understand the concept of ERP in detail
- ERP Questionnaires and User Manual for further ERP research

Contents

Abbreviations, Notations and Nomenclature

APS – Advanced Planning and Scheduling
BBP – Best Business Practices
BPR – Business Process Reengineering
CAGR – Compound Annual Growth Rate
CEO – Chief Executive Officer
CFFs – Critical Failure Factors
CFs – Critical Factors
CIO – Chief Information Officer
CM – Change Management
CRM – Customer Relationship Management
CS – Computer Systems
CSFs – Critical Success Factors
EFA – Exploratory Factor Analysis
EH – Exploratory Hypothesis
ERP – Enterprise Resource Planning
ERPII – Enterprise Resource Planning II
ES – Exploratory Statements
H0 – Null Hypothesis
H1 – Alternative Hypothesis
IS – Information System
IT – Information Technology
KCFFs – Key Critical Failure Factors
KCSFs – Key Critical Success Factors
KMO – Kaiser-Meyer-Olkin
LE – Large Enterprise
MES – Manufacturing Execution System

MIS	–	Management Information System
MNCs	–	Multinational Corporations
MRP	–	Material Requirements Planning
MRPII	–	Manufacturing Resource Planning
N	–	Number of respondents in each questionnaire
No.	–	Number
PAC	–	Production Activity Control
PMI	–	Project Management Institute
RCMV	–	Rotated Component Matrix Value
RCSF	–	Ranking of Critical Success Factors
ROI	–	Return of Investment
SaaS	–	Software-as-a-Service
SAP	–	Systems, Applications, and Products
SCM	–	Supply Chain Management
SMEs	–	Small-Medium Size Enterprise
SPSS	–	Statistical Package for the Social Sciences
TF	–	Theoretical Framework
TQM	–	Total Quality Management
TVE	–	Total Variance Explain
V	–	Version
WH	–	Working Hypothesis

Introduction

"For successful ERP implementation enterprise should learn from yesterday's failure, work for today and hope for tomorrow, the important thing is not to break the continuity of efforts"

—Elarbi, 2001

This chapter begins with a presentation for the background of the research along with an introduction of ERP concepts. The presentation thereafter followed by the problem discussion those results in the statement of purpose (Research Gap—Research Questions—Research Objectives—(SOP) Research Statements/Research Hypotheses—Research Answer). It includes the needs, importance and scope of the study. It justifies, highlight and define the aim and scope of the work presented in this book in detail. It also highlight the significant contribution from this study in brief.

BACKGROUND

This research examines Critical Success Factors (CSFs) in Enterprise Resource Planning (ERP) implementation focussing on Indian small to mid-sized firms (SMEs). Much of the research on ERP implementation addresses the critical success factors and best practices used in large-scale implementations at large organizations. Little research deals with ERP implementation in SMEs. Yet, as the largest firms complete ERP implementations, ERP software vendors are focussing on the SMEs market (Gable and Stewart, 1999). SMEs face many of the same competitive problems as larger organizations, but have limited resources, experience and staffing skills (Nelson, 2007). As with the larger enterprises, ERP implementation is becoming critically important to

SMEs in streamlining business processes, improving operational performance, and integrating data. Understanding the CSFs in ERP implementation is more critical to SMEs than larger organizations due to their more limited resources. SMEs may not be able to withstand the financial impact of the partial failures and project abandonments that have impacted many of their larger counterparts (Muscatello *et al.*, 2003).CSFs can be defined as "the limited number of areas in which results, if they are satisfactory, will ensure successful competitive performance for the organization" (Rockart,1979).CSFs methodology has been applied to many aspects of information systems research including ERP systems implementations (Williams and Ramaprasad, 1996; Parr and Shanks, 2000). Information technology has been a force multiplier for the organizations desirous of gaining a competitive edge in a global business environment. The need to share large quantities of data effectively and efficiently between suppliers, customers, geographically dispersed units, and internal functional departments necessitated the development of integrated information systems (Monk and Wagner, 2009). ERP systems are examples of the most strategic tools a business can employ. They help integrate company operations by creating a computing environment that includes a central database for sales and marketing, production and materials management, accounting, finance, and human resource functional business data (Monk and Wagner, 2009). Implementing ERP in developing countries is faced by several obstacles that delay implementation compared with developed countries. The challenges faced by developing countries vary. On the organizational level, organizations working in developing countries find the ERP cost is a major barrier for implementing ERP systems especially for SMEs. Thus, most of the implementation done in ERP is for large scale companies which can afford the costs. This includes multinational organizations (Seethamraju and Seethamraju, 2008).

Another barrier for ERP implementation is related to the IT maturity in both national and organizational levels. In developing countries, IT infrastructure has many weak issues related to the IT penetration such as internet and computer penetration in organizations and social levels. This is in addition to the lack of number of computer and internet users on both national and organizational levels. Other factors which lead to lack of implementation are related to cultural factors and lack of knowledge of ERP systems (Seethamraju and Seethamraju, 2008). ERP systems are widely used to extract and process data from different functional areas across the enterprise (Gore, 2008). ERP systems are therefore called 'Cross-Functional' systems as they integrate business processes across different functional areas of an organization. These systems are sought after to improve the visibility of information across the organization and to allow a better access to information in a borderless environment (Ignatiadis and Nandhakumar, 2007).

Hence, ERP systems are used by large scale companies as well as SMEs. The challenges accompanied by the implementation of ERP systems are not limited to the size of the organization, but go further to where the organization is implementing its ERP systems. Developed countries are widely accepting and applying ERP systems in their organizations in comparison with developing countries. Statistics show that 88 per cent of ERP market is in North American and European countries while the rest of market goes to the rest of the world (*www.amrresearchcorp.com*). This gap in ERP implementation is directly related to the economic and technological status of each respective country. Developing countries are facing many challenges in applying information systems/information technology projects due to the poor and unstable economic status which is reflected in the delay of the ERP implementation (Huang and Palvia, 2001). The enhancement in the performance leads to the reduction in costs which eventually leads organizations to achieve competitive advantage. Even more, the organizations' vision recently is focusing on how to sustain competitiveness via implementing ERP systems (Gore, 2008). These organizations find sustaining the competitive advantage over their competitors as a major motive for ERP implementation (Adhikari, 2007; Heeks, 2007).

Porter's Model for the five 'Competitive Forces' on any organization; identifies technology as a driving factor for competency in enterprise organizations. Also, Porter's 'Competitive Advantage Theory' identifies four main determinants affecting a company's competitiveness in its business field. (Heeks, 2007) uses the Porter's 'Competitive Advantage Theory' as a tool to analyze the IT sector in developing countries and explained how ERP systems can gear up the competitive advantages for organizations functioning in such countries. As for an organization to obtain a sustained competitive advantage states that an ERP system implementation has to be of 'value creating strategy' where no other competitors are using as an advantage of their independent strategies. ERP implementation was not deployed by large scale companies alone, but also many SMEs have started the process of implementing ERP systems to have a competitive advantage in their respective market share. SMEs seek to reorganize and streamline their internal and external operations via implementing ERP systems. SMEs were, in many cases, enforced by large scale companies to implement ERP systems in order to be linked with external organizations and being able to continue working with them. This is done as part of the Supply Chain Management (SCM) systems or Customer Relationship Management (CRM) systems. Although the importance of applying ERP systems in both SMEs and large organizations are equal, SMEs normally face challenges in terms of limited resources and lack of appropriate infrastructure (Seethamraju and Seethamraju, 2008). For a long time, companies struggled with extremely long project timelines in order to develop information systems that met their specific requirements. Organization had to develop a custom code which tedious process was requiring many programmers as well as significant end-user involvement.

Moreover, after implementation most of these programmers needed to be retained for the maintenance of custom programming. Project timelines were dragged out because often business owners didn't know what they wanted until they saw it (Hurst and Nowak, 2000). Many companies had departmentalized systems, which did not share information and thus became the 'information silos' within an organization. This resulted in data discrepancies which resulted in companies taking a long time to close the books for quarter and year-end reporting. These unconnected and multiple systems also created a need for many distinct interfaces between systems that were not designed to talk with each other. In order to eliminate these problems, a new breed of software systems, called Enterprise Resource Planning (ERP), was created. These systems provide integration between different functional modules (for example, Accounting, Sales and Distribution, Materials Management, Production, Planning, etc.). These ERP systems are customized which provide a common set of data source to the whole organization.ERP has been defined by various researchers but with few differences.(Kumar *et. al.*, 2000) defined Enterprise Resource Planning (ERP) systems as configurable information systems packages that integrate information and information based processes within and across functional areas in an organization. (O'Leary, 2000) also defined ERP systems are computer based systems designed to process an organization's transactions and facilitate integrated and real-time planning, production, and customer response. A method for the effective planning and controlling of all the resources needed to take, make, ship and account for customer orders in a manufacturing, distribution or service company. ERP comprises of a commercial software package that promises the seamless integration of all the information flowing through the company—financial, accounting, human resources, supply chain and customer information (Davenport, 1998).

ERP covers the techniques and concepts employed for the integrated management of business as a whole, from the view point of the effective use of management resource, to improve the efficiency of an enterprise. ERP integrates various functions of an enterprise such as sales, marketing, human resource, MIS(Management Information System), accounting, finance, production, operations , strategy, quality, logistics(SCM, Supply Chain Management), maintenance, CRM(Customer Relationship Management), research and development etc by BPR(Business Process Reengineering), information technology and change management for better utilization, planning, control and integration of enterprise resource so that an enterprise can achieve its long term as well as short term objectives. Modern information technology is oriented towards business processes and communications between persons using these processes, and is therefore called process and information technology (Ould, 1995). It must be stressed that IT applications have the strongest impact on the standardization or elimination of process variations. For that reason, BPR and IT infrastructure strategies, both of which are derived from organizational strategy, are in need of effective alignment to ensure the success of the BPR initiative (Al-Mashari and Zairi, 1999).ERP implementations usually involve broad organizational transformation processes, with significant implications on the organization's management model, structure, management style, culture, and particularly, on people (Caldas and Wood, 1999).The implementation consists of the configuration of the ERP system and the introduction of corresponding organizational and technical changes, like the definition of new responsibilities or the design of new interfaces (Keller and Teufel, 1998). (Sumner, 2000) also argued that ERP causes significant cultural transformation to the organization and tends to reset organizational values in terms of discipline, change and processes. Evaluating and selecting an ERP offering includes a complex process that should be a 'fact-based' process that brings the organization to the point where comfortable well-informed decisions can be made (Donovan, 2001).One key characteristic of accountability for ERP software selection and implementation lies to varying degrees with organizational (i.e. internal) decision makers and external consultants (Caldas and Wood, 1998; Wood and Caldas, 2000; Donovan, 2001).

(Zeng *et al.*, 2003) thought that an ERP system should be:

- *Flexible:* An ERP system has to be able to react to the changing needs that the organization can have in future. This is facilitated by the fact that ERP systems are constructed on client/server technology that makes it possible to run them on various database servers.
- *Comprehensive:* An ERP system should be able to support a variety of organizational processes. Consequently, ERP systems cover different modules.
- *Modular and Open:* An ERP system ought to allow any module to be interfaced or disconnected whenever needed without disrupting other modules.
- *Beyond the Company:* A good ERP system is not restricted by the organizational boundaries; it should support connection to entities outside the organization.

(O'Leary, 2000) lists the most important dimensions of the ERP systems:

- ERP affects the predominant corporations in the market
- ERP affects many small and medium companies
- ERP affects competitors' behaviour
- ERP affects business associates necessities
- ERP changes the character of consulting companies
- ERP provides one of the most important tools for reengineering
- ERP changes the characteristics of jobs in all areas
- ERP cost is high
- ERP increases its market share incredibly

Indian ERP Market will have a great opportunity when they explore into the untapped areas of the SMEs segment with innovative practices tuned to mid size organizations processes and business needs. Companies like Sage Software has focussed on this segment in a major way, by offerings various product for SMEs (www.sagesoftware.co.in). *Adoption of ERP as a Service (SaaS,* Software-as-a-Service)-based Enterprise Resource Planning (ERP) is an on-demand deployment of ERP software, where the user can access the software through licence as a web-based service. It provides an alternative to implementation or maintaining ERP software. SaaS-based ERP includes finance, order management, inventory control, purchasing and manufacturing functionality. The increasing popularity of the SaaS-based applications account for the growth of ERP, as the enterprise resources are maintained by a service provider. There needs to be no doubt in the promising opportunities and prospects of ERP in the future in both software and non software sectors. Whether growth plans include buying and selling in the global marketplace, adding more talent to team, or expanding services, ERP has the tools and the flexibility to successfully accelerate business expansion , streamline existing business and operational processes thereby improving efficiency and productivity. (www.sagesoftware.co.in).

MAIN FUNCTIONS AND MODULES

ERP software is made up of various different ERP modules which ultimately help to run business in a more efficient and effective manner. A module is basically a part of an ERP system that can purchase individually to meet business needs. While vendors may point out that it is more costly to purchase them individually over the long run, it may be less costly in the short run, by giving flexibility and the opportunity to work with a vendor without a massive investment. An ERP system can include module for order entry, accounts receivable and payable, general ledger, purchasing, warehousing, transportation and human resources. ERP implies the use of packaged software rather than proprietary software written by or for one customer. ERP modules may be able to interface with an organization's own software with varying degrees of effort, and, depending on the software, ERP modules may be alterable via the vendor's proprietary tools as well as proprietary or standard programming languages. The following is a list of different elements or modules that are contained in most of today's ERP systems (Kapp, Latham and Latham, 2001).

- Business and Strategic Planning Module
- Resource Planning Module
- Executive Decision Support Module
- Sales and Operations Planning Module
- Forecasting Module
- Customer Relationship Management (CRM) Module
- Order Entry, Quoting, and Product Configuration Modules
- Master Production Schedule Module
- Rough Cut Capacity Planning Module
- Material Requirements Planning (MRP) Module
- Detailed Capacity Planning Module
- Production Activity Control (PAC) Module
- Manufacturing Execution System (MES) Module
- Issuing Material to Jobs Module
- Advanced Planning and Scheduling (APS) Module
- Finance Module
- Costing Modules
- Engineering Modules
- Human Resource Modules
- E-Commerce Modules

ADVANTAGES AND DISADVANTAGES

A typical ERP implementation is complex with the high cost. Organizations might have difficulties in integrating the ERP software with the hardware, operating systems, database management systems, and telecommunications suited to their organizational needs (Markus *et al.*, 2000). (Markus and Tanis, 2000) have presented three main reasons (high costs, risk of losing competitive advantage, and resistance to change) for organizations not to acquire successful ERP implementation. Therefore, organizations must carefully analyze the advantages and disadvantages of ERP implementation before starting ERP system. The implementation and integration of ERP systems can leads to major benefits, such as reaching more vendors, cost reduction, time reduction, reduction of data redundancy, and improvement of communication between departments (Holsapple and Sena, 2005).

Although the implementation of ERP systems can lead to benefits, it also has disadvantages, such as extremely high costs (software, hardware and training) and low level of customization.ERP systems may cause problems in companies as well, such as stress (Smith *et al.*, 1999) and resistance from employees (Sumner, 1999).The benefits of ERP in any organization are beyond doubt. Some of the key benefits are listed below (Garg *et al.*, 2006)

- Reduced planning cycle time
- Reduced manufacturing cycle time
- Reduced inventory
- Reduced error in ordering
- Reduced requirement of manpower
- Enables faster response to changing market situations
- Better utilization of resources
- Increased customer satisfaction
- Enables global outreach

Other benefit includes:

- Cooperation between managers and employees
- Consolidation of finance, marketing and sales, human resource, and manufacturing applications
- IT infrastructure, involving building business flexibility, IT cost reduction, and increased IT infrastructure capability
- Organisational, relating to supporting organizational changes, facilitating business learning, empowering, and building common visions
- A primary benefit of ERP is easier access to reliable, integrated information (information availabe for all deparments like materials management/ inventory/production control etc)
- Elimination of redundant data and the rationalization of processes, which results in substantial cost savings.
- It enables decision-makers to have an enterprise-wide view of the information they need in a timely, reliable and consistent fashion (real-time information available anywhere; anytime).

- The system provides consistency, visibility and transparency across the entire enterprise.
- The integration among business functions facilitates communication and information sharing, leading to dramatic gains in productivity and speed.

Disadvantages

- Personnel turnover; companies can employ new managers lacking education in the company's ERP system, proposing changes in business practices that are out of synchronization with the best utilization of the company's selected ERP.
- Customization of the ERP software is limited. Some customization may involve changing of the ERP software structure which is usually not allowed.
- Re-engineering of business processes to fit the 'industry standard' prescribed by the ERP system may lead to a loss of competitive advantage and the system may be over-engineered relative to the actual needs of the customer.
- ERP vendors can charge sums of money for annual license renewal that is unrelated to the size of the company using the ERP or its profitability.
- Technical support personnel often give replies to callers that are inappropriate for the caller's corporate structure. Computer security concerns arise, for example when telling a non-programmer how to change a database on the fly, at a company that requires an audit trail of changes so as to meet some regulatory standards.
- ERPs are often seen as too rigid and too difficult to adapt to the specific workflow and business process of some companies—this is cited as one of the main causes of their failure. The system can suffer from the 'weakest link' problem—inefficiency in one department or at one of the partners may affect other participants and systems can be difficult to use.
- Many of the integrated links need high accuracy in other applications to work effectively. A company can achieve minimum standards, and then over time 'dirty data' will reduce the reliability of some applications. Once a system is established, switching costs are very high for any one of the partners (reducing flexibility and strategic control at the corporate level).
- The blurring of company boundaries can cause problems in accountability, lines of responsibility, and employee morale.

Resistance in sharing sensitive internal information between departments can reduce the effectiveness of the software. ERP systems can be very expensive to install. There are frequent compatibility problems with the various legacy systems of the partners (www.gleez.com).

MAJOR VENDORS AND ERP MARKET

SAP AG founded in 1972 is the world's largest Enterprise Resource Planning (ERP) software with 82,000 customers / 91,500 installations / 12 million users in 120 countries as of year 2009 (www.sap.com).The SAP system comprises of a number of fully integrated modules. These modules or solutions, as SAP would like to call them, cover virtually every aspect of business management. SAP provides standard business application software which reduces the amount of time and money spent on developing and testing all the programs.SAP AG is at the beginning of a new growth curve similar to the one it experienced in the early 1990s. SAP is the world's largest business-software maker by revenue, ahead of U.S.-based rivals Oracle Corp and Microsoft Corp. It took the top position with its so-called enterprise resource, or ERP, software product R/3, which was launched in the early 1990s. SAP last year, set a target to triple its customer base to 100,000 by 2010, as it aims to sell more software to smaller companies with annual revenues below $1 billion. Traditionally, SAP sells software to major firms like Wal-Mart Stores Inc. in the U.S. or German BMW AG. SAP has set its hopes on a new software product for smaller companies. The ERP market is a very competitive and fast growing market. According to (*www.amrresearchcorp.com*) the leading

Table 1.1: Worldwide ERP Application Licences, Maintenance and Subscription Revenue by Customer Segments, Based on Key Forecast Assumption, 2008-2013 ($)

Classification of Enterprise According to Size	2008	2009	2010	2011	2012	2013	2008-2013 (CAGR* %)
Small Business (< 1000 Employees)	9,347.4	9,677.0	10,068.0	10,581.0	11220.0	11925.0	5.0
Medium-size Business (1000-4999 Employees)	9,551.6	9,938.0	10,439.0	11,004.0	11736.0	12475.0	5.5
Large Business (5000+ Employee)	14,064.1	13,880.0	14,089.0	14,650.0	15362.0	16019.0	2.6
Total	**32,963.0**	**33,495.0**	**34596.0**	**36235.0**	**38318.0**	**40419.0**	**4.2**

*CAGR—Compound Annual Growth Rate *Source:* IDC, October 2009

industry and market analysis firm specializing in enterprise application and enabling technologies, the ERP software market will grow at a compound annual growth rate of 37 per cent over the next five years. To sustain their rapid growth, ERP vendors have to sell more licenses into their installed base so ERP vendors will try to sell more licences into their installed base. Currently, ERP vendors have a 10-20 penetration (i.e. percentage of total employees using the ERP system). This will grow to 40-60 per cent within the next five years. While ERP originated in the manufacturing market, ERP usage has spread to nearly every type of enterprise including retail, utilities, the public sector and healthcare organization. Most will purchase new ERP system over the next five years, often for the first time (Lakdawla, 2009)

CURRENT SCENARIO

The Indian ERP market experienced compounded annual growth rate of 25.2 per cent during the period 2004-2009. The market was $83 million in 2004, and is projected to be around $160-180 million in 2010 (www.articlesbase.com). In India, SMEs are the backbone of the economy and are today faced with global competition. Therefore it becomes imperative for them to look for means of responding to the dynamic markets. ERP systems have become the most common IT strategy for most large companies. SMEs too are moving towards ERP systems. They need to adopt a proactive approach towards ERP and consider it as a business solution rather than a mere IT solution. Though the ERP market is growing and ERP vendors have shifted their focus to the SMEs segment, there are several issues to be solved. The need of ERP systems is understood in SMEs but ERP adoption is not yet as penetrated as it is in less. Like many other technological advances, ERP systems were initially implemented mostly at large organizations. Their relative absence from SMEs has probably been the main reason for the research focus on large companies (Somers and Nelson, 2001; Mabert *et al.*, 2003b; Mandal and Gunasekaran, 2003; Umble *et al.*, 2003; Nah and Delgado, 2006). More recently, however, vendors began to provide SMEs specific ERP (Bingi *et al.*, 1999; Bell and Orzen, 2007; Deep *et al.*, 2008). ERP implementation at SMEs has been catching up with large companies (Van Everdingen *et al.*, 2000; Mabert *et al.*, 2003a). (Laukkanen *et al.*, 2007) indicate that significant differences exist between SMEs (medium-size, small, micro enterprises) and LEs in ERP implementation. Specifically, the findings suggest that SMEs experience more knowledge constraints than LEs in ERP implementation. Also, SMEs differ from LEs in important ways affecting their information-seeking practices that impact information and technology (IT) implementation. These differences include lack of information systems management, concentration of information-gathering responsibilities to a small number of individuals, lower levels of resources available for information-gathering, and in the quantity and quality of available environmental information (Buonanno *et al.*, 2005). Thus, SMEs need different characteristics from ERP systems.

Today, some ERP vendors have taken up the gauntlet and have been moving their attention toward SMEs (Gable and Stewart, 1999) by offering simplified and cheaper solutions from both the organizational and technological points of view, preconfigured systems based on best-practices at a fraction of the cost originally required and promising short implementation times. Large IT projects such as ERP implementations have more chance to be failures than most people expect. In the last decades, many studies have identified that the success rate is approximately 25 per cent, the failure rate is also about 25 per cent, and partial successes and failures exist around 50 per cent (Holland, 2007). According to (Johansson, 2007a) a major problem with the existing ERP systems is the misfit between the delivered functionality from the vendor and the needed functionality in the receiving end-customer organization, this despite aforementioned the focus on 'best practices'. This gap causes high project implementation costs due to the need for further customization and non-realized business value. According to (Johansson, 2007a) this has lead to an increasing interest amongst vendors to improve future ERP systems to support the end-customer organization even better. This quest is even more pressing when focusing on the small and midsized organizations that up until now have faced relatively higher ERP system costs. 51 per cent of ERP projects are considered failures and a full 30 per cent far exceed budget and miss their completion dates by a wide margin (Caruso, 2007).

ERP has become the latest buzzword in the IT industry and almost every company is trying to follow the trend but not without reason. An ERP package can be of great benefit in implemented properly (Henderson, 2007). (Andersen and Johansen, 2007) further note that the vision behind the next generation of ERP-systems (what could be called the third generation of ERP-systems) specialized for the small and midsized-market, is to develop comprehensive global ERP system, that can be localized to all types of organizations with a minimum of initial and on-going costs. In that sense it is of great interesting to find out exactly what areas use when developing the future ERP-systems. Now-a-days, in the emerging ERP research area, the definition and measurement of ERP Implementation success is a thorny issue. (Markus and Tanis, 2000) states that success means different things depending on who defines it. Thus, for instance, project managers and implementation consultants, often define success in terms of completing the project on time and within budget. But people whose job is to adopt ERP systems and use them to achieve business results tend to emphasize having a smooth transition to stable operations with the new system, achieving intended business improvements like inventory reductions, and gaining improved decision support capabilities (Markus and Tanis, 2000).With hundreds of companies implementing the ERP systems to make their business more efficient only few are very successful in implementing them. According to a survey done by Gartner (www.gartner.com) only 60 per cent of companies implementing ERP system claim they got expected benefits (Dignan, 2007). Every year, according to the Project Management Institute (PMI), nearly 70-80 per cent of all enterprise resource planning implementation projects fail, go over-budget or go live past the original deadline (Roman, 2005). Failure has been common among ERP implementations these are not new to the business world. The business world has seen ERP implementations fail in big companies like Hershey and the result of it being lawsuits against ERP software vendors (Kimberling, 2006). According to the market analytic enterprise resource planning, 2004-2009 report, ERP market revenues increased 14 per cent in 2004 which was very impressive. The report goes on to reveal that nearly one-third of the growth in the overall ERP market was due to fluctuations in forex exchange rates (Reilly, 2005). ERP systems thus incorporate values and practices that will not necessarily match all environments. For example, (Soh *et al.*, 2000) surveyed 'misfits' observed in ERP implementations and found that these tend to be higher in Asian companies because of differences from European and US business practices.

The critical factors approach is widely prevalent in ERP systems literature. Many failures and near failures of ERP system deployments have been attributed to the lack of a critical factors approach to ERP implementation (Buckhout *et al.*, 1999; Umble and Umble, 2002).In this globally competitive environment companies need to constantly improve business performance by improving their business processes. Since the 1990's more and more companies are turning to enterprise resource planning to replace obsolete process and improve business performance. Now the IT implementation dynamics have changed such that companies expect a breakeven ROI of two to three years. Doing the ERP implementation right can be rewarding; failing can be devastating. Therefore, it is very important to know the critical success factors of ERP implementation and make sure full emphasis are put on these. ERP implementation is a lengthy and complex process, and there have been many cases of unsuccessful implementations which have had major impacts on business performance (Parr and Shanks, 2000).

There have been many reports of unsuccessful ERP implementations within business, including accounts of the inability of Hershey to ship candy at Halloween, Nike losing shoe orders, and FoxMeyer's failure to process orders (Cotteleer, 2003). Majed (2000) reported that 70 per cent of ERP implementations did not achieve their estimated benefits. In other studies, the percentage of ERP implementations that can be classified as 'failures' ranges from 0 per cent to 60 per cent or higher (Langenwalter, 2000), and failures of ERP system implementation projects have been known to lead to problems as serious as organizational bankruptcy (Bulkelery, 1996; Davenport, 1998; Markus *et al.*, 2000). However, there have been various definitions of failure of ERP implementation. Failure has been defined as an implementation that does not achieve a sufficient Return on Investment (ROI) identified in the project approval phase. Using this definition, it has been found that failure rates are in the range of 60–90 per cent (Ptak, 2000). Enterprise Resource Planning (ERP) systems have always been highly complex information systems. ERP implementation is a very difficult and expensive project an organization can ever take. It was reported that 75 per cent of the ERP projects are classified as failures (Smith, 1999). Due to globalization, SMEs today operate in a wider arena. Majority of them have MNCs as their clients. These MNCs require SMEs to implement the same ERP system as them to allow for tighter integration in their supply chain, which permits them to design and plan the production and delivery so as to reduce the turnaround time. Considering the growth in ERP implementation in the SME segment, several SMEs are implementing ERP systems as their peers have done so. While in the past many SMEs were active in local markets, currently the technologies and networks are changing the basis of competition. SMEs are now exposed to the forces of global business. From this point of view, it is crucial that SMEs change focus in the market, lower operation cost, and improve their competitiveness. ERP helps companies gain a competitive edge by streamlining business processes, integrating business units, and providing organizational members greater access to real-time information (Jones and Price, 2004; Van, Van and Waarts, 2000).

Most of the existing studies that investigate the success factors for ERP implementations focus on the projects that have been carried out in North America and Western Europe (Davison, 2002).In recent years, researchers such as (Martinsons, 2004; Davison, 2002; Soh et al., 2000; Molla and Loukis, 2005) have examined ERP implementations in other countries. Considering that most ERP systems are designed by western information technology (IT) professionals the structure and processes embedded in these systems reflect western culture. As a result, fundamental misalignments are likely to exist between foreign ERP systems and Indian SMEs. These factors can result in design with undesirable reality gaps, which tend to lead to underperforming systems (Heeks, 2001; Walsham, 2001).

According to Gartner research group (www.gartner.com), the rapid evolution of ERP has already leaded to a new corporate ERP II, which is supposed to help businesses gain more competitive edge in the future. The major difference is that ERP II involves collaborative commerce, which enables business partners from multiple companies to exchange information posted on ecommerce exchanges.

STATEMENT OF THE PROBLEM

Despite the benefits that can be achieved from a successful ERP system implementation, there is already evidence of high failure risks in ERP implementation projects. Too often, project managers focus mainly on the technical and financial aspects of the implementation project, while neglecting or putting less effort on the nontechnical issues. Therefore, one of the major research issues in ERP systems today is the study of ERP implementation success. Prior research has shown that conflict with ERP consultants is one of the main managerial problems during the implementation period of ERP system (Themistocleous *et al.*, 2001). ERP Consultants can bring to the organization specialized skills, experience, and know-how that the organization needs when it is both time consuming and expensive for it to build internally (Gable, 2003). They can also offer a firm wide view, encourage unity between members, and they are usually neutral (Davenport, 1998). ERP Consultants can perform the role of change facilitator and are involved in very important knowledge transfer (Gable, 2003). (Soh, Yap and Raman, 1992) investigated the importance of consultants on computerization success in small businesses. They concluded that the level of computer system usage of small businesses with consultants is higher than that of small businesses without consultants. Therefore there is a need to understand ERP Implementation success from consultant's point of view.

Traditionally, large organizations adopt packaged software to address their information systems requirements. One such popular example is Enterprise Resource Planning (ERP) systems. In the year 2000, it was reported that over 70 per cent of Fortune 1000 companies had or were in the process of implementing an Enterprise Resource Planning (ERP) system (Hillegerberg and Kumar, 2000). As the demand from large corporations plateau ERP vendors shifted their emphasis to Small and Medium size firms (Piturro, 1999). Prior research studies in the ERP context mainly focused on large organizations with ERP systems, ignoring the importance of small and medium organizations (SMEs). However, this shift in focus by the ERP vendors was not projected in research activities in recent years. Given that SMEs are significantly different from large organizations (Lee and Oakes, 1995; Ghobadian and Gallear, 1996), and that more and more SMEs are implementing ERPs, the relevant question would be, "What factors may contribute in the success and failure of ERP implementation at Indian SMEs?"In this study, investigations had been made for critical success and failure factors that may contribute in the success and failure of ERP Implementation at Indian small and medium size enterprise (SMEs) from the perspectives of the Indian ERP consultants involved in ERP implementation. Critical Success Factors (CSFs) define as the key aspects (areas) where 'things must go right' in order for the ERP implementation process to achieve a high level of success and Critical Failure Factors (CFFs) define as the key aspects (areas) where 'things must go wrong' in order for the ERP implementation process to achieve a high level of failure. A typical critical factors approach used to understand ERP implementation success and failure at Indian SMEs.

"A Study on Critical Success Factors for Successful ERP Implementation at Indian SMEs"

Along this line, in this research researcher seeks to contribute to understanding of the critical success and failure factors of ERP implementations at Indian SMEs and how these factors can be put into practice to facilitate the process of ERP implementations at Indian SMEs. Researcher had tried to build a consensus from previous research and had derived unified models and guidelines of critical success and failure factors for the successful ERP implementations at Indian SME.

The following research questions (investigative questions) were addressed as primary and secondary research objectives:

- What are the CSFs (Critical Success Factors) that contribute in the success of ERP implementation at Indian SMEs?
- What are the KCSFs (Key Critical Success Factors, most preferred CSFs) that should be taken into high priority for the successful ERP implementation at Indian SMEs?
- What are the CFFs (Critical Failure Factors) that contribute in the failure of ERP implementation at Indian SMEs?
- What are the KCFFs (Key Critical Failure Factors, most preferred CFFs) that should be taken into high priority to avoid the failure of ERP implementation at Indian SMEs?
- Is it possible to categories the CSFs for the successful ERP implementation at Indian SMEs?
- Is it possible to categories the CFFs for the failure of ERP implementation at Indian SMEs?
- Do thirty CSFs of the large enterprise also contribute in the success of ERP implementation at Indian SMEs?
- Do twenty CFFs of the large enterprise also contribute in the failure of ERP implementation at Indian SMEs?
- Is it possible to develop a reliable survey instrument (standard survey tool) to explore the CSFs for the successful ERP implementation at Indian SMEs?

- Is it possible to develop a reliable survey instrument (standard survey tool) to rank the CSFs for the successful ERP implementation at Indian SMEs?
- Is it possible to develop a reliable survey instrument (standard survey tool) to explore the CFFs for the failure of ERP implementation at Indian SMEs?
- Is it possible to develop a statistically proved checklist based on the CSFs and CFFs for the successful ERP implementation at Indian SMEs?
- Is it possible to develop guidelines and recommendation based on the gap analysis between CSFs and CFFs in order to facilitate the formulation of strategy on how to make successful ERP implementation at Indian SMEs?
- Is it possible to develop a common theoretical framework to cover both the aspects of ERP implementation (i.e. success and failure of ERP implementation at Indian SMEs) for current and future research?
- Is there anything common among CSFs and CFFs for the ERP implementation at Indian SMEs in order to explore the dimensions for the customized survey instruments (questionnaires) in future research?
- Is it possible to develop the user manual for the customized survey instruments (questionnaires) for the current and future research?
- Is it possible to map the Indian ERP consultant's perception towards CSFs and CFFs for the successful ERP implementation at Indian SMEs?

RESEARCH OBJECTIVES AND EXPLORATORY HYPOTHESES (EXPLORATORY STATEMENTS)

Primary (specific) objectives of this research were as below:

- To explore the CSFs for the successful ERP implementation at Indian SMEs
- To rank the CSFs based on their importance for successful ERP implementation at Indian SMEs
- To explore the CFFs for the failure of ERP implementation at Indian SMEs
- To rank the CFFs based on their importance for the failure of ERP implementation at Indian SMEs
- To categorize the CSFs in order to form a unified structure for the successful ERP implementation at Indian SMEs

- To categorize the CFFs in order to form a unified structure for the failure of ERP implementation at Indian SMEs
- To find out the reliability of instrument in totality for exploring and defining the CSFs for the successful ERP implementation at Indian SMEs
- To find out the reliability of instrument in totality for ranking the CSFs for the successful ERP implementation at Indian SMEs
- To find out the reliability of instrument in totality for exploring and defining the CFFs for the failure of ERP implementation at Indian SMEs
- To find out the validity of instrument in totality for exploring and defining the CSFs for the successful ERP implementation at Indian SMEs
- To find out the validity of instrument in totality to rank the CSFs for the successful ERP implementation at Indian SMEs
- To find out the validity of instrument in totality for exploring and defining the CFFs for the failure of ERP implementation at Indian SMEs
- To develop a strategic ERP implementation model for the successful ERP implementation at Indian SMEs.
- To provide a checklist for the successful ERP implementation at Indian SMEs.
- To provide the guidelines and recommendations for the successful ERP implementation at Indian SMEs.
- To develop a theoretical framework for the future research in the area of successful ERP implementation and adoption at India SMEs
- To find out the possible dimensions for both the customized survey instruments (questionnaires) in order to facilitate the standardization process of survey instruments in future research.
- To prepare the user manual for the customized survey instruments (based on pilot survey results) for final research.

Secondary (general) objectives of this research were as below:

- To develop a common ERP model for ERP implementation at Indian SMEs
- To develop ERP implementation success model for Indian SMEs
- To develop ERP implementation failure model for Indian SMEs
- To validate CSFs of LEs for ERP implementation at Indian SMEs

- To validate CFFs of LEs for ERP implementation at Indian SMEs
- To perform gap analysis between CSFs and CFFs for the successful ERP implementation at Indian SMEs

Exploratory Hypotheses (Exploratory Statements)

Literature Review-Research Gap-Research Questions-Research Objectives (SOP) – Research Statements/Research Hypotheses- Research Answer

- *ES01:* The perception (response) of the Indian ERP consultant's does not support the statement that "all the 30 CSFs of the LEs also contribute in the success of ERP implementation at Indian SMEs"
- *ES02:* The perception (response) of Indian ERP consultant's does not support the statement that "all the 20 CFFs of the LEs also contribute in the failure of ERP implementation at Indian SMEs".
- *ES03:* There are no KCSFs for the successful ERP implementation at Indian SMEs because all the 30 CSFs have same ranks (and hence importance) given by the Indian ERP consultants.
- *ES04:* There are no KCFFs for the failure of ERP implementation at Indian SMEs because all the 20 CFFs have same mean value (and hence importance) given by the Indian ERP consultants.
- *ES05:* All the 30 CSFs can't be categorized to form a unified structure for the successful ERP implementation at Indian SMEs because of their independent nature from each other and hence the exploratory factor analysis is not valid
- *ES06:* All the 20 CFFs can't be categorized to form a unified structure for the failure of ERP implementation at Indian SMEs because of their independent nature from each other and hence the exploratory factor analysis is not valid
- *ES07:* The customized survey instrument to explore the CSFs for the successful ERP implementation at Indian SMEs can't be used as reliable survey tool for the current and future research because of the low construct reliability of the survey instrument (questionnaire).
- *ES08:* The customized survey instrument to rank the CSFs for the successful ERP implementation at Indian SMEs can't be used as reliable survey tool for the current and future research because of the low construct reliability of the survey instrument (questionnaire).
- *ES09:* The customized survey instrument to explore the CFFs for the failure of ERP implementation at Indian SMEs can't be used as

reliable survey tool for the current and future research because of the low construct reliability of survey instrument (questionnaire).

- *ES10:* The customized survey instrument to explore the CSFs for the successful ERP implementation at Indian SMEs can't be used as validate survey tool for the current and future research because of the low construct validity of the survey instrument (questionnaire).
- *ES11:* The customized survey instrument to rank the CSFs for the successful ERP implementation at Indian SMEs can't be used as validate survey tool for the current and future research because of the low construct validity of the survey instrument (questionnaire).
- *ES12:* The customized survey instrument to explore the CFFs for the failure of ERP implementation at Indian SMEs can't be used as validate survey tool for the current and future research because of the low construct validity of the survey instrument (questionnaire).
- *ES13:* No dimensions can be identified for the survey instrument (questionnaire) related to the identification (exploring) of the CSFs for the successful ERP implementation at Indian SMEs to facilitate the standardization process of the survey instrument (questionnaire) in future research.
- *ES14:* No dimensions can be identified for the survey instrument (questionnaire) related to the identification (exploring) of CFFs for the failure of ERP implementation at Indian SMEs to facilitate the standardization process of the survey instrument (questionnaire) in future research.

IMPORTANCE OF THE STUDY

- It appears from the previous studies that organizational conditions at SMEs differ from that of large organizations. This suggests that the relative importance of CSFs and CFFs in ERP implementation may also differ. Since literature on ERP implementation at Indian SMEs is relatively sparse, this study may helps to narrow this knowledge gap by investigating success and failure factors for the successful ERP implementation at Indian SMEs.
- It may become easier to formulate the exact integrated strategies to analyze and understand ERP Implementation at Indian SMEs.
- It may provide a platform to the future researchers for the successful ERP implementation at Indian SMEs.
- It May help to predict how ERP Implementation may response to Indian SMEs.

- It may support ERP vendors, consultants, customers, end users, employees, marketers, corporate, investors, and other stakeholders for the successful ERP Implementation at Indian SMEs. It may facilitate them to identify their target segment that they can influence and which can work in their favor during all the phases of ERP implementation at Indian SMEs.

SCOPE OF THE STUDY

- This study has been conducted in India to identify and rank the CSFs along with the CFFs for the successful ERP Implementation at Indian SMEs.
- Analysis has been done from the Indian ERP consultants/ vendor point of view only.
- This study was restricted for ERP implementation at Indian SMEs only
- This study was restricted to Indian scenario only
- Focus of the study was to analyze Indian ERP consultants/vendors perceptions (opinion) those who implement ERP rather than the customer/client (Indian SMEs) those who enjoy the ERP services.
- Its results are more specific to service provider (vendor/consultant) rather than service receiver (customer/client).
- Small and medium enterprises (SMEs) have been receiving less focus from the software vendors than large enterprises (LEs). Research on the implementation of ERP in certain European countries shows that the job of implementing an Enterprise Resource Planning (ERP) package is a riskier business for SMEs than for LEs. This research presents a critical success and failure factors approach for the successful ERP implementation at Indian SMEs therefore in future it may help to ERP consultants/vendors/Indian SMEs.
- ERP implementation related models were presented along with the proposed implementation guidelines were specific to Indian SMEs only
- Only one dimension of ERP systems (i.e. implementation of ERP systems at Indian SMEs) were taken in to consideration. This study does not cover the adoption part of the ERP systems at Indian SMEs
- Furthermore, this researcher limits the inclusion of literature to the time period from 1979 to 2009. This date range was chosen to provide the most up-to-date and relevant information concerning

approaches to ERP implementation. Another reason for selecting this date range was the difficulty of locating ERP resources online prior to 1979 because of the frequency of web site updates.

- The steps taken in this project, if it will be proven on some additional projects along with an Indian SMEs in future, it could become basis for a more formalized set of activities, or even a methodology for the further advance research.

NEED AND RATIONAL BEHIND THE STUDY

Technology has had a major impact on every organization. Whether it is a small or large organization, being competitive is the key to success. Issue in dealing with a new ERP system is not solely technology, but it involves high degree of planning and commitment too. SME's face many of the same competitive problems as larger organizations, but have limited resources, experience and staffing skills (Nelson and Millet, 2001). As with the larger enterprises, ERP implementation is becoming critically important to SMEs in streamlining business processes, improving operational performance, and integrating data. Understanding the CSFs and CFFs for the successful ERP implementation is more critical to SMEs than larger organizations due to their more limited resources. SMEs may not be able to withstand the financial impact of the partial failures and project abandonments that have impacted on many of their larger counterparts (Muscatello *et al.*, 2003). Most of the existing studies that investigate the success factors for the successful ERP implementations focus on the projects that have been carried out in North America and Western Europe. In recent years, researchers such as (Martinsons, 2004), have examined ERP implementations in other countries. Considering that most ERP systems are designed by western information technology (IT) professionals, the structure and processes embedded in these systems reflect western culture. As a result, fundamental misalignments are likely to exist between foreign ERP systems and Indian companies requirements. These factors can result in design with undesirable reality gaps, which tend to lead to underperforming systems (Walden and Browne, 2002). Over the past years, the global economic crisis has put the spotlight on many business organizations of any size. With India not being spared of the impact, large establishments have attempted to tackle this crisis in their own ways. SMEs are increasingly being brought into focus on account of their huge growth potential. Various researchers have recommended research into the implementation and use of ERP at SMEs (Huin, 2004; Jacobs and Bendoly, 2003; Muscatello *et al.*, 2003). (Huin, 2004) argues that unless differences between small and large firms are understood, managing ERP projects in SMEs will continue to be slow, painful and at times even unfruitful. Thus, it appears from previous studies that organizational conditions at SMEs differ from that of large organizations. This suggests that the relative importance of CSFs in ERP implementation may also differ. Since literature on ERP implementation at Indian SMEs is relatively sparse, this research helps to narrow this knowledge gap by investigating ERP implementation at Indian SMEs.

This research study conducted to assess the Indian ERP consultant's perception for the critical success and failure factors in ERP implementation at Indian SMEs. It is done in order to know how to make successful ERP implementation at Indian SMEs by exploring 30 CSFs and 20 CFFs so that these CSFs can be promoted and CFFs can be avoided to increase the probability of successful ERP implementation at Indian SMEs. Efficient and effective management of these factors along with the guidelines supported by checklist and recommendation can helps to ERP consultants, vendors and Indian SMEs in managing ERP project in better way at Indian SMEs. It may provide an insight of various strength and weakness related to ERP implementation at Indian SMEs in terms of CSFs and CFFs. ERP implementation success model, ERP implementation failure model and Strategic ERP model supported by gap analysis (recommendation and check list) may helps to simplify the process of successful ERP implementation at Indian SMEs. All the outcomes of this research in terms of models, guidelines etc may helps to ERP consultants, vendors and Indian SMEs to chalk out the strategies to avoid the failure of ERP implementation at Indian SMEs.

ORGANIZATION OF THE BOOK AND CHAPTER SCHEME

- Chapter I Introduction
- Chapter II Review of Literature
- Chapter III Theories and Research Models
- Chapter IV Research Design
- Chapter V Analysis of Data
- Chapter VI Research Findings and Discussions
- Chapter VII Summary and Conclusions
  - Bibliography

This Book consists of seven chapters. Chapter 1 introduces background information by providing the general concept of ERP systems and motivation for the research in the area of ERP implementation at Indian SMEs. Chapter 2 reviews the previous efforts and findings in related areas. It presents an overview of previous research on ERP implementation in information systems. Chapter 3 has two main sections. In the first section, previous research, theories and fundamentals of project management in ERP implementation were presented to form the theoretical background of the research model. The second section provides the conceptual research models, describing factors and components along with their definitions and causal relationships. Chapter 4 presents the research design, showing survey instruments and their descriptions. The results of the pilot survey were examined by reliability, validity test etc, to know that whether the survey instruments were developed properly or not. Chapters 5 and 6 contain the analysis and interpretation of main research findings. Chapter 7 summarizes the study and concludes by examining the contributions of the completed research models and presents the recommendations for further advance research in this work. Figure 1.1 shows the organization of this book.

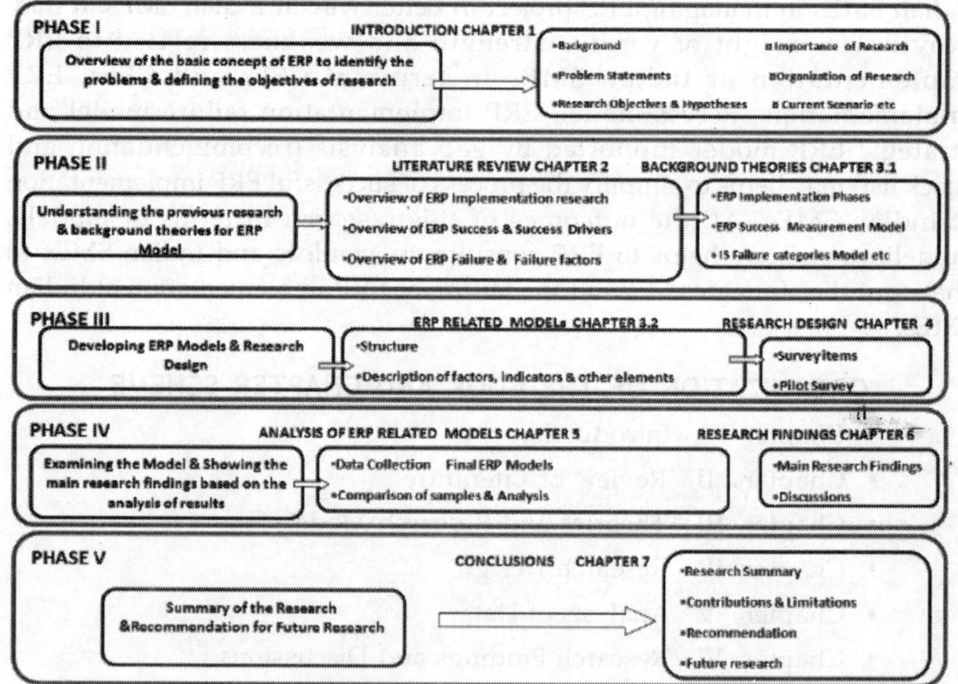

Fig. 1.1 : Organization of Book and Chapter Scheme
(*Source:* Author, MS PowerPoint)

Chapter Summary

This chapter has provided an overview of the ERP Systems. It reviews ERP systems in general including background information, advantages, disadvantages, and major vendors along with the functional modules. In background information section basic concept, definition and characteristics of ERP systems were described. This study attempts to identify the critical success and failure factors for ensuring the successful ERP implementation at Indian small and medium scale enterprise (SMEs). The significance of this research has been discussed and research questions have been identified (Literature Review-Research Gap-Research Questions-Research Objectives (SOP) – Research Statements/Research Hypotheses- Research Answer). A justification for the undertaking of this research project has been given. From the initial literature review, it can be concluded that ERP systems have many benefits mostly from integrated functions and standardization, but also have disadvantages due to their high cost and long implementation periods. Finally, outlines of the remaining chapters within this book have been presented. A thorough literature review on important concepts to this research is presented in the next chapter.

Review of Literature

"ERP Implementation sometimes demands to see what everybody else has seen and to think what nobody else has thought"

– Monk *et al.*, 2009

The purpose of this chapter was to present the previous efforts and findings in related areas. It presents an overview of previous research on ERP implementation in information systems. In the first part of this chapter evolution of ERP along with the literature reviews for the ERP implementation phases were presented. Second part of this chapter deals with the various critical success and failure factors of the LEs (Large Enterprise) as identified by the various researchers along with the definitions of SMEs (Small Medium Size Enterprise). Thorough literature review of all the factors has been taken as the theoretical frameworks for this study. It presents a critical appraisal of the previous work published in the literature pertaining to the area of ERP implementation at LEs.

EVOLUTION OF ERP

The focus of manufacturing systems in the 1960's was on inventory control. Most of the software packages then (usually customized) were designed to handle inventory, based on traditional inventory concepts. In the 1970's the focus shifted to MRP (Material Requirement Planning) systems. In the 1980's the concept of MRP-II (Manufacturing Resources Planning) evolved which was an extension of MRP to shop floor and distribution management activities. In the early 1990's, MRP-II was further extended to cover areas like engineering, finance, human resources, projects management etc i.e. the complete gamut of activities within any business enterprise. Hence, the term ERP (Enterprise Resource Planning) was coined.

Table 2.1: Evolution of ERP

Decade	Label	New Concept
60	Inventory Control Systems, Forecast	Computer in Business Applications
70	Material Requirement Planning(MRP)	Bills of Material(BOM) and Material requirement calculations and procurement
80	Manufacturing Resource Planning (MRP /II)	Closed loop Planning and capacity constraints
90	Enterprise Resource Planning (ERP)	Integrated Database, HRM and Quality Management
00	Enterprise Resource Planning (ERP /II)	Inter organizational collaboration

(**Source:** www.erppandit.com)

ERP/II (ERP-2) systems is a new concept introduced by Gartner group (www.gartner.com) in 2000 in order to label the latest extension of the ERP systems.

Table 2.2: Generation's of ERP

Particulars	First Generation ERP	Second Generation ERP	Third Generation ERP
Scope	Single company	Single company	Multiple companies
No. of Sites	Single	Multiple	Multiple sites from different companies
Methodology Focus	Streamline business processes	Global integration of Enterprise	Integration of supply chain
Technology Focus	Business process efficiency	Interoperability across the globe	Interoperability across platforms
Organization Focus	Business process	Seamless integration across multiple sites	Product/Market channel
Process Focus	Enterprise-wide closed loop	Global enterprise-wide closed loop	E-business, SCM, CRM

(**Source:** Siau, 2004)

ERP Implementation

Considering the radical business changes required for the implementation of ERP systems, combined with the inherent complexity of these packages, it is not surprising that making the transition to ERP is neither easy nor quick. ERP is indeed often identified with out-of-control budgets and questionable returns (Schneider, 1999). (Appleton,1997) claims that about half of ERP projects fail to achieve hoped-for benefits because managers significantly underestimate the efforts involved in managing change. (Hammer and Champy, 1993) define a business process as a collection of activities that take one or more kinds of input and create an output that is of value to the customer. (Shanks and Parr, 2000) defined ERP implementation as the process of developing the initial business case and planning the project, configuring and implementing the packaged software, and subsequent improvements to business processes. ERP implementation is considerably different from any traditional information system implementation for many reasons: (1) the integrated nature of ERP applications causes dramatic changes on work flow, organizational structure and on the way people do their jobs; (2) ERP systems are not built but adopted, this involves a mix of business process reengineering and package customization, (3) ERP implementation is not just a technical exercise but it is a socio-technical challenge as it poses new set of management procedures. In that sense, it has become clear that ERP implementation differs from traditional systems development where the key focus has shifted from a heavy emphasis on technical analysis and programming towards business process design and human elements (Gibson, 1999)

ERP Implementation Phase

Implementing an ERP system is generally an extensive challenge. Performance of the enterprise will often get worse before it gets better and enterprises are expected to encounter the resistance throughout the phases of ERP system implementation. Several researchers have developed different ERP project lifecycle (Shanks *et al.*, 2000; Ross, 1999; Markus and Tanis, 2000).ERP project lifecycle produced a four phase implementation phase. The planning phase includes both the business concentration of Markus and Tanis' chartering phase and technical concentration of Ross' design phase. The improvement phase includes both incremental and radical improvements to business process corresponding to the Markus and Tanis' onward and upward phase.

In summary, although each researcher has presented different ERP implementation phases, some phases are very similar to others. For example, Ross' implementation phase covers Bancroft *et al.,* several phases: as is, to be, construction, testing, and actual implementation. Markus and Tanis' project and shakedown phases are very similar to Ross' implementation and stabilization phases. Markus and Tanis' onward and upward phase have involved Ross' continuous improvement and transformation phases. Ross also mentioned that large ERP system implementation might require different cycles through the process model for each separate module within the ERP system. In this book, author decided to adopt (Shanks *et al.*, 2000) synthesized ERP project lifecycle as a major ERP implementation process model to understand the concept of ERP implementation phase.

ERP Implementation at SMEs

Various researchers have recommended research into the implementation and use of ERPs at SMEs (Bernroider and Koch, 2001; Huin *et al.*, 2003; Jacobs and Bendoly, 2003; Mabert *et al.*, 2003a; Muscatello *et al.*, 2003; Sun *et al.*, 2005). (Huin, 2004) argues that unless differences between small and large firms are understood, managing ERP projects in SMEs will continue to be slow, painful and at times even unfruitful. However, not many studies appear to have tackled this challenge yet. (Loh and Koh, 2004) review of the literature identified 10 CSFs, which were then confirmed by interviews across eight SMEs from the UK. (Soja, 2006) ERP survey in Poland identified 16 factors at large organizations but at only two firms with less than 300 employees. (Muscatello *et al.*, 2003) studied four US manufacturing SMEs, however they were all subsidiaries of large firms and they all had annual revenues greater than US$ 50 million. (Buonanno *et al.*, 2005) explored the antecedents of ERP adoption in Italian large firms and SMEs. These and a few other studies, (Adam and O Doherty, 2000; Shin, 2006) provided valuable insights into the dynamics of ERP implementation at SMEs. Thus, it appears from previous studies that organizational conditions at SMEs differ from that of large organizations. This suggests that the relative importance of CSFs in ERP implementation may also differ. Since literature on ERP implementation at SMEs is relatively sparse, this research helps to narrow this knowledge gap by investigating ERP implementation at Indian SMEs.

ERP Implementation Success and Failure

The literature on ERP implementation success and failure is inconclusive. While some analysts report positive impacts and outcomes of ERP application, others have revealed ERP failures. One of the reasons behind these different views lies in the multidimensionality of the concept of success and the difficulty of developing a single success and failure measurement. Based on review of both ERP and IS success and failure literature (Al-Mashari *et al.*, 2003; Bingi *et al.*, 1999; Davenport, 1998; Gable *et al.*, 2003) two dimensions of ERP success and failure were identified. As the success and the failure of ERP systems can be classified into two categories; the success and failure of ERP adoption (end user or customer point of view) and the success and failure of ERP implementation (consultant or vendor point of view). The ERP Implementation dimension looks at the success and failure of ERP implementation process. Implementing an ERP system often constitutes a company's largest-ever IS investment, and in many cases the largest-ever corporate project (Sumner, 2000). There are a variety of 'cost' factors that may escalate the initial budget. These include implementation assistance cost, cost of system integration, reengineering cost, cost of changing a companies' IT architecture to support ERP technology, etc. (Cotteleer *et al.*, 2003; Shang and Seddon, 2002). Furthermore, depending on the implementation strategy a company adopts, ERP projects are often long and intense (Cotteleer *et al.*, 2003).

According to one survey, the average time for implementing an ERP system is 23 months (Umble and Umble, 2002). Process success and failure gauges whether an ERP project is completed inside the time and budget schedule.

SMALL AND MEDIUM SIZE ENTERPRISE (SMEs)

The literature points out significant differences between SMEs and large organizations. SMEs top management is usually involved in day-to-day activities (Quinn and Carson, 2003). However, managers may have limited formal training (Lee and Oakes, 1995). Absence of long-term planning is another dominant factor (Gunasekaran *et al.*, 1996). On the other hand, SMEs have relatively informal structures and culture (Mintzberg *et al.*, 2003), which increase cross-functional exchanges, and small management teams, which results in efficient decision-making (Ghobadian and Gallear, 1996; McAdam, 2000). These later issues have been considered particularly advantageous for major projects (Lee and Oakes, 1995). One major disadvantage of SMEs is lack of human and financial resources (Ghobadian and Gallear, 1996; Gunasekaran *et al.*, 1996; McAdam, 2002; Achanga *et al.*, 2006). (Achanga *et al.*, 2006) stressed that staff shortages at SMEs might even require production to halt during training. Skills upgrading may be needed, however SMEs often cannot afford extensive training (Raymond *et al.*, 1998). Furthermore, they may face challenges in paying for major consulting (Kinni, 1995). (Sun *et al.*, 2005) indicated that such resource shortages might hinder project success. Regarding IT, SMEs seldom have dedicated IT staff, let alone a formal department (Adam and O Doherty, 2000; Mabert *et al.*, 2003a). Major projects face increased external and internal risks when compared to large organizations. Externally, SMEs are more fragile than large companies (Rao, 2000; Shin, 2006) and face greater difficulty in obtaining credit (Lu, 2006). Such external risks can lead to project delays or even abandonment (Serafeimidis and Smithson, 1999). Internally, SMEs may find it difficult to implement reengineering projects due to limited spare resources (Eshelman *et al.*, 2001; McAdam, 2002). Overall, they may face greater challenges in adopting technology (Raymond *et al.*, 1998; Shin, 2006). Finally, the cost of an ERP implementation may be proportionally higher for SMEs than for large organizations (Mabert *et al.*, 2000), and SMEs may be more severely impacted by unsuccessful implementations (Muscatello *et al.*, 2003).Resource constraints, limitations of the infrastructure and capability are most likely the major challenges facing an SMEs to adopt ERP systems. However, the factors that are influencing ERP in large organizations vary from those influencing the Small- Medium- Enterprises (Laukkanen et al. 2007). Large organizations benefits from adopting and implementing ERP systems range from simple organized operational level business processes to strategic decision taking capabilities (Seethmraju and Seethmraju, 2008;Mabert *et al.*, 2003).The updated IT infrastructure play a vital role in ERP implementation in large organizations. The basic functional areas (human resources, production and manufacturing, sales and marketing, finance and accounting) do exist in the large organizations. While taking into consideration that the financial ability of large scale companies enables the large investment in IT/IS and can support the risks attached to such investment.

In their book (Laudon and Laudon ,2009) define the most favorable ERP systems implemented in large organizations in order to be, Customer Relationship Management (CRM) system, Supply Chain Management (SCM) system, Enterprise Resource Planning (ERP) System, and Knowledge Management System (KMS). Major vendors for such systems are international vendor who excel worldwide such as Oracle, SAP, BAAN, Microsoft Great Plains, etc. In line with (Seethmraju and Seethmraju, 2008), there is no clear identification of what defines the critical success factors for ERP implementation in large enterprises.

Quiet literally, the reason for this is that not only the implementation takes responsible for the ERP's success or failure; it is the whole adoption process which identifies implementation as part and different stages of implementations pre- and post preparations, standardization and integration with other implemented ERP systems (Huang *et al.*, 2004). Thus, CSFs have different weigh of significance over different organizations working in different places of the world. There is a difference between size of the organization when it comes to the time it takes between the organization starts to implement an ERP to its implemented ERP go live. The claim is that small businesses have a shorter time than midsized and large organizations (Cuddy, 2007).

ERP systems used to be a domain of large companies but there are a still increasing number of small and mid-sized enterprises adopting them as well. There are some reasons for this trend, including a saturation of the market, as most large organizations have already implemented an ERP system, increasing possibilities and need for the integration of systems between organizations and the availability. SMEs have been defined on the basis of various criteria such as the number of workers employed, volume of output or sales, value of assets employed, and the use of energy, etc. Organization for Economic Cooperation and Development (OECD) defines establishments with up to 19 employees as 'very small', between 20 and 99 employees as 'small, from 100 to 499 employees as medium, and over 500 employees as large enterprises. However, many establishments in some developing countries with 100 to 499 employees are regarded as relatively 'large' firms. Multilateral Investment Guarantee Agency (MIGA) has recently developed a guarantee programme, called the Small Investment Programme (SIP) that is specifically designed for SMEs. MIGA defines SMEs, for coverage under this program, as firms with not more than 300 employees, value of assets not exceeding US $ 15 million and annual sales not exceeding US $ 15 million. The European Union defines SMEs as enterprises that have employees of less than 250, with a turnover not exceeding Euro 50 million. In India the SMEs are not well defined. The internal group set up by the Reserve Bank of India has recently recommended that the units with investment in plant and machinery in excess of Small Scale Industries (SSI) limit and up to Rs. 10 crores may be treated as medium enterprises .The US Small Business Act 1953 states that a small business concern is one that is independently owned and operated and which is not dominant in its field of operation. SBA has a section called Office of Size Standards that defines the appropriate size for a small business. The size standards are broken by NAICS industry classification and are based on two things (*a*) size standards in millions of dollars; and (*b*) by number of employee. In most industries, 500 is the maximum for small businesses, though there are industries where a business can have 1000-1500 employees yet still considered 'small business'. The European Union makes a general distinction between self-employment, micro, small and medium sized businesses based on the following criteria:

Table 2.3: Number of employees, (Effective Policies for Small Business: A Guide for the Policy Review Process and Strategic Plans for Micro, Small and Medium Enterprise Development) (2004, UNIDO and OECD)

0	Self-employed
2-9	Micro business
10-49	Small business
50-249	Medium-size business

The definition, this research used, In the Indian context for micro, small and medium enterprises as per the MSME Development Act, 2006 that defined based on their investment in plant and machinery (for manufacturing enterprise) and on equipments for enterprises providing or rendering services. According to the Ministry of Micro, Small and Medium Enterprises, recent ceilings on investment for enterprises to be classified as micro, small and medium enterprises are as follows:

Table 2.4: Definition of Indian SMEs

Classification	Manufacturing Enterprises*	Service Enterprises**
Micro	Rs. 2.5 million/ Rs. 25 lakh (US$ 50,000)	Rs. 1 million/ Rs. 10 lakh (US$ 20,000)
Small	Rs. 50 million/ Rs. 5 crore (US$ 1 million)	Rs. 20 million/ Rs. 2 crore (US$ 40,00,000)
Medium	Rs. 100 million/ Rs. 10 crore (US$ 2 million)	Rs. 50 million/ Rs. 5 crore (US$ 1 million)

* Investment limit in Plant and Machinery
** Investment limit in Equipments
(**Source:** MSME Development Act, 2006)

Small and Medium sized Enterprises (SMEs) are of critical importance to many economies. SMEs are integral part of economies, they also face numerous challenges in implementing technologies such as Enterprise Resource Planning (ERP) systems, including a lack of human and financial resources to support such initiatives (McAdam, 2002; Achanga *et al.*, 2006). Like many other technological advances, ERP systems were initially implemented mostly at large organizations. Their relative absence from SMEs has probably been the main reason for the research focus on large companies (Somers and Nelson, 2001; Mabert *et al.*, 2003b; Mandal and Gunasekaran, 2003; Umble *et al.*, 2003; Nah and Delgado, 2006).

More recently, however, vendors began to provide SME specific ERP (Bingi *et al.*, 1999; Bell and Orzen, 2007; Deep *et al.*, 2008). ERP adoption at SMEs has been catching up with large companies (Van Everdingen *et al.*, 2000; Mabert *et al.*, 2003a). There is some suggestion that smaller type businesses are unaware of the advantages of ERP technology and how the technology has become necessary for global interaction is an issue, if not addressed, may eventually push these businesses out of the market. ERP systems adoption several criteria have been proposed for small and mid-size business to select and implement an appropriate ERP system solution that includes affordability, supplier knowledge, local support, technical upgradeability and the availability of the latest technology (Rao, 2000).

According to Saccomano (2003) the initial target market for ERP vendors was big companies that could afford solutions costing millions of dollars at project start up. In recent times, many multinational companies have restricted their operations to partnering only those midsize companies that are using compatible ERP software. Hence, it becomes essential for many Indian SMEs to adjust their business model and adopt ERP software that is compatible with the large enterprises with which they deal (Rao, 2000). Thus, Indian SMEs are increasingly finding themselves attracted to ERP solutions and the associated benefits. Additionally, ERP systems are becoming a necessity in order to maintain relations with larger enterprises (Rao, 2000).

CRITICAL SUCCESS FACTORS (CSFs) OF LEs (LARGE ENTERPRISES)

Critical Success Factors (CSFs) approach was first used by (Rockhart, 1979) in IS (Information Systems) area. It has been applied to many aspects of IS including project management, manufacturing systems implementation, reengineering, and, more recently, ERP systems implementation (Bancroft, 1996; Brown, 1999; Gibson, 1999). Within ERP implementation context, CSFs are defined as factors needed to ensure a successful ERP project (Gibson, 1999). Several studies identified the critical factors needed to enable project managers and management boards to improve their ERP implementation projects. Implementing successful ERP systems is investigated by many researchers. Their general focus was on identifying CSFs that need to exist in any organization to have successful ERP implementation. These factors have been tested in different organizations in many developed and developing countries by many researcher; (Al-Mashari *et al.*, 2003; Akkermans and Helden, 2002; Bancroft *et al.*, 2001; Bradford and Florin, 2003; Holland and Light, 1999; Jarrar *et al.*, 2000; Mabert, at al 2003; Parr and Shanks, 2000; Skok and Legge, 2002;Somers and Nelson, 2003; Umble *et al.*, 2002; Welti, 1999; Zhang *et al.*, 2002). These factors include, but not limited to, clear objectives, user involvement, effective communications, change management, project team, project champion, consultants, architecture choices, minimal customization, excellent project management, top management support, data analysis and conversion, business process re-engineering and user training and education. The findings showed that top management commitment and leadership, customer focus, information and analysis, training, supplier management, strategic planning, employee involvement, human resource management, process management, teamwork, product and service design, process control, benchmarking, continuous improvement, employee empowerment, quality assurance, social responsibility, and employee satisfaction were the most commonly extracted factors across these 76 studies(Sila, Ismail and Ebrahimpour, 2000). According to (Esteves and Bohórquez, 2007) most of the research studies about ERP impact has been in the form of individual case studies, while experiences on the field of Small and Medium-sized Enterprises (SMEs) often fail in recognizing the economic and organizational impacts related to their ERP implementation and use.

Following is the finding of thorough literature reviews that shows a list of critical success factors along with brief description that had been identified in previous research as CSFs for successful ERP implementation in large enterprise. This list has been identified and used as a theoretical framework for the study to identify and rank the critical success factors for the successful ERP implementation at Indian SMEs.

Top Management Commitment and Support

Top management advocacy, provision of adequate resources, commitment to the project, and commitment of senior management with their own involvement and willingness to allocate valuable resources to the implementation effort (Dawson and Owens, 2008). Top management should understand the degree of the changes and supports (Muscatello and Chen, 2008). Cooperation of top management with the steering committee and the development of communication makes top management support become visible. (Bueno,2008). The positive commitment, enthusiasm, and support of senior management for ERP project (Shanks *et al.,* 2000). Top management support has been thought to be the most important factor and confirmed by many western countries and Chinese researchers (Bingi *et al.,* 1999; Parr and Shanks, 2000; Somers and Nelson, 2001; 2004; Nah *et al.,* 2001; Akkermans and Helden, 2002; Umble *et al.,* 2003; Jiang, 2005; Zhang *et al.,* 2002 and 2005; ZhouSivunen, 2005; Yusuf *et al.,* 2006).

Top management support has been identified as the most important success factor in ERP system implementation projects. According to (Zhang *et al.,* 2002) top management support in ERP implementation has two main aspects: providing leadership and providing the necessary resources. (Duchessi, *et al.,* 1989) concludes that commitment from top management and adequate training is critical success factors for implementation. The commitment of top management should be emphasized throughout an organization. In particular, no more important factor than the support of the management is critical in the project's life. The roles of top management in IT implementation include developing an understanding of the capabilities and limitations of IT, establishing reasonable goals for IT systems, exhibiting strong commitment to the successful introduction of IT, and communicating the corporate IT strategy to all employees (McKersie and Walton 1991; Umble *et al.,* 2003). Senior management must be involved, including the required people and appropriate time to finish and allocate valuable resources to the implementation effort. The shared vision of the organization and role of the new system and structures should be communicated between managers and employees. Policies made by the manager will come with the new systems in the company. In case of conflict, the proper mediation will be based on that standard (Brown and Vessey 1999).

Change Management Process

Organizations exist of different structures depending on the different characteristics of the organization and the environment that they are competing in (Mintzberg, 1979). (Groth, 1999), has indicated that the introduction of information technology into these organizational structures impact on the existing organizational configurations. There have been strong indications that the benefits from an ERP implementation is actually derived from the change in the organization and that the ERP system is just an enabler for these changes (Martin, 1998). Refers to the knowledge is used to ensure that a complex change, like that integrated with a new big information system, gets the right results, in the right timeframe, at the right costs. The change management approach will ensure the acceptance and readiness of the new system, allowing the organization to get the benefits from using ERP (EstevesSousa and Pastor Collado, 2000). Change management has been studied as one of the important factors by researchers (Shanks *et al.*, 2000; Nah *et al.*, 2001; Umble *et al.*, 2003; Somers and Nelson, 2001 and 2004; Nah and Delgado, 2006). Change management was mostly identified in the western countries context.

BPR and Software Configuration

Re-engineering of business process activities invloves identifying and improving the efficiency of critical operations, restructuring important non-value-adding operations, eliminating inefficient processes while re-engineering business processes: a uniform response, common goals and homogenous vision should be created, so uncertainty and failure rate is minimized (Muscatello and Chen, 2008). Consideration of the adoption of a new enterprise system as an opportunity to improve the way it does business, rather than an interruption of the status quo (Caruso, 2007). It is critical for ERP implementation success. It is inevitable that business process is molded to fit the new system (Bingi *et al.*, 1999). Installing an ERP system includes re-engineering the old business processes into the best business process standard followed in the industry (Bingi *et al.*, 1999). All business processes must agree to the ERP package. Organizations should be willing to change the business to fit the software with minimal customization. Modifications should be avoided to reduce errors and to take advantage of newer versions of the ERP systems.

Almost every analyst of ERP implementation experience strongly advises companies to avoid modifying the software (Markus *et al.*, 2000). However, it is not easy to get everyone to agree to the same process, and adopters often intend to request the vendors to modify the ERP software instead of re-engineering their own business process. Business process re-engineering and minimal customization has been discussed by different researchers (Bingi *et al.*, 1999; Parr and Shanks, 2000; Shanks *et al.*, 2000; Nah *et al.*, 2001; Somers and Nelson, 2001 and 2004; Jiang, 2005; Zhang *et al.*, 2002 and 2005). (Hammer and Champy, 2001) defined Business Process Re-engineering (BPR) as the fundamental rethinking and radical redesign of business processes to achieve dramatic improvements in critical, contemporary measures of performance, such as cost, quality, service and speed. (Somers and Nelson, 2004) stated that BPR plays a significant role in the early stages of implementation. it is important in the acceptance stage and tends to be less important when the technology becomes routine. Furthermore, (Davison, 2002) argued that ERP implementation often requires changes in job descriptions and essential skills. It is inevitable that business processes are molded to fit the new system (Bingi *et al.*, 1999). Aligning the business process to the software implementation is critical (Holland *et al.*, 1999). Organizations should be willing to change the business to fit the software with minimal customization (Holland *et al.*, 1999). However, adapters very often intend to request the vendors to modify the ERP software instead of re-engineering their own business process. Implementing an ERP system involves re-engineering the existing business processes to the best business process standard (Holland *et al.*, 1999; Bingi *et al.*, 1999; Motwani *et al.*, 2002). Nevertheless, companies usually trust and are not willing to give up their own business tradition. They can easily declare that the software simply did not fit business rules around commissions, royalties and that these rules could not be changed without serious negative business implications (Markus and Tanis, 2000).

Project Champion

The project champion should be a high-level executive sponsor who has the power to set goals and legitimize change. Project champion work as an advocate for the system who is unswerving in promoting the benefits of the new system (Dawson and Owens, 2008). It refers to an individual, not always a senior manager, who consistently advocates the benefits of the ERP system. The success of technological innovation has often been related to the presence of a champion who performs the crucial functions of transformational leadership, facilitation, and marketing the project to the users. This champion usually owns the role of change champion for the project life and understands both the technology and business context (Somers and Nelson, 2001). This factor has been included in many previous studies (Parr and Shanks, 2000; Nah *et al.*, 2001; Somers and Nelson, 2001 and 2004; Akkermans and Helden, 2002). The success of technological innovations has often been linked to the presence of a champion who performs the crucial functions of transformational leadership, facilitation, and marketing the project to the users (Toni and Nelson, 2001). By appointing an executive level individual with extensive knowledge of the organization's operational processes, senior management can monitor the ERP system implementation, because the champion has direct responsibility for and is held accountable for the project outcome.

Championship is a critical enabling factor if ERP stands a chance of succeeding (Willcocks and Sykes, 2000).

Business Plan, Vision

A clear business plan and vision to steer the direction of the project A clear business model, a justification of investment, a project mission and identified goals and benefits (Dawson and Owens, 2008). Organizational preparedness with respect to technology such as computers and network connections, 'soft factors' such as education, training, maturity of current processes, commitment to release the right people as well as the top management's commitment (Helo, 2008). (Nah, 2003) stated that one of the biggest problems ERP project leaders face comes not from the implementation itself, but from expectations of board members, senior staff, and other key stakeholders. It is important to set the goals of the project before even seeking top management support. Many ERP implementations have failed as a result of lacking clear plans (Somers and Nelson 2004). ERP domain knowledge is important for creative development (Legare, 2002). When more is known about the potential of ERP systems in terms of what they can do and what their impacts are, then group members are better able to creatively develop and apply this knowledge within the organizational context (Legare, 2002). With other words, the development and implementation of ERP systems can be improved by acquiring team members with significant depth and breadth of knowledge concerning the potential ERP capabilities and tasks (procedures, processes, and context) (Legare, 2002).Furthermore, the clear business plan and vision has been commonly accepted as one of the critical success factor to ERP implementation (Akkermans and Helden, 2002; Buckhout *et al.*, 1999). (Buckhout *et al.*, 1999) asserted that a clear business plan and vision to steer the direction of the project is needed throughout the ERP life cycle. A business plan that outlines proposed strategic and tangible benefits, resources, costs, risks and timeline is critical (Wee, 2000). This will help keep focus on business benefits (Nah *et al.*, 2001). The success factor of clear vision will translate later into needs requirement, into measures checks and balances control, and a means of calculating a return on investment. These are crucial to guide an ongoing organizational effort for ERP implementation as it sometimes exceeds the time framework for a typical business project (Gunson *et al.*, 2001). It is vital to set the project goals before seeking top management support. The organization must carefully define why the ERP system is being implemented and what critical business needs the system will address (Bhatti, 2005). Clear goals and objectives have been noted by researchers as one of the important factors (Parr and Shanks, 2000; Somers and Nelson, 2001 and 2004; Akkermans and Helden, 2002; Umble *et al.*, 2003; Nah and Delgado, 2006; ZhouSivunen, 2005), Clear goals and objectives have been thought to be very important in the first stage of the ERP implementation process.

Effective Communication Plan

The formal promotion of project teams and the advertisement of project progress to the rest of the organization should be communicated well may be by monthly bulletins, newsletters, weekly meetings, and frequent e-mail updates (Nah, Islam and Tan, 2007). Communication of expectations from upper managers to bottom operators, creating awareness of ultimate business process changes (Dawson and Owens, 2008). Information about how the system will help employees do their jobs better will eliminate conflict between the logic of the system and the logic of business processes, cooperation to eliminate resistance to change (Muscatello and Chen, 2008). In ERP projects, companies that pay particular attention to educating employees and communicating future changes to the entire company tend to have much better chance of achieving project success.

For a cross-functional system such as ERP to work, users from all departments must feel that they know and own the system (Scavo, 1995). This prerequisite has a direct impact on the user expectations of the ERP system. Although a number of these prerequisites can be categorized into other disciples, such as change management, project management concepts play an important role in the success of ERP implementations. ERP implementation success as an ERP system is tightly integrating different business functions. The communication and cooperation between different departments in an organization will have a large effect on the smooth flow of the required information and expertise among the departments. This factor has been illustrated by researchers (Somers and Nelson, 2001 and 2004; Nah *et al.*, 2001; Al Mashari *et al.*, 2003; Nah and Delgado, 2006; Woo, 2007).

Post-Implementation Evolution

Any project is not complete without the allowance for some kind of post-evaluation (Nah *et al.*, 2001; Al-Mashari *et al.*, 2003; Tarafdar and Roy, 2003; Holland and Light, 1999). (Mandal and Gunasekaran, 2003) also suggest that there should be an allowance for a feedback network. The post assessment will be difficult to complete, however, unless there had been established metrics (Ross and Vitale, 2000) or focussed performance measures (Umble *et al.*, 2003). (Ross and Vitale, 2000) stress the need for continued management support.

Risk Management

Risks are inherent in projects (Gray and Larson, 2000). ERP implementation risks can be categorized as technical, business or organizational. Furthermore, risks from each category appear throughout the entire project, from making a decision to going live (O'Leary, 2000). Because of this, risk management really should cover all five problem areas of project management. Having a concrete action plans beforehand is important to mitigate risks (Kulik, 1997). Active risk management is also required because risks change constantly (Welti, 1999).Every information technology implementation project carries important elements of risk; hence it is probable that progress will deviate from the plan at some point in the project life cycle. ERP implementation project risks are described as uncertainties, liabilities or vulnerabilities that may cause the project to deviate from the defined plan. Risk management is the competence to handle unexpected crises and deviation from the plan (Slevin and Pinto, 1996). The implementation of ERP system project is characterized as complex activity and involves a possibility of occurrence of unexpected events. Therefore, risk management is to minimize the impact of unplanned incidents in the project by identifying and addressing potential risks before significant consequences occur. It is understood that the risk of project failure is substantially reduced if the appropriate risk management strategy is followed.

Focused Performance Measure

Is a very important factor for ERP success and must be constructed to measure the achievements against project goals. The performance measure includes on time deliveries, usability, availability, gross profit margin, cost and saving measures, and user satisfaction, etc. Performance measure has been argued by researchers (Nah *et al.*, 2001; Akkermans and Helden, 2002; Umble *et al.*, 2003; Al Mashari *et al.*, 2003).

In order to ensure effective uptake and use of ERP following the implementation of a new system, the management and on-going evaluation of the system's performance are needed to ensure expected outcomes are achieved; and to enable effective measurement of the business efficiency and effectiveness improvement provided by the ERP (Ellis ,2005).

Quality Improvement Measures

Crucial points to take into consideration are the data accuracy, consistency, frequency of use, data redundancy, data relevancy, data cleansing, consolidation, transformation, validation (Caruso, 2007). (Xu *et al.*, 2002) identifies critical factors such as top management support, training, communication, employee relations, project teams, quality controls, and change management as crucial in achieving high ERP information quality. Researchers such as (Vosburg and Kumar, 2001; Madapusi and Kuo, 2007; Madapusi *et al.*, 2007) also focus on the importance of adopting a quality improvement measure as a critical factors for ERP implementation. Past research indicates that researchers focussed on identifying different dimensions of information quality. (Wand and Wang, 1996) used an 'internal' and 'external' view of data to identify information dimensions. (Wang and Strong, 1996) used a 'fitness of use' of approach to postulate four information dimensions—internal, contextual, representational, and accessible. (Ballou *et al.*, 1998) used an information product approach to identifying information quality dimensions.

Organizational /Corporate Culture

Open, supportive, and learning organizational culture encourages involvement/participation, adaptation leads top management to learn, to accept, to adapt to the new, and help them more likely convince and persuade the rest of the organization. It helps ERP cross-functioanal team members understand, appreciate the different strengths, skills that each member brings to the teams encourages increased interaction and improved communication throughout the organization (Nah, Islam and Tan, 2007). Corporate Culture is a combination of two things: the type of people who are employed by a company, their personal values, skills, habits etc and the way the organization works, the focus, decision making process, attitude to staff, stability, etc. Both feed off one another. To successfully take on an ERP system, an organization needs to change its 'Corporate Culture'. It may need to change from being highly flexible and not paying a lot of attention to consistency or accuracy, to one of being almost obsessed with detail, of being prepared to have business practices that are actually adhered to rather than just being documented and forgotten. People need to change from focusing on turnover to focusing on profit. Staff needs to change their focus from their own job, to the whole organization. What they do in their area has impacts in places they may never have envisaged. None of this is easy, and in many cases will be un-achievable. Some people will not be prepared to make the change and will either leave of their own volition or be asked to leave. This is the cost of ERP. Another dimension to 'Cultural Change' is the timeframe in which the change is to be made (Wang, 2001). ERP potential cannot be leveraged without strong ordination of time, effort and goals across business and IT personnel (Toni and Nelson 2001). This category could effectively be considered a subcategory of change management; however, given the number of citations that dealt specifically with the issue of cultural change, it was decided to consider it as a separate CSF. (Davison, 2002) suggests that there is a critical need to be consciously aware of the cultural differences and preferences from both organizational and geographical perspectives. Therefore, it is necessary to understand the business characteristics (Tarafdar and Roy, 2003) and the need for a culture that is conducive to change (Nah *et al.*, 2001).

Adoption costs from the perspectives of all stakeholders must be reduced as much as possible (Aladwani, 2001). Finally, consideration must be given to the identification and usage of strategies that are necessary to implement cultural change (Skok and Legge, 2002).

Implementation Cost

It is important to know up front exactly what the implementation costs will be and dedicate the necessary monies (Trimmer *et al.*, 2002; Bingi *et al.*, 1999; Somers and Nelson, 2001 and 2004). However, the nature of ERP implementations are such that there are usually unforeseen and unexpected occurrences that increase the overall costs (Holland and Light, 1999; Al-Mudimigh *et al.*, 2001). Therefore, a loose budget policy is recommended (Ribbers and Schoo, 2002). Empirical studies also indicate that both ERP vendors and ERP clients are starting to team up to identify, model, and evaluate cost factors contributing to the ERP return-on-investment equation (Davenport, 2000). Costs with ERP implementation include not only software, but also items such as training, hardware, and consulting (Willis *et al.*, 2001). The lack of a formal budget at some companies left them without the ability to compare actual versus budgeted costs, as described in the literature (Hong and Kim, 2002; Mabert *et al.*, 2003*b*).

Software Development, Testing, Trouble Shooting and Crises Management

Scott and Vesey (2001) have emphasized the need to be flexible in ERP implementations and to learn from unforeseen circumstances. Similarly, (Mandal and Gunasekaran, 2003) echoed the need to prepare to handle unexpected crises situations. The need for troubleshooting skills will be an ongoing requirement of the implementation process (Al-Mashari *et al.*, 2003; Holland and Light, 1999; Nah *et al.*, 2001). During the final stages of the implementation process, the project team should consider the inclusion of testing exercises (Kumar *et al.*, 2002; Nah *et al.*, 2001; Al-Mashari *et al.*, 2003) as well as simulation exercises before the system 'goes live' (Yusuf *et al.*, 2004).

IT Infrastructure

It is critical to assess the IT readiness of the organization, including the architecture and skills (Tarafdar and Roy, 2003; Somers and Nelson, 2001; Somers and Nelson, 2004; Bajwa *et al.*, 2004; Siriginidi, 2000*a, b*). If necessary, infrastructure might need to be upgraded or revamped (Kumar *et al.*, 2002; Palaniswamy and Frank, 2002). Al-Mashari (2002) Yasser (2000) argued that adequate IT infrastructure, hardware and networking are crucial for an ERP system's success. It is clear that ERP implementation involves a complex transition from legacy information systems and business processes to an integrated IT infrastructure and common business process throughout the organization. Hardware selection is driven by the firm's choice of an ERP software package. The ERP software vendor generally certifies which hardware (and hardware configurations) must be used to run the ERP system. This factor has been considered critical by the practitioners and as well as by the researchers.

Selection of ERP Package

Ensuring software fit, A systematic requirements assessment is a must. Make use of knowledgeable outside consultants for the assessment, if there is a lack of internal knowledge of ERP systems (Muscatello and Chen, 2008).

The choice of the package involves important decisions regarding budgets, timeframes, goals, and deliverables that will shape the entire project. Choosing the right ERP packaged software is critical to ensure minimal modification, successful implementation and use (Toni and Nelson 2001). The selection of the specific ERP package is one that requires careful attention (Kraemmergaard and Rose, 2002; Yusuf *et al.*, 2004; Al-Mashari *et al.*, 2003; Somers and Nelson, 2001 and 2004). It is also necessary to keep in mind that the system must match the business processes (Chen, 2001).

Data Conversion and Integrity

A fundamental requirement for the effectiveness of ERP systems is the availability and timeliness of accurate data. Data problems can cause serious implementation delays, and as such, the management of data entering the ERP system represents a critical issue throughout the implementation process (Toni and Nelson, 2001). There are different names of master data quality, but the meaning is rather similar. For example, (Somers and Nelson, 2001) used data analysis and conversion, (Zhang *et al.*, 2002 and 2005) used data accuracy, which means data loaded from existing legacy systems or documents must be of high quality. Timely and accurate data in a single consistent format is thought a fundamental requirement for the effectiveness of ERP system implementation. This factor has been considered critical by researchers (Shanks *et al.*, 2000; Somers and Nelson, 2001 and 2004; Umble *et al.*, 2003; Zhang *et al.*, 2002 and 2005; Jiang, 2005; Yusuf *et al.*, 2006). Much of the success of the implementation process and ultimately the success of the system relies on the ability of the team to ensure data accuracy during the conversion process (Umble *et al.*, 2003; Bajwa *et al.*, 2004; Somers and Nelson, 2001 and 2004; Xu *et al.*, 2002). This stage of the implementation might also involve the cleaning up of suspect data (Yusuf *et al.*, 2004).

Legacy System Consideration

The existing business and legacy systems determine the IT and organizational change required for success (Dawson and Owens, 2008). Another challenge is internal staff adequacy, software and hardware expertise should be gained. ERP systems selection based on the current technology and business process may be a mistake since it is very limiting (Muscatello and Chen, 2008). Awareness of the amount of process and technology change, the degree of difficulty in getting users to modify behaviour and ultimately the cultural change required to fully tap the potential of the software's tools and processes(Caruso, 2007). Legacy system sum up the existing business processes, organization structure, culture and information technology, therefore, they cannot be controlled by a company in the same way as the other variables (Holland and Light, 1999). Legacy system determines the amount of organization change that will be required for successful ERP system implementation and it will also dictate the starting point for the implementation (Holland and Light, 1999). Evaluating the existing legacy system, organization should be able to define the nature and scale problems that might be likely to meet during implementation (Holland and Light, 1999). There must also be consideration of the current legacy system in place as this will be a good indicator of the nature and scale of potential problems. This could directly affect the technical and organizational change required (Nah *et al.*, 2001; Al-Mudimigh *et al.*, 2001; Al-Mashari *et al.*, 2003; Holland and Light, 1999). Whether or not there is a reasonably well working manual system in place is another consideration (Siriginidi, 2000b).

Vanilla ERP

A minimum customization and an uncomplicated implementation strategy change in the business to fit the software with minimal customization. Purchase the package that fits best into its business processes (Dawson and Owens, 2008). The concept of vanilla ERP means that organizations should be committed to the idea of implementing the 'vanilla' version of an ERP. This is the basic version with no or minimal customization (Siriginidi, 2000*a*, *b*; Somers and Nelson, 2001 and 2004; Nah *et al.*, 2001, Palaniswamy and Frank, 2002, Mabert *et al.*, 2003, Shanks and Parr, 2000).

System Documentation

This is important so that the creation of the documentation can be seen as part of the implementation process and so that the two teams can share resources as necessary. Well-designed and well-built documentation can save company time and money on support costs after the ERP system is in place. It is important to create the entire set of documentation (Holland and Light, 1999; Nah *et al.*, 2001; Kuruppuarachchi *et al.*, 2002; Umble *et al.*, 2003).

Project Team

A cross-functional flexible team consisting of the best people in the organization which will deal with the problems as they arise in the implementation process. A mix of consultants and internal staff so the internal staff can develop the necessary technical skills for design and implementation. Managers should be assigned full time to the implementation. Partnerships should be managed with meetings scheduled regularly (Dawson and Owens, 2008). Involvement of potential users in the main stages of the ERP implementaion (Bueno, 2008). The ERP team should involve of the best people in the organization (Loh and Koh 2004;Al-Mashari *et al.,* 2006).The success of projects is related to the knowledge, skills, abilities, and experiences of the project manager as well as the selection of the right team members. Also, team should not only be technologically competent but also understand the company and its business requirements (Remus 2006). The ERP team should consist of the best people in the organization (Buckhout *et al.,* 1999; Bingi *et al.,* 1999; Rosario, 2000; Wee, 2000). Building a cross-functional team is also critical. Both business and technical knowledge are essential for success (Bingi *et al.,* 1999; Sumner, 1999). (Wee, 2000) stressed that the ERP project should be the top and only priority to the ERP team and their workload should be manageable. He also asserted that the team should be co-located together at an assigned location to facilitate working together is important for ERP project. An ERP project involves all of the functional departments and demands the effort and cooperation of technical and business experts as well as end users. The team should be balanced or cross functional and usually comprise a mix of internal staffs and external experts. The internal staff can learn the necessary knowledge and skills for ERP system from external consultants (Bhatti, 2005). ERP teamwork and composition has been considered as one of the important factors and discussed by different researchers (Shanks *et al.,* 2000; Nah *et al.,* 2001; Umble *et al.,* 2003; Somers and Nelson, 2001 and 2004; Nah and Delgado, 2006). Especially, (Nah *et al.,* 2001) have ranked this factor as the No. 1 position among their CSFs list.

Implementation Strategy and Timeframe

Several researchers iterated the need to address the implementation strategy and to, specifically, implement the ERP under a phased approach (Mandal and Gunasekaran, 2003; Scott and Vessey, 2000; Cliffe, 1999; Robey *et al.,* 2002; Gupta, 2000; Motwani *et al.,* 2002). Other researchers addressed the question of whether the implementation should be centralized versus decentralized (Siriginidi, 2000a, b). Finally, this concept also considers implications of multi-site issues (Umble *et al.,* 2003) and the benefits of introducing a Greenfield site (Siriginidi, 2000b). The ERP implementation strategy should be reviewed in this level to determine the impact of ERP system implementation on the enterprise. (Trepper, 1999) argues that the organization's executive managers must understand how ERP system implementation will impact on the organization to ensure a smooth transition.

(Davenport, 1998*a*) argues that the logic of an ERP system could conflict with the logic of the business, and either the implementation will fail, wasting large sums of money and causing a great deal of disruption, or the system will weaken important sources of competitive advantage, hobbling the company. Therefore, the company has to have a clear understanding of the business implications to avoid potential perils of failures. (Holland and Light, 1999) suggest that the propensity of an organization for change should influence the choice of ERP implementation project strategy. There are two main technical options to implement an ERP system: modify the ERP system package to suit an organization's requirements or the implementation of a standard package with minimum deviation from the standard settings. Companies that do not select the second option are liable to face major difficulties (Bancroft, 1998; Martin, 1998; Gibson *et al.*, 1999). This includes management decisions concerning how the software package is to be implemented (Holland *et al.*, 1999). There are different approaches to ERP implementation strategy ranging from 'skeleton' to 'big-bang' implementations (Gibson *et al.*, 1997). While 'skeleton' implementations are phased and provide usable functionality incrementally, 'big-bang' ones offer full functionality all at once at implementation end. The advantages and disadvantages of these extreme approaches should be measured, especially at a functionality level.

Consultant Selection

While they may seem expensive (Brown, 2001), external consultants possess a great deal of specialized knowledge about the ERP system (Welti, 1999). They also bring along a lot of implementation experience. Therefore, having good external consultants on the project team can help solve technical problems quickly, resulting in shortened implementation time and higher quality (Somers and Nelson, 2001). They are important for ERP implementation. These experts and consultants are normally from ERP vendors and ERP consulting companies. They are experienced and important for a company to implement the ERP system during the whole ERP implementation process and after the implementation phase. This factor has been discussed as one of the factors which impacted the ERP implementation success by researchers (Bingi *et al.*, 1999; Parr and Shanks, 2000; ZhouSivunen, 2005; Yusuf *et al.*, 2006).

Vendor/Customer Relationship

Many researchers have advocated the need to include an ERP consultant as part of the implementation team (Trimmer *et al.*, 2002; Bajwa *et al.*, 2004; Kraemmergaard and Rose, 2002; Al-Mudimigh *et al.*, 2001; Bingi *et al.*, 1999; Skok and Legge, 2002; Kalling, 2003; Willcocks and Stykes, 2000; Motwani *et al.*, 2002).

However, as part of this relationship, it is imperative to arrange for knowledge transfer from the consultant to the company (Al-Mashari *et al.*, 2003) so as to decrease the dependency on the vendor/consultant (Skok and Legge, 2002). Therefore, the ERP phenomenon is driven by both software vendors and adopting organizations. ERP systems could not be a solution to an adopting organization's problems, if it were not addressed properly by the software companies selling ERP systems (Oliver and Romm, 2000).

Project Management

Establishment of the scope of the ERP implementation project, determining the involvement of business units, the amount of project reengineering, definition of milestones, critical paths, deadlines within the schedule and budget is necessory (Dawson and Owens, 2008). Defining the change control procedures and holding everyone to them (Muscatello and Chen, 2008). Establishment of a disciplined Programme Mangement Office (PMO) which will create business value within IT and concern not only with deadlines and plans but also with strategic alignment, or achieving tangible business improvement (Caruso, 2007). ERP systems implementation is a set of complex activities thus organizations should have an effective project management strategy to control the implementation process (Zhang *et al.*, 2002). Project management activities span from the first stage of the ERP life cycle to losing it. Project planning and control is a function of the project's characteristics such as project size, experiences with the technology, and project structure (Somers and Nelson, 2004). Involves the use of skill and knowledge in coordinating the scheduling and monitoring of defined activities in order to achieve the stated objectives of implementation projects. The formal project implementation plan defines project activities, commits personnel to those activities, and promotes organizational support by organizing the implementation process (Bhatti, 2005). Therefore, a detailed project plan related to project goals and objectives must be defined. Project management has been thought as one of the important factors by many researchers (Somers and Nelson, 2001 and 2004; Nah *et al.*, 2001; Al Mashari *et al.*, 2003; Umble *et al.*, 2003; Nah and Delgado, 2006; Jiang, 2005; Zhang *et al.*, 2002 and 2005; Woo, 2007).

Client Consultations

Al-Mashari *et al.*, (2003); Al Mudimigh *et al.*, (2001) mention the need for communication and consultation with various key stakeholders, but in particular with the client. Organizations need to keep its clients apprised of its projects to avoid misconceptions (Al-Mudimigh *et al.*, 2001). Holland and Light (1999); Mandal and Gunasekaran (2003) also support this CSF. Slevin and Pinto (1987) define client consultation as the communication and consultation with, and active listening to all affected parties, mainly the client. It is essential for an organization to keep its clients aware of its future project to avoid misconception. Slevin and Pinto (1987) argued that the consultation with clients should occur early in the process; otherwise the chance of subsequent client acceptance will be lowered. In general, this factor has not been thoroughly discussed in the literature reviewed.

User Involvement

User involvement is one of the most cited critical success factors in ERP implementation projects. User involvement increase user satisfaction and acceptance by developing realistic expectations about system capabilities (Esteves *et al.,* 2003). User involvement is essential because it improves perceived control through participating in the whole project plan.

According to Zhang *el at.,* (2002) there are two areas for user involvement when the company decides to implement an ERP system: user involvement in the stage of definition of the organization's ERP system needs, and user participates in the implementation of ERP systems. If the employees who are not on the project team are excluded from the entire ERP implementation process, they may resist or fear the new system (Mendel, 1999). On the other hand, involved users are not only more motivated to adopt the new system, but they can also help identify and resolve potential issues early, thereby improving implementation quality (Brown, 2001). As they try out the system, user expectations can be better gauged and met during implementation.

User Education and Training

Sufficient and timely training for fundamental ERP systems, education, technical training in the usage of the ERP software in international cases additional cultural and language training are critical for ERP (Muscatello and Chen, 2008). Managers must be proactive in securing the technology training to insure that their technical employees can run the ERP system effectively. Educating and training users to use ERP is important because ERP is not easy to use even with good IT skills (Woo, 2007). Nah *et al.,* (2003) argued that sufficient training can assist increase success for ERP systems. However, lack of training may lead to failure. According to Zhang *et al.,* (2002) the main reason for education and training is to increase the expertise and knowledge level of the users within the company. User training should be emphasized, with heavy investment in training and re-skilling of developers in software design and methodology (Sumner, 1999). However, education and training are frequently underestimated and are given less time due to schedule pressures, and less understanding of cross-functional business process is often reported. The author found in the studies that some of the managers are not totally aware what exactly ERP is, what it can bring and how to do it. More seriously, some of the managers might not even realize the high costs, risks, and the relevant changes and conflicts to implement the ERP system. This causes the incapable support from the management. Successful ERP implementation depends on successful training (McAlary, 1999). Training teaches new skills, which makes employees feel more confident and more enthusiastic about the possibilities with the new system (Plotkin, 1999). Appropriate timing for training varies by company. The key is to balance the needs of current work and the new system (O'Leary, 2000). Like user involvement, training helps to improve quality of ERP project results and to meet user expectations. It include technical knowledge of ERP system, its reference models, knowledge of ERP operation and use for IT and business people (Shanks *et al.,* 2000). In ERP implementation process many projects fail in the end due to lack of proper training. Many researchers have considered user training and education to be an important factor of the successful ERP implementation (Bingi *et al.,* 1999; Somers and Nelson, 2001 and 2004; AlMashari *et al.,* 2003; Umble *et al.,* 2003; Jiang, 2005; Zhang *et al.,* 2002 and 2005; ZhouSivunen, 2005; Yusuf *et al.,* 2006; Woo, 2007). The main reason of user training and education for ERP implementation is to make the user comfortable with the system and improve knowledge level of the people. ERP related concept, features of ERP system, and hands on training are all important for ERP implementation. Training is not only using the new system, but also in new processes and in understanding the integration within the system, how the work of one employee influences the work of others (Bhatti, 2005).

Personnel/Staff

Taking into account the new organizational, interdepartmental, and personnel aspects of work organizations managers must considerd the skill development needed by employees. Sufficient training and education of current employees or hiring of outside consulting also help (Muscatello and Chen, 2008) .The personnel resource has been discussed as one of the factors which impact the success of ERP implementation. However, this issue hasn't got enough prior attention; Lack of such resources often emerges as an important issue (Soh *et al.,* 2000). Individuals in the organization should have domain relevant skills (task knowledge), creativity-relevant skills (cognitive abilities), and task motivation (intrinsic and extrinsic) in order to achieve the creativity to contribute to the successful implementation of ERP system (Hong and Kim, 2002). Lack of personnel resources has become a serious problem in ERP implementation. A typical ERP project requires many internal personnel resources for the project completion (Soh *et al.,* 2000).

Employee Attitude and Morale

This CSF is related to the need for the project manager/champion to nurture and maintain a high level of employee morale and motivation during the project (Trimmer *et al.*, 2002; Willcocks and Stykes, 2000; Bingi *et al.*, 1999). It is imperative that the team leader creates a stimulating work environment (Mandal and Gunasekaran, 2003) and recognizes the work of the members (Barker and Frolick, 2003). Ultimately, this should result in a high level of staff retention (Skok and Legge, 2002). The possibility of losing staff because of their marketability externally is a very real, but often overlooked, cause of project failure.

Empowered Decision Makers

While not widely cited, this CSF deserves special consideration because it is felt to be a factor that might be overlooked if included within another category. This concept refers to the need for the team to be empowered to make necessary decisions (Shanks and Parr, 2000; Chen, 2001) in due time, so as to allow for effective timing with respect to the implementation (Gupta, 2000).

CRITICAL FAILURE FACTORS (CFFs) OF LARGE ENTERPRISES (LEs)

ERP implementations have been found to be difficult projects to undertake and success is not assured (Goodhue and Haines, 2000). The ways to fail an ERP implementation outnumbers the ways to succeed it, claims (Martin, 1998). A number of papers in academic journals and newspaper articles report on ERP implementation projects failures with negative economic impacts on the organizations that implemented the systems (Stedman 1999a; Levinson 2001; Fitzsimmons, 2002). A survey of one hundred executives of leading organizations found that only one in three ERP initiatives was considered a success .As ERP implementation failure rates are so high and the consequent impacts are so detrimental to business, there is a compelling reason for opening the 'black box' to investigate the factors causing failure. Previous research has focused on IS implementation for the definition of IS failure (Lyytinen, 1988). However, the majority of studies have failed to take into account the richness of the ERP failure phenomenon. In this study an investigations conducted for ERP failure from the perspectives of CFFs involved in ERP implementation at Indian SMEs. Critical Failure Factors (CFFs) as the key aspects (areas) where things must go wrong in order for the ERP implementation process to achieve a high level of failure.

Thorough literature reviews had been done to identify CFFs for ERP failure in the large enterprise. Following is the list of 14 Critical Failure Factors (CFFs) had been identified by the (Wong *et al.*, 2005) for the failure of ERP Implementation in the Large Enterprise (LEs). Along with this list few more CFFs were also identified and used as a theoretical framework, to identify and rank the critical failure factors for the failure of ERP implementation at Indian SMEs.

Poor Consultant Effectiveness

In study of few LEs ERP Implementation consultant ineffectiveness was one of the major CFF. Wong *et al.*, (2005) had found that consultants were considered by their project team members to be inexperienced with ERP systems and unable to provide a professional level of advice on EPR project planning. Consultants communicated ineffectively during the project phase due to language barriers, and they copied the ERP configuration directly from the branch office and only suggested workarounds without applying professional skills to conduct BPR to bridge the gap between ERP systems and business processes. A detailed test plan and guidelines were not suggested to the project team. The consultants delivered poor quality of training (very brief and like a pre-sales demonstration), conducted BPR to a poor quality and delivered poor quality management reports due to insufficient industrial experience. Consultants spent only two days on training the project team and configuring the ERP systems. They did not provide any consulting service on BPR, project management, or ERP implementation. The project team commented that the service was insufficient and unprofessional. The consultants were inexperienced in using the ERP system, they followed their formal implementation methodology during only the first two months, and BPR was poorly conducted as they were not satisfied with the consulting fee received from the project. Also, the user requirement analysis document produced was too wordy (all business process flow charts for clarifying how to conduct BPR were absent) and the training material (prepared by the consultants) was found to be too brief and unhelpful (Wong *et al.*, 2005).

Poor Quality of BPR

The project team members disclosed that they had an unclear vision of why or how to conduct BPR, and their consultants provided unprofessional advice for conducting BPR. They commented that the consultants provided lots of workarounds to resolve problems associated with business process mismatch. Project team members found it difficult to collaborate and contribute to BPR, and the poor quality of BPR led to incorrect system configuration problems. Business processes were not successfully re-engineered to fit with the ERP systems, and the project teams were unready for the adaptation of new business processes and they did not have the mind-set for implementing or using the ERP system. Moreover, during the BPR process, consultants did not conduct mapping analysis to map the software functionalities with business requirements, and this led to a mismatch between ERP and business processes. Users and the business process were not ready for ERP implementation, and thus, the ERP system could not provide support for business. Their ERP vendor adopted a customization strategy and provided a two-day consulting service (all BPR expertise, ERP implementation process and testing advice were absent), it took more than eighteen months for vendors to complete the customization programming (mapping the ERP functions with the business processes). The project team mentioned that mapping analysis was conducted in a rush. The high level business process flow diagram was missing, and thus, project team members and users were unsure of how to re-engineer the business process to fit with the ERP system. The wordy BPR documents which were free from diagrams were insufficient for the project team to understand how to reengineer the business process for a better adaptation to the new business process and ERP system usage (Wong *et al.*, 2005).

Poor Project Management Effectiveness

Due to limited ERP knowledge, capability and poor project management skills, none of the companies' project managers could exercise effective project management of ERP implementation. They agreed that a failure to plan, lead, manage and monitor the project was a core factor that resulted in their implementation failure, because the ERP system was complex, and project teams were required to collaborate with top management, different departments, users and consultants during implementation process. The ERP project was considered by the project managers to be challenging and demanding, as it involved managing systems, people (project team, users and external consultant) as well as re-designing business processes. The over-tight and unrealistic project time schedule and insufficient human resource exhausted the project team members and users in coping with the ERP implementation. Activities of the different phases could not be conducted thoroughly (e.g., systems configuration and testing were conducted in a rush). Users could not understand the new system or adapt to the new business process within the over-tight schedule. None of the project managers in these studies were able to exercise effective project management control, especially in managing consultants, and reporting implementation problems to top management whenever necessary. It is important for the project manager to effectively manage the consultants, for example, in evaluating their communication and training performance, when conducting BPR, and when testing system performance. Indeed, in this study, most of the companies' project team members lacked ERP experience (including top management, the project manager, middle level management and operational staff). However the external consultants were not able to provide professional advice and so led a failed implementation. Top management and project managers need to ensure sufficient knowledge and expertise for ERP implementation before the start of ERP implementation (Wong *et al.,* 2005).

ERP Software Misfit

Due to poor ERP selection and evaluation process, ERP software was found to be ill-fitting with the business requirements. For example, the ERP was inefficiently managing a high volume of product master files, and unable to design complicated bills of materials and production planning formulation. Research results indicate the ERP system was utilized in a very limited way due to the problem of misfit. Project teams relied on heavy customization (for example, changing the system program, or writing many management reports, or conducting data transfer as workarounds) to solve problems (Wong *et al.,* 2005).

High Turnover Rate of Project Team Members

As project team members suffered from high work stress and tremendous workload when coping with the implementation, some members resigned from their jobs. This contributed to the insufficient ERP knowledge and skill transfer among project team members during the ERP implementation life cycle. In the end, users and project team members had insufficient ERP knowledge for performing their daily tasks when using the ERP system (Wong *et al.,* 2005).

Over-Reliance on Heavy Customization

Due to software mismatch, heavy customization was required in the areas of program customization and report customization. Customization could cause project delays, overspent budget and an unreliable system (due to poor quality of customization, unresolved system bugs and insufficient testing). Customizing the ERP to fit with business processes might lead to sacrificing 'best practices' embedded in the ERP system (Wong *et al.,* 2005).

Poor IT Infrastructure

Due to top management's insufficient financial resource provided for the implementation budget, a low performance IT infrastructure hardware was proposed by the consultants and project manager so as to reduce the costs of ERP implementation. The poor IT infrastructure contributed to the slow processing capability of the ERP system (Wong *et al.,* 2005).

Poor Knowledge Transfer

Consultants were found to be inexperienced in the use of the ERP system (as they tried to practice during training sessions), and they could not deliver professional ERP training to the users. Their training material and user documentation were found to be too brief and unhelpful by the users. Project team members mentioned that the knowledge transfer process was ineffective, the project team members and project manager could not acquire sufficient knowledge or skills to use, maintain and support the ERP system. (Wong *et al.*, 2005).

Unclear Concept of the Nature and Use of the ERP System from the Users' Perspective

Due to the poor quality of training provided by the consultants and insufficient education delivered by the top management and project team, users were not given a clear idea of the nature and use of the ERP system. They did not understand the rationale for implementing the ERP system or the process of implementation. Thus, they were not prepared for the implementation, and had high resistance to change, which led to political problems, poor quality of BPR and a resistance to using the system. (Wong *et al.*, 2005).

Unrealistic Expectations from Top Management Concerning the ERP Systems

Top management assumed that ERP implementation could provide great solutions without considering the complexity of the ERP system, the possible implementation process complications and the associated risks. This gave the whole project team and users unrealistic expectations. This misconception also led to superficial project planning and an underestimation of budget and resource allocation, and resulted in a failure of ERP implementation from a project management perspective. (Wong *et al.*, 2005).

Too Tight Project Schedule

Top management and the project manager would like to reduce the budget of the ERP project, and thus they set too tight project schedule. Implementation activities were conducted in a rush (e.g., project planning, BPR, training, testing and so on) in order to meet the project deadline. The project team and users were overloaded and thus they might have had higher resistance to change. Some users were absent from training as they were too exhausted. It resulted in poor knowledge transfer. (Wong *et al.*, 2005).

Users' Resistance to Change

Due to a limited knowledge of formalized business processes and ERP systems, as well as work overload during the implementation process, users were resistant to change. This contributed to user resistance to participating in BPR, a lack of use of the ERP system, and poor quality of data entered into the system. (Wong *et al.*, 2005).

Poor Top Management Support

Top management is expected to provide support in the areas of committing to the ERP project, sufficient financial and human resource, and the resolution of political problems if necessary. Limited financial support contributed to a rushed ERP implementation process, project team members were overloaded and thus high staff turnover rate, ineffective knowledge transfer, and political problems occurred. Insufficient commitment could lead to political problems which hindered the implementation process (causing poor BPR, widespread user resistance to change and low user satisfaction) (Wong *et al.*, 2005).

Poor Quality of Testing

Due to the over-tight project schedule and insufficient knowledge in testing ERP systems, it was conducted in a rush and was of low quality. It was agreed by the project team that the ERP testing result was an indicator for revealing the readiness of the ERP system to 'go live' from the perspectives of examining IT infrastructure capacity, correct configuration of ERP system, people (including users and project team) were equipped with sufficient knowledge and skills, and data was of good quality. They mentioned that they should not expect that all problems could be resolved after the systems goes live, as problems had become more complicated than they had predicted. They pointed out that workload of project team members and users had increased tremendously in order to fix the problems and cope with daily operations (Wong *et al.*, 2005).

Other than above study few more critical failure factors of the LEs have been identified in the literature review were as below

Lack of Formal Communication

Previous studies (Mabert *et al.*, 2003b; Mandal and Gunasekaran, 2003, Nah and Delgado, 2006) suggested that stakeholders should be provided with a detailed implementation plan including target business objectives, and should be kept informed about project progress.

All of the successful cases appeared to place minimal or no effort towards formal communication, but no implementation challenges could be directly associated with that decision. What did seem to influence success was the ability to 'interact' (*i.e.* two-way) with staff to obtain input and feedback. Communication on the project's progress to staff is not as important as letting them know time frames of go live and dates that are needed for the project. Communicating with staff regarding their requirements is much more important (Soja, 2006).

Software Modifications

Achieving a proper fit between processes and software has been considered critical for ERP success (Fan *et al.*, (2000); Gattiker, (2002); Bendoly and Jacobs, (2004); Quiescenti *et al.*, (2006); Poba-Nzaou *et al.*, (2008). Soh *et al.*, (2000) Gattiker and Goodhue (2002), among others, stated that such fitting could be achieved by either modifying company chose to significantly modify their software. This was somewhat surprising because of the limited resources and IT skills available to the companies. Inevitably, companies faced additional challenges in testing and simply understanding how the software operated after the modifications. As stated by a team member, "Where we had those software problems of fixing one thing and unfixing another—we thought the two things were totally unrelated. We would not even have thought of testing it." It appears that company chose to adapt software to processes rather than *vice-versa* to avoid failures in processes that were considered either strategic or reliable before the implementation. The downside was that software integration and testing turned more difficult as staff lacked time and technical expertise, and external consultants often lacked business-specific knowledge. The only approach that would appear satisfactory would be gathering the internal team and consultants to test the software together rather than assigning this responsibility to a single party (Soja, 2006).

Informal Strategy

(Soja, 2006) found that 'linking with strategy' and 'implementation goals' were not significant factors. This seems to be opposed to findings from large organization studies (Stratman and Roth, 2002; Al-Mashari *et al.*, 2003; Umble *et al.*, 2003) that identified strategic visioning or planning as a CSF. Other authors have stressed the informal nature of business (Mintzberg *et al.*, 2003) and their lack of proactive planning (Gunasekaran *et al.*, 1996). Contrary to expectations, the business strategy was not formalized or communicated to the team. Project decisions were based on current business requirements and expected growth. This approach appeared to have a short-term focus (Soja, 2006).

Part-time Dedications

The literature suggests that the internal team should be dedicated to the project full-time, away from everyday operations (Shanks *et al.*, 2000; Mabert *et al.*, 2003b; Umble *et al.*, 2003). However, team members in the cases (including the project leader) were generally expected to carry on with functional tasks during the implementation. Moreover, that practice did not appear negatively associated to project success.

One of the explanations for this counter-intuitive finding might come from the 'hard-working' culture of the companies, as employees were expected to be flexible and take on additional responsibilities as needed. (Soja, 2006) similarly found that 'work time schedule' (i.e. time exclusively dedicated to the project) did not significantly influence success. "Due to the size of firm, it very clear that this project was over and above their regular duties and that we expected them to do whatever it takes, such as overtime and working weekends." (Soja, 2006)

Functionality Problems with the Systems

According to (Brown, 2002; Madden,2002; Moodie, 2002*b*) if proper functionality is not provide by the system after ERP implementation as excepted company had to take funding from other source that was aimed for other areas to support the implementation project. Staff reported that it was hard to get information. Staff had problems accessing information too.

Cost Overruns

It is expensive to take people out of normal positions and backfill with other staff—if this had not been budgeted for. Staff will not be happy with the benefits of the systems *vs.* the cost. (Lawnham, 2001) had also found that due to over budget because of unexpected costs staff was not happy with ERP implementation that resulted into ERP failure.

Chapter Summary

This chapter has provided an overview for the evolution of ERP system along with the introduction of ERP implementation phases. The significance of critical factors has been discussed through thorough literature review and survey items have been identified for research. A justification for the undertaking of various factors has been given. Finally, based on the review of CSFs and CFFs of the ERP implementation in LEs, the general concepts (survey items—CSFs and CFFs) for the success and failure of ERP Implementation at Indian SMEs were derived to use it as a theoretical framework in order to develop and test the conceptual ERP implementation research models. With these conceptual research models possible factors that can lead to the failure and success of ERP implementation at Indian SMEs may be explore and understand to some extent. Remaining part of literature review to form the strong theoretical framework along with the conceptual research models for this research was presented in the next chapter.

Early investigations of CSFs as Holland and Light (2003) were based on general case studies of the LEs. Later Nah *et al.,* (2001), Somers and Nelson (2001) and Al- Mashari *et al.,* (2003) investigated CSFs for the different phases of ERP. Implementation in the LEs While this research investigated CSFs for specific settings as *e.g.* Indian SMEs and All phases of ERP implementation.

This study covers 30 CSFs and 20 CFFs, which discussed implementation issues of ERP systems at Indian SMEs.

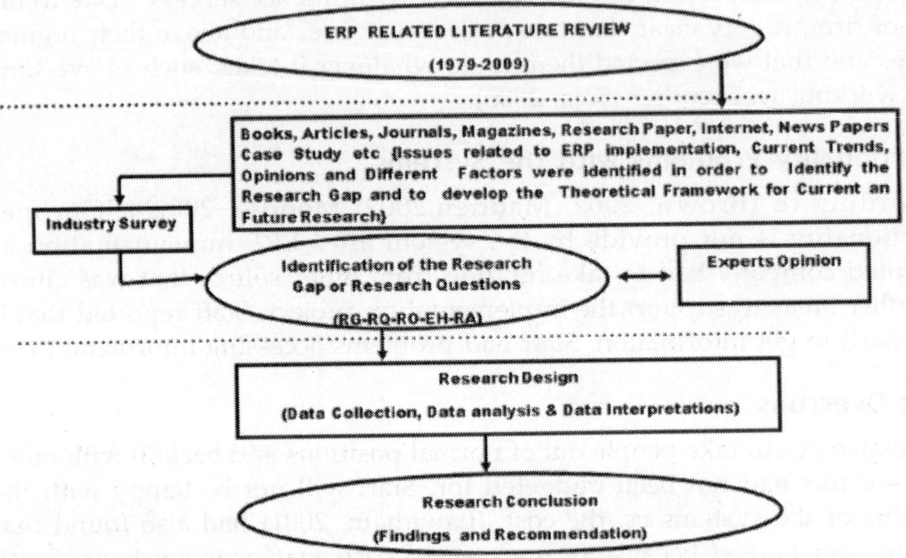

Fig. 2.1 : ERP Related Literature Review Process

(**Source:** Author, MS PowerPoint)

3 Theories and Research Models

"Somewhere, something incredible is waiting to be known, to steal ideas from one person is plagiarism; to steal ideas from many is research"

– Herzog, 1996

In order to research into the critical success and failure factors for the successful ERP implementation at Indian SMEs and to have a guidance framework to collect research data, a theoretical framework has been developed to aid the research process. This chapter introduces how the models have been arranged. The different factors that were addressed in the chosen models were already described in detail in literature review part (chapter two), a description of the use of the model was presented and finally a summary of the main points followed.

THEORETICAL FRAMEWORK

In order to develop a useful theoretical framework that can aid the data collection process and to assess specific success and failure factors for implementing an ERP system at Indian SMEs it was important to assess existing frameworks that have been used to classify ERP Implementation success and failure in the literature. Following section discussed the existing frameworks present in the literature and also examines the usefulness that these frameworks offer to the research questions that this book investigates.

Existing ERP Critical Success Factors Frameworks and Theories

Failures and success as discussed in Chapter Two—Literature Review, a number of ERP implementation projects have been reported as 'failed' because of reportedly substantial economical difficulties (Donovan 2000; Mearian 2000; Stedman 2000; Coffin and G. 2001). Within the ERP research field, a number of researchers have looked at ERP success and how to ensure ERP implementation success (Brown and Vessey 1999; Bonner 2000; Smyth 2001*a*). Following this, the field has focussed specifically on critical success factors in trade, research publications and a number of non-industry specific CSFs have been introduced as an aid to assist these failures and future ERP projects (Bingi *et al.*, 1999; Holland and Light 1999; Markus and Tanis 1999; Sumner 1999; Wee 1999; Robinson 2000; Trimble 2000; Al-Mudimigh *et al.*, 2001; Gable *et al.*, 2001*a*; Kuang *et al.*, 2001; Smyth 2001*b*; Gunasekaran *et al.*, 2002). Consequently, few of the newest CSFs established have focused on more specific issues, such as vendors related ERP system types (Clegg *et al.*, 2001; Esteves 2002) and country specific differences (Corbitt *et al.*, 2000). Recent publications have also focussed on measuring and attempting to predict the return of investment (ROI) that the ERP system will bring (Dinn 1999; Rosemann and Wiese 1999; Donovan 2000; Gable *et al.*, 2001b; Stensrud 2001; Sommer 2002).

Holland and Light's Critical Success Factors and Leavitt's System Model

Holland and Light's Model (1999) and Leavitt's System Model(1973) as shown in Figures 3.1 and 3.2 below, was taken as a base to create the new CSFs group(enterprise, technology, vendor and employee related CSFs) in conceptual ERP implementation success model. Holland and Light's Model (1999) was derived from Pinto and Slevin's (1987) earlier work on strategy and tactics. This model can be seen as important as it focuses on the actual organization, strategic, tactical, people and technology aspects that can exist in an ERP implementation process from a management perspective.

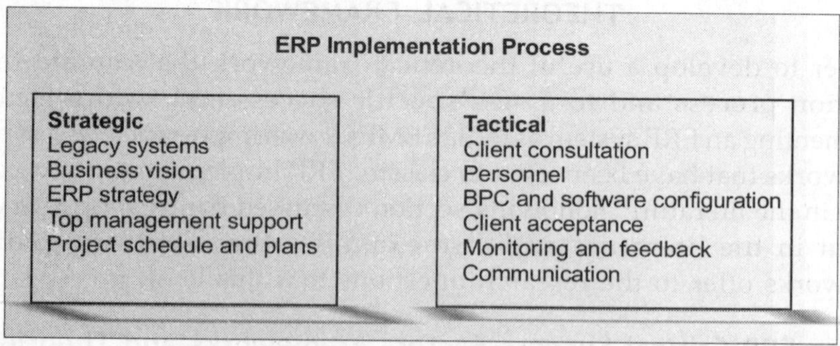

Fig. 3.1 : Critical Success Factor Model with Strategic and Tactical Factors
(**Source:** Holland and Light, 1999)

Leavitt *et al.*, (1973) proposed that change may focus on 1 of 4 subsystems in an organization:

- *Structure*—levels of hierarchy, spans of authority, centralization
- *Technology*—complexity, degree of employee usage, operator control and responsibility
- *People*—values, beliefs, attitudes, motives, drives, competencies
- *Task*—job design, repetitiveness, physical and cognitive demands, autonomy and discretion.

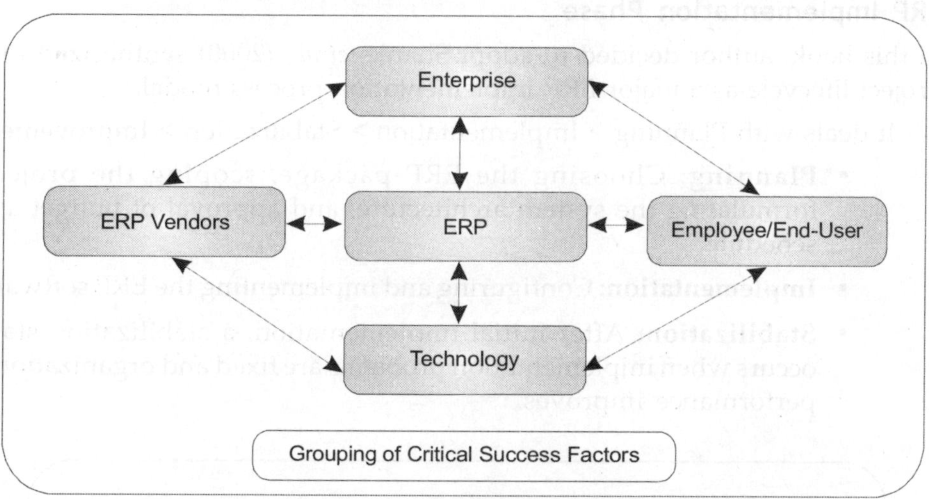

Fig. 3.2 : Grouping of CSFs, Based on Leavitt's System Model, 1973

Project Management Success Factors for ERP Implementation

What is considered a large project varies from one context to another depending on determinants including complexity, duration, budget and quality of the project? In ERP projects, the complexity depends on the project scope, including the number of business functions affected and the extent to which ERP implementation changes business processes. ERP projects achieving real transformation usually take from one to three years in duration. Resources required include hardware, software, and consulting, training and internal staff, with estimates of their cost ranging from $0.4 million to $300 million, with an average of about $15 million (Koch, 2002). Therefore, by viewing ERP implementation as a large project in general, CFs can adhere to the fundamentals of project management for achieving the success of ERP implementation. Several researchers have developed sets of fundamental project success factors which can significantly improve project implementation chances (Pinto and Slevin 1987; Shenhar *et al.*, 2002). In addition, several researchers have identified the best practices and risks related to IS projects such as ERP implementation. (Akkermans *et al.*, 2002) provided success factors for ERP implementation based on a broad literature review followed by a rating of the factors by 52 senior managers from the U.S. firms that had completed ERP implementations. (Ewusi-Mensan, 1997) identified reasons why companies abandon IS projects based on surveys of canceled projects in fortune 500 companies in the U.S. (Keil, 1998) proposed significant software project risks based on a Delphi study of experienced software-project managers in Hong Kong, Finland, and the U.S.

ERP Implementation Phase

In this book, author decided to adopt Shanks *et al.*, (2000) synthesized ERP project lifecycle as a major ERP implementation process model.

It deals with Planning > Implementation > Stabilization > Improvement

- **Planning**: Choosing the ERP package, scoping the project, formulating the system architecture, and approval of budget and schedule.
- **Implementation:** Configuring and implementing the ERP software.
- **Stabilization:** After initial implementation, a stabilization stage occurs when implementation problems are fixed and organizational performance improves.

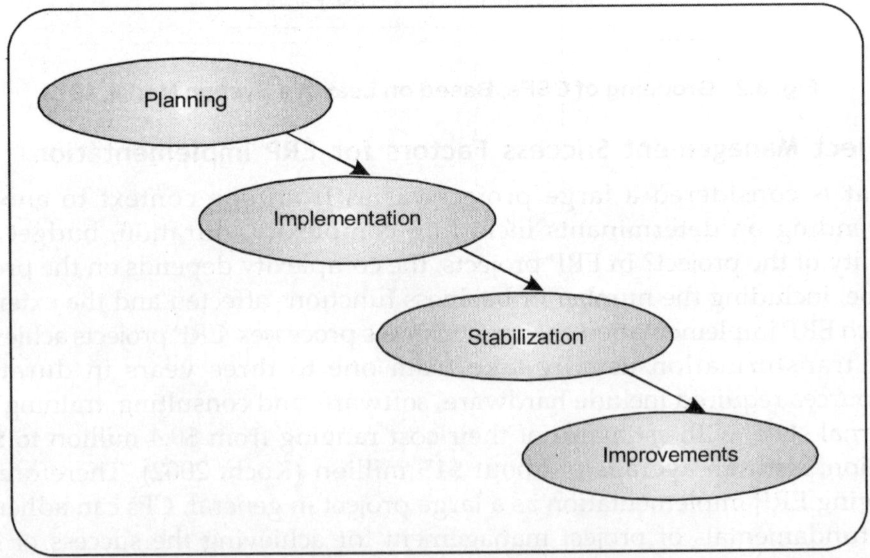

Fig. 3.3: Synthesized Process Model for ERP Implementation Phases

(Source: Shanks *et al.*, 2000)

- **Improvement**: Achieving the benefits, updating new modules, focussing on continuous improvement and transformation.

Shanks *et al.*, (2000) notes that success is mainly concerned with completion of the ERP project on time and within budget for acceptable standards in the first two phases (Planning and implementation phases) of ERP process model. Furthermore, success is more concerned with the perceived contribution of the system to organizational performance in the last two phases (stabilization and improvement phases) of ERP process model.

ERP Success Measurement Model

(Ifinedo, 2006) proposed an extended ERP system success measurement model to include Workgroup Impact (WI) not included in the Gable *et al.*, model. The author argues that any ERP success measurement model should include a dimension related to WI because ERP systems are often adopted to enhance efficient cross-functional operations .Here, "workgroup" refers to the sub-units and/or functional departments of an organization. A version of the extended ERP success measurement model proposed by (Ifinedo, 2006) is illustrated in Figure 3.4.

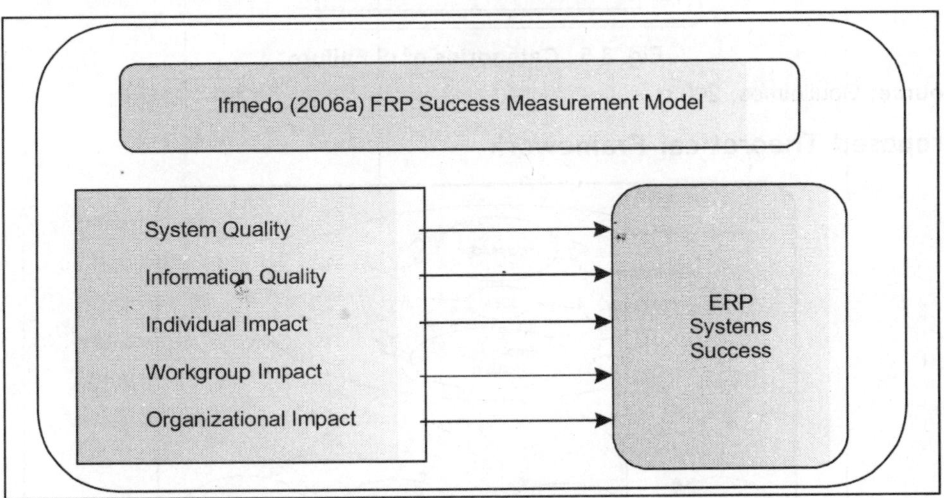

Fig. 3.4 : ERP Success Measurement Model

Source: Ifinedo, 2006

Categories of IS Failure

The author believes that it would be unjust to create an absolute definition of failure. It is more plausible to have a number of degrees of failures. A number of authors define four major categories of IS failure (Lyytinen and Hirschheim, 1987; Yeo, 2002; Goulielmos, 2003).

Table 3.1: Categories of IS Failure

Category of Failure		Description of Failure
1.	Correspondence failure	The IS fails to meet its design objectives
2.	Process failure	The IS overruns it's budget or time constraints
3.	Interaction failure	The users maintain low or non-interaction with the IS
4.	Expectation failure	The IS does not meet stakeholders' expectations

Source: Goulielmos, 2003

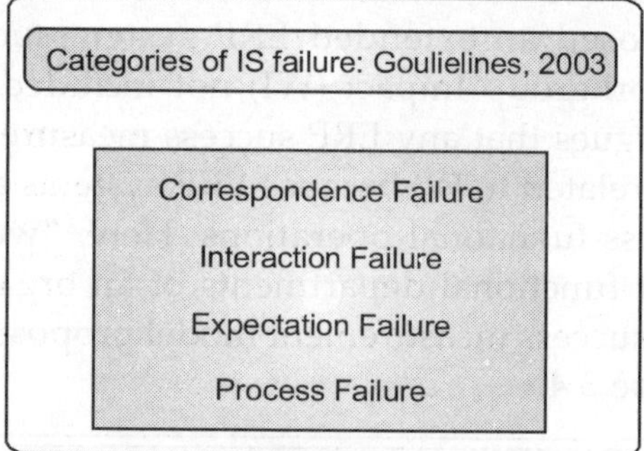

Fig. 3.5 : Categories of IS Failure

Source: Goulielmos, 2003

Proposed Theoretical Framework

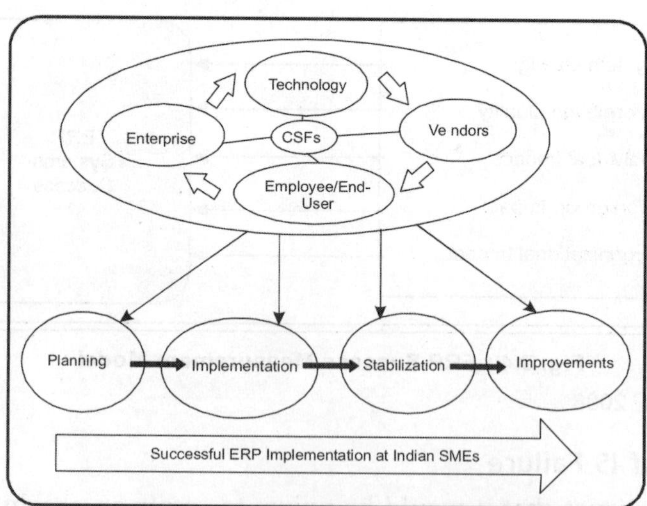

Fig. 3.6: Proposed Theoretical Framework for Successful ERP Implementation at Indian SMEs

Source: Author, MS PowerPoint

The theoretical framework (Figure 3.6) is represented by four main sets of factors, namely enterprise related factors, technology related factors, vendor related factors and employee/end user related factors. No attempts have been made in the academic literature to link any soft critical success factors to the various ERP implementation related phases together for the successful ERP implementation at Indian SMEs. A theoretical implementation process was identified by (Ibrahim, 2007) such that it is suggested that there is an explicit linkage between factors and ERP implementation phases. Figure 3.6, 3.7 and 3.8 shows the proposed theoretical framework for ERP implementation at Indian SMEs.

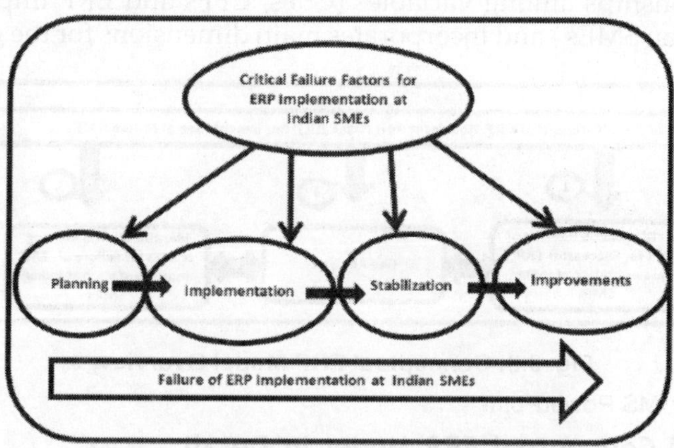

Fig. 3.7: Proposed Theoretical Framework for Failure of ERP Implementation at Indian SMEs

Source: Author, MS PowerPoint

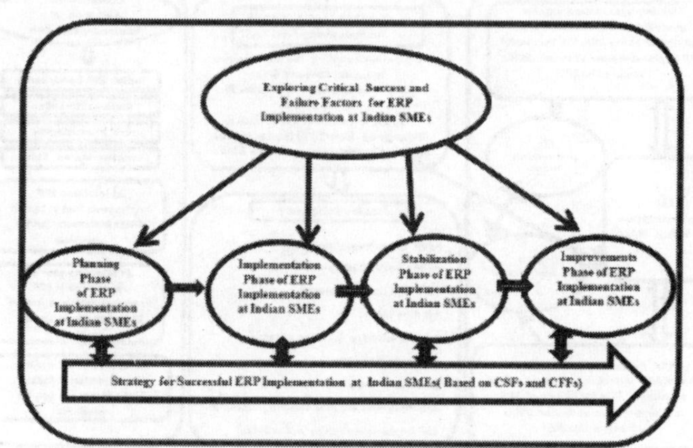

Fig. 3.8: Proposed Theoretical Framework for ERP Implementation at Indian SMEs

Source: Author, MS PowerPoint

CONCEPTUAL ERP MODEL FOR ERP IMPLEMENTATION AT INDIAN SMEs

Figure 3.9 and 3.10 shows the proposed ERP model, referred to as the conceptual ERP Model. As discussed in the previous sections, the success and failure of ERP systems can be classified into two categories; the success and failure of ERP adoption and the success and failure of ERP implementation. For the successful ERP Implementation this research uses already proven models for ERP success such as ERP success measurement model and categories of IS failure model for ERP implementation failure. Based on these combined theoretical backgrounds the models hypothesizes the rationale for the relationships among variables (CSFs, CFFs and ERP implementation phases at Indian SMEs) and incorporates main dimensions for the gap analysis.

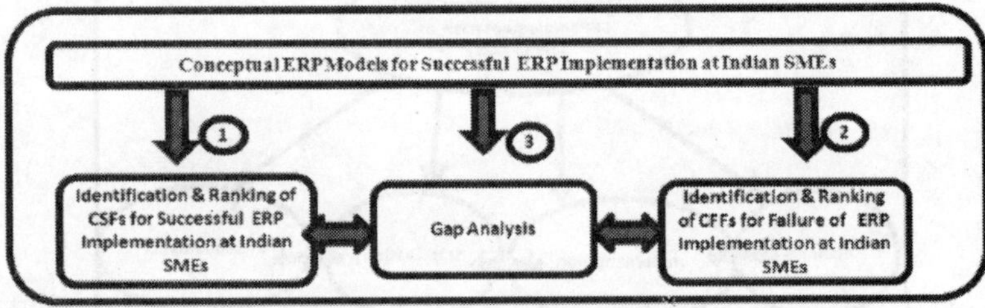

Fig. 3.9: Conceptual ERP Model Overview

Source: Author, MS PowerPoint

Structure of Conceptual ERP Model in Detail

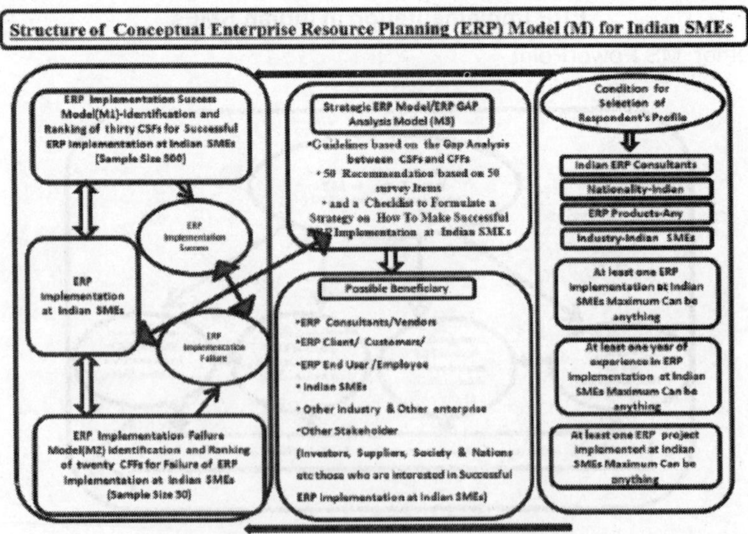

Fig. 3.10: Structure of Conceptual ERP Model (M) in Detail,

Source: Author, MS PowerPoint

Structure of ERP Implementation Success Model

Figure 3.11 *(See on next page)* and 3.12 *(See on p. 69)* shows the proposed model, referred to as the conceptual ERP implementation success model. As the success of ERP systems can be classified into two categories; the success of ERP adoption and the success of ERP implementation. The model also considers in the success of ERP implementation based on the reviews related to the fundamentals of project management. The success factors for the large enterprise as suggested by the various researcher in literature review were used in the model because these were already validated in previous research and confirmed by several experts interviewed for large enterprise. This research hypothesizes these factors directly contribute in the success of ERP implementation at Indian SMEs. Based on the proposed model, this research developed the initial instrument (two close ended questionnaires) to identify and rank the 30 CSFs for the successful ERP implementation at Indian SMEs.

Criteria Grouping and Prioritization

For the sake of ordering, it was useful to group the previously stated CSFs of the LEs under 4 titles; Enterprise-related, Technology-related, Vendors-related and Employees/End-user-related. These four main groups with their related sub factors can be seen in Table 3.2 *(See on next page)*. In fact, the user-related criteria can also be listed under the technology-related title since technology related criteria can affect the user friendliness of the system. But it was better to make a distinction between these two titles. The cost-related title also includes the enterprise-related criteria. It was needless to form a fifth group since any factor of the enterprise influences the total cost of the system; so there was no misleading in taking cost-related criteria as enterprise-related. During the rest of the project, these four groups and their related sub-criteria will be used. Please note that these criteria grouping was based on Leavitt's System Model (1973) and according to personal opinions improved by the previous studies, and are subject to change from person to person, according to the point of view.

- **Enterprise:** In the computer industry, an enterprise is an organization that uses computers. A word was needed that would encompass corporations, small businesses, non-profit institutions, government bodies, and possibly other kinds of organizations. (www.searchwinit.techtarget.com).
- **Technology:** the most general definition of technology is the application of science or knowledge to commerce and industry (www.yourdictionary.com).
- **Vendor:** The sellers of goods, services, or real property are considered as vendor. (www.yourdictionary.com).

- **Employee/End-user:** A person who receives compensation for performing services subject to the will and control of an employer with regard to what shall be done and how it shall be done (www.yourdictionary.com).

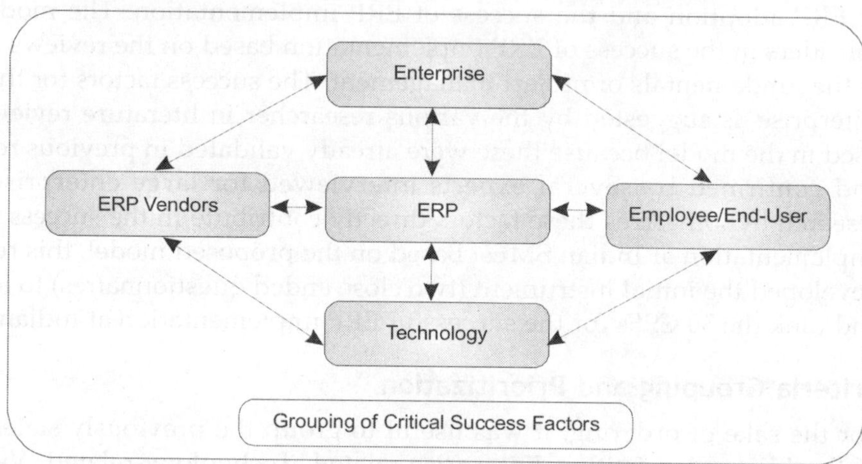

Fig. 3.11: Framework for Grouping of CSFs

Source: Author, MS PowerPoint

Table 3.2: Grouping of CSFs

Enterprise Related CSFs	Technology Related CSFs
Top Management Commitment and Support Change Management Process BPR and Software Configuration Project Champion Business Plan, Vision Effective Communication Plan Post Implementation Evolution Risk Management Focussed Performance Measure Quality Improvement Measure Organization/Corporate Culture Implementation Cost	Software Development, Testing, Trouble Shooting and Crises Management IT Infrastructure Selection of ERP Package Data Conversion and Integrity Legacy System Consideration Vanilla ERP System Documentation
Vendor Related CSFs	**Employee/End-User Related CSFs**
Project Team Implementation Strategy and Timeframe Consultant Selection Vendor/Customer Relationships Project Management Client Consultations	User Involvement User Education and Training Personnel/Staff Employee Attitude and Morale-empowered Decision Makers

Source: Author, MS Word

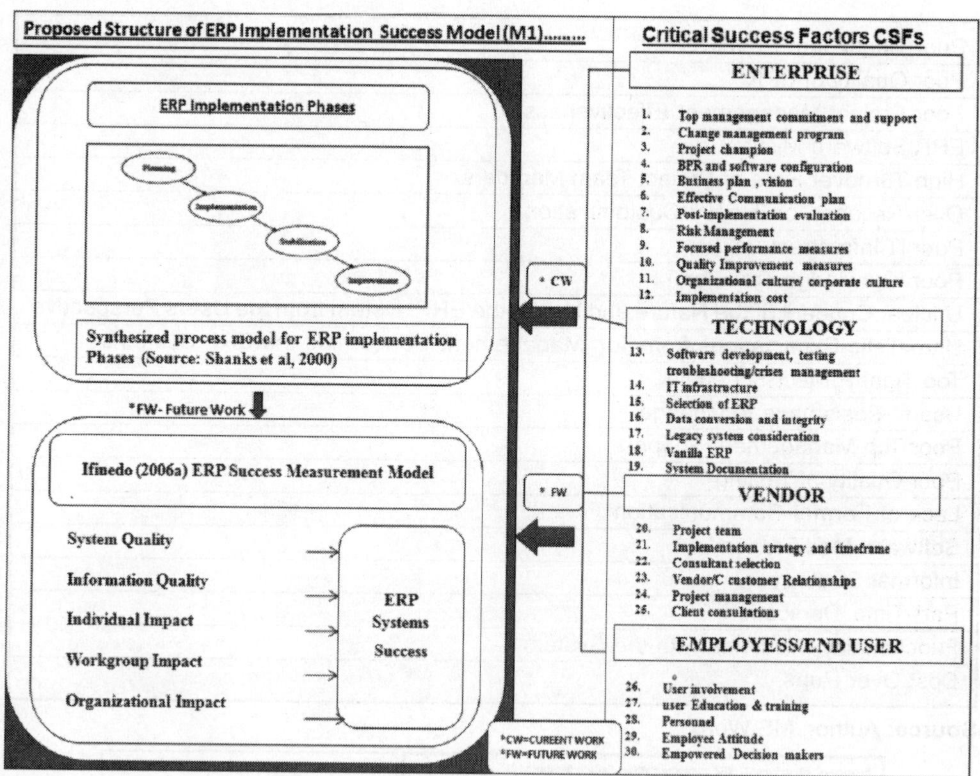

Fig. 3.12: Structure of ERP Implementation Success Model (M1)

Source: Author, MS PowerPoint

Structure of ERP Implementation Failure Model

Figure 3.13 *(See on next page)* shows the proposed model, referred to as the conceptual ERP implementation failure model. As the failure of ERP systems can be classified into two categories; the failure of ERP adoption and the failure of ERP implementation The failure factors for the large enterprise as suggested by the various researcher in literature review were used in the model because these were already validated in previous research and confirmed by several experts interviewed for large enterprise. This research check whether these factors directly contribute in the failure of ERP implementation at Indian SMEs or not. Based on the proposed model, this research developed the initial instrument (one close ended questionnaire) to explore and rank the CFFs for the failure of ERP implementation at Indian SMEs. Following is the list of CFFs of the LEs taken into consideration for this research purpose.

Table 3.3: Critical Failure Factors

Critical Failure Factors
Poor Consultant Effectiveness
Poor Quality of BPR
Poor Project Management Effectiveness
ERP Software Misfit
High Turnover Rate of Project Team Members
Over-Reliance on Heavy Customization
Poor IT Infrastructure
Poor Knowledge Transfer
Unclear Concept of the Nature and Use of the ERP system from the Users Perspective
Unrealistic Expectations from Top Management Concerning the ERP Systems
Too Tight Project Schedule
Users' Resistance to Change
Poor Top Management Support
Poor Quality of Testing
Lack of Formal Communication
Software Modification
Informal Strategy
Part-Time Dedication
Functionality Problems with the System
Cost Over Runs

Source: Author, MS Word

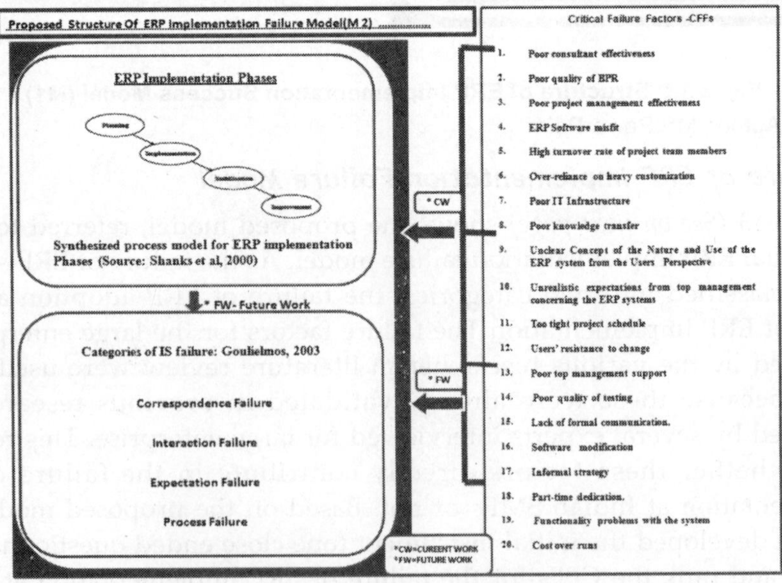

Fig. 3.13: Structure of ERP Implementation Failure Model (M2)

Source: Author, MS PowerPoint

Structure of ERP GAP Analysis/ Strategic ERP Model

Figure 3.14 shows the proposed model, referred to as the ERP GAP analysis mode/Strategic ERP model. As the failure and the success of ERP systems can be classified into two categories; the failure and the success of ERP adoption and the failure and the success of ERP implementation. The model also study the success and the failure factors for the ERP implementation at Indian SMEs as suggested by the various researcher in the literature review of the LEs because these were already validated in previous research and confirmed by several experts interviewed for the large enterprise. This research check whether these factors contribute to the success and failure of ERP implementation at Indian SMEs or not. Based on the proposed model, this research developed the initial guidelines for the successful ERP implementation at Indian SMEs supported by recommendations and checklist that can be used as a strategic tool for successful ERP implementation at Indian SMEs.

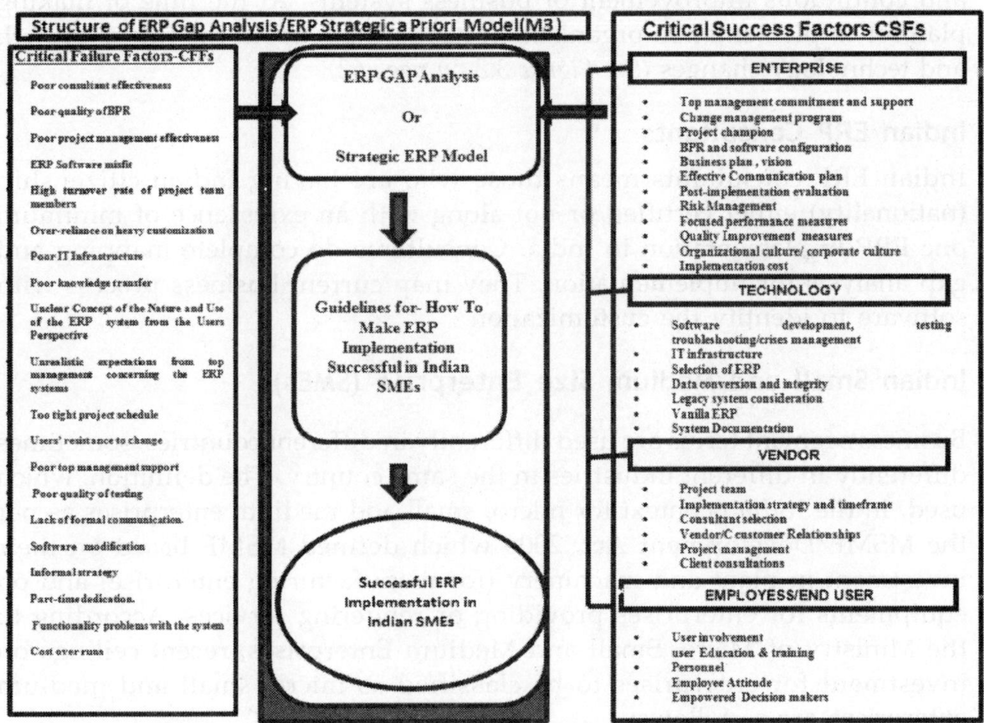

Fig. 3.14: Structure of ERP Gap Analysis Model (M3)

Source: Author, MS PowerPoint

OPERATIONALIZATION

Operationalization is the process of defining a fuzzy concept so as to make the concept measurable in form of variables consisting of specific study/ observations. In a wider sense it refers to the process of specifying the extension of a concept.

Enterprise Resource Planning (ERP)

ERP systems are highly integrated enterprise-wide standard information systems (software packages) that automate core corporate activities (business processes) such as finance, human resources, manufacturing, supply chain management and customer relationship management.

ERP Implementation Phases

ERP Implementation should be divided in steps. Major focus should be on pre-implementation readiness work, implementation project management and continuous improvement of business systems. At the time of making plan for implementation organization has to think about the future growth and technology changes *(See Figure 3.3 on page 62)*.

Indian ERP Consultants

Indian ERP consultants means those who are having Indian citizenship (nationality) either certified or not along with an experience of minimum one ERP implementation in India. Consultants do complete mapping and gap analysis for implementation. They map current business process with software to identify the customization.

Indian Small and Medium Size Enterprise (SMEs)

Business segment terms are used differently in different countries, sometimes differently in different industries in the same country. The definition, which used, In the Indian context for micro, small and medium enterprises as per the MSME Development Act, 2006 which defined MSME based on their investment in plant and machinery (for manufacturing enterprise) and on equipments for enterprises providing or rendering services. According to the Ministry of Micro, Small and Medium Enterprises, recent ceilings on investment for enterprises to be classified as micro, small and medium enterprises are as follows:

Critical Success Factors (CSFs)

Critical Success Factors (CSFs) is the term for elements that are necessary for an organization or project to achieve its mission. It is a critical factor or

Table 3.4: Definition of Indian SMEs

Classi-fication	Manufacturing Enterprises*	Service Enterprises**
Micro	Rs. 2.5 million/ Rs. 25 lakh (US$ 50,000)	Rs. 1 million/ Rs. 10 lakh (US$ 20,000)
Small	Rs. 50 million/ Rs. 5 crore (US$ 1 million)	Rs. 20 million Rs. 2 crore (US$ 40,00,000)
Medium	Rs. 100 million/ Rs. 10 crore (US$ 2 million)	Rs. 50 million/ Rs. 5 crore (US$ 1 million)

(**Source**: MSME Development Act 2006)
* Investment limit in Plant and Machinery
** Investment limit in Equipments

activity required for ensuring the success of a company or an organization or project. The term was initially used in the world of data analysis and business analysis.

Table 3.5: Operationalization of Critical Success Factors

Critical Success Factors (CSFs)	Operationalization
1	2
Top Management Commitment and Support	The commitment of top management should be emphasized throughout an organization. Senior management must be involved, including the required people and appropriate time to finish and allocate valuable resources to the implementation effort.
Change Management Process	Change management is a structured approach to transitioning individuals, teams, and organizations from a current state to a desired future state.
BPR and Software Configuration	It is very important to consider the extent to which the company needs to re-engineer its current business processes in order to be compatible with the ERP software. The integrative design of ERP systems increases the complexity involved in source code modification, most companies significantly underestimate the effort required for modifications. Therefore, do not change basic software code as far as possible.
Project Champion	The project champion should be an individual who can make things happen and ensure that management stake in the project is conveyed to all

...(Contd.)

1	2
	levels, top management support is maintained throughout the project, necessary resources are provided at critical junctures, parties at loggerheads are brought together. Decisions and compromises are enforced.
Business Plan, Vision	Well defined objectives help to keep the project constantly focused, and are essential for analyzing and measuring success. They must clearly define objectives, they must be measurable and controllable, and the savings must be quantified for each objective
Effective Communication Plan	Organization should have a communication plan. The communication plan has to detail several areas including the rationale for the ERP implementation, details of the business process management change, demonstration of applicable software modules, briefings of change management strategies, tactics, and establishment of contact points.
Post Implementation Evolution	A Post-Implementation Review (PIR) is an assessment and review of the completed working solution. It will be performed after a period of live running, sometime after the project is completed.
Risk Management	The process of determining the maximum acceptable level of overall risk to and from a proposed activity, then using risk assessment techniques to determine the initial level of risk and, if this is excessive, developing a strategy to ameliorate appropriate individual risks until the overall.
Focussed Performance Measure	Performance measures describe how success in achieving the project goals will be measured and tracked. Performance measurement targets provide the quantifiable answer to the question: "How to know when has been successful in achieving goal?"
Quality Improvement Measure	Good quality implies happy users. However, quality is hard to define, impossible to measure, easy to recognize. Nevertheless, most frameworks specify a measurable (process) quality indicator from which process quality can be inferred.

...(Contd.)

1	2
Organization/Corporate Culture	Basically, organizational culture is the personality of the organization. Culture is comprised of the assumptions, values, norms and tangible signs (artifacts) of organization members and their behaviours. Members of an organization soon come to sense the particular culture of an organization. Culture is one of those terms that are difficult to express distinctly, but everyone knows it when they sense .The concept of culture is particularly important when attempting to manage organization-wide change. Practitioners are coming to realize that, despite the best-laid plans, organizational change must include not only changing structures and processes, but also changing the corporate culture as well.
Implementation Cost	It often dictates whether the approach is financially feasible. There are considerable cost differences among the frameworks, making some impossible for smaller organizations to adopt. The implementation of certain processes or process management practices may not be as cost-effective for small organizations as for large ones. However, the exact impact of organization size on cost is not obvious. It will be impossible to provide exact numbers in this characteristic. However, rough estimates should be provided where such numbers can be obtained, Cost estimates can be influenced by organization specific attributes such as size, as well as inconsistent use of cost models.
Software Development, Testing, Trouble Shooting and Crises Management	This factor is related with the problem and risk areas that exist in every implementation. Trouble-shooting mechanisms should be included in the implementation plan. Two important aspects are the adaptation and transfer of old data and the 'go live' moment. The time and effort involved in the transfer of data from previous systems should not be under-estimated.
IT Infrastructure	It conforms to critical technology standards and is equipped with full communication and network infrastructure, meeting all the attributes. A standardized IT infrastructure. Suitable business and IT legacy systems.
Selection of ERP Package	Management must make a careful choice of an ERP package that best matches the legacy systems, e.g. the hardware platform, databases and operating systems along with business requirement.

...(Contd.)

1	2
Data Conversion and Integrity	This effort often involves translating or amalgamating existing data to conform to the specifications required by the ERP system.
Legacy System Consideration	Legacy systems are the business and IT systems prior to the ERP that encapsulate the existing business processes, organization structure, culture and information technology .They are a good source of information for ERP implementations and the possible problems that can be found during the implementation. Another aspect is to decide which legacy systems will be replaced and the need to interface with those legacy systems for which the ERP does not provide an adequate replacement.
Vanilla ERP	Vanilla software is computer software that is not customized from its delivered form. It is used without any customizations applied to it. Vanilla software can become a widespread de facto industry standard, widely used by businesses and individuals.
System Documentation	Documentation understood as document is any communicable material (such as text, video, audio, etc., or combination thereof) used to explain some attributes of an object, system or procedure. It is often used to mean engineering documentation or software documentation, which is usually paper books or computer readable files (such as HTML pages) that describe the structure and components, or on the other hand, operation, of a system/ product.
Project Team	It is responsible for creating the initial, detailed project plan or overall schedule along with complete project team with full talent for the entire project, assigning responsibilities for various activities and determining due dates. A great deal of know-how is essential for the complex implementation of an integrated standard software package.
Implementation Strategy and Timeframe	This includes management decisions concerning how the software package is to be implemented. There are different approaches to ERP implementation strategy. The advantages and disadvantages of these extreme approaches should be measured, especially at a functionality level.

...(Contd.)

1	2
Consultant Selection	The success of a project depends strongly on the capabilities of the consultants because the consultant is the only one with in-depth knowledge of the software. Usually, in many cases the time dedicated to the implementation project is shared with other activities. It is also important to ensure that the staff believes in the project success. Consultants should be involved in a way that helps the implementation process while also sharing their expertise with the internal staff involved.
Vendor/Customer Relationships	During the implementation phases there are different partners involved such as consultants, customers, clients, software and hardware vendors. An adequate partnership between them will ease achievement of the goals defined.
Project Management	In order to successfully accomplish the decision to implement an ERP system, the effective project management comes into play to plan, coordinate and control such an intricate project.
Client Consultations	The client consultation is an extremely important element of the process. It is at implementation time that determines what the client wants, what their history is, and how implementation is going to perform their massage.
User Involvement	Participating in the system development and implementation, the users go through a transition period that gives them time to better understand the project's consequences.
User Education and Training	When the ERP system is up and running it is very important that the users be capable to use it, hence they should be aware of the ERP logic and concepts and should be familiar with the system's features through proper education and training.
Personnel/Staff	Project work is very demanding and a complex project requires people with a high learning potential and at least all key project members must be available full-time along with required skills and knowledge to ensure project continuity and progress.
Employee Attitude and Morale	Positive attitude and high morale of employee reduces resistance to change and increase the probability of ERP acceptance during ERP implementation.

...(Contd.)

1	2
Empowered Decision Makers	Empowerment is the process of enabling or authorizing an individual to think, behaves, take action, control work and decision making in autonomous ways. It is the state of feeling self-empowered to take control of one's own destiny.

(**Source**: Author, MS Word)

Critical Failure Factors (CFFs)

Critical Failure Factors (CFFs) can be defined as the key aspects (areas) where things must go wrong in order for the ERP implementation process to achieve a high level of failure.

Table 3.6: Operationalization of Critical Failure Factors

Critical Failure Factors (CFFs)	Operationalization
1	2
Poor Consultant Effectiveness	Inexperienced consultants with ERP systems will unable to provide a professional level of advice on EPR project planning. Consultants will communicate ineffectively during the project phase. Without applying professional skills to conduct BPR to bridge the gap between ERP systems and business processes. A detailed test plan and guidelines will not be suggested to the project team. Consultants will delivered poor quality of training will conduct BPR to a poor quality and delivered poor quality management reports due to insufficient industrial experience. They will not be able to provide any consulting service on BPR, project management, or ERP implementation.
Poor Quality of BPR	Unclear vision of why or how to conduct BPR, and unprofessional advice for conducting BPR. Project team will found it difficult to collaborate and contribute to BPR, and the poor quality of BPR led to incorrect system configuration problems. Business processes will not be successfully reengineered to fit with the ERP systems.
Poor Project Management Effectiveness	Wrong information regarding the scope, size, and complexity of an ERP implementation, As a

...(Contd.)

1	2
	result, management sometimes does not initiate the necessary level of detailed project management planning and control. Due to limited ERP knowledge, capability and poor project management skills, none of the project managers could exercise effective project management of ERP. Project management control, especially in managing consultants, and reporting implementation problems to top management is necessary. It is important for the project manager to effectively manage the consultants.
ERP Software Misfit	If the implementation is treated as simply an IT project, the ERP system will never realize its full capabilities. In such cases, it is likely that the technology will be deployed in a vacuum, business processes will not be properly reengineered and aligned with the software requirements, and staff will resist using it. Due to poor ERP selection and evaluation process, ERP software will found to be ill-fitting with the business requirements.
Poor IT Infrastructure	Every ERP implementation will encounter a certain number of problems. These difficulties can include bugs in the software, problems interfacing with existing systems, and hardware difficulties. Normally, such problems simply contribute to the organization not achieving its target goals. However, if technical problems go unresolved or are poorly managed, they can doom the implementation.
Poor Knowledge Transfer	Top managers and all system users must be fully educated so they understand how the ERP system should be integrated into the overall company operation. All users must be trained to take full advantage of the system's capabilities. A failure to educate and train all relevant personnel will guarantee implementation problems.
Unclear Concept of the Nature and Use of the ERP system from the Users Perspective	Due to the poor quality of training provided by the consultants and insufficient education delivered by the top management and project team, users will not get a clear idea of the nature and use of the ERP system. They will not

...(Contd.)

1	2
	understand the rationale for implementing the ERP system or the process of implementation. Thus, they will not prepared for the implementation, and will have high resistance to change, which led to political problems, poor quality of BPR and a resistance to using the system.
Unrealistic Expectations from Top Management Concerning the ERP Systems	Many companies grossly underestimate the amount of resources, time, and outside assistance required to implement and run the new system. Moreover, managers and workers frequently assume that performance will begin to improve immediately because the new system is complex and difficult to master; organizations must be prepared for an initial decline in productivity after the new software is put into operation. As familiarity with the new system increases, the expected improvements will come. But management must be prepared for initial waves of frustration.
Too Tight Project Schedule	Top management and the project manager will like to reduce the budget of the ERP project, and thus they set too tight a project schedule. Implementation activities will conducted in a rush (e.g., project planning, BPR, training, testing and so on) in order to meet the project deadline. The project team and users will be overloaded and thus they might have higher resistance to change. Some users will absent from training as they will be too exhausted. It resulted in poor knowledge transfer.
Poor Top Management Support	If top management is not strongly committed to the system, does not foresee and plan for the profound changes necessitated by ERP, or does not actively participate in the implementation, the implementation has a high likelihood of failure. The implementation of ERP must be viewed by top management as a transformation in the way the company does business.

...(Contd.)

1	2
Poor Quality of Testing	Data entered into an ERP system may be used throughout the organization. Because of the integrated nature of ERP, if inaccurate data is entered into the common database, the erroneous data may have a negative domino effect throughout the enterprise. Inaccurate data can lead to errors in market planning, production planning, material procurement, capacity acquisition, and the like. If a company with inaccurate data just forges ahead under the assumption that data errors will be corrected when they are spotted, the ERP will lose credibility. This encourages people to ignore the new system and continue to run the company under the old system.
Lack of Formal Communication	Informal communication contains facts, deceptions, rumors and unclear data. The informal channels of communication may transmit completely imprecise information that may harm rather than help an organization.
Software Modification	Some of the biggest ERP system implementation failures occur because the new software's capabilities and needs are mismatched with the organizations existing business processes. An ERP system that is not designed to meet the specific business needs of the company can cause tremendous problems. A significant mismatch between the technological imperatives of the system and the existing structure, processes, or business needs of the organization will generate widespread chaos. Less severe mismatches between business processes and software requirements will merely create significant problems for implementers and users.
Informal Strategy	A way of tackling problem based on intuitive understanding. Informal strategies may use idiosyncratic methods of recording the work
Part-Time Dedication	Employment that is less than a full-time organizational commitment on the part of the employee for ERP implementation leads to ERP failure because of less commitment and involvement

...(Contd.)

1	2
Functionality Problems with the System	Problem to perform required function as expected and if the problem does not recur, proceed with the rest of the troubleshooting steps leads to ERP failure.
Cost Over Runs	Cost overrun is defined as excess of actual cost over budget. Cost overrun is caused by cost underestimation and is sometimes called 'cost escalation'.

(**Source**: Author, MS Word)

ERP Success

To determine how successfully an implementation project has been completed, the degree of project success should be assessed in terms of time, cost, quality, and scope as usual project management contexts applied. ERP implementation project was completed on time, on budget, with good quality, and finally whether the scope of the system was well matched with the company's needs. Success of an ERP program is two-fold. On one hand the impact of the resulting information system on the organization is of interest. On the other hand the execution of the ERP program is of interest as a measure of efficiency. The former is named 'Program Objectives', the latter 'Project Objectives' in research.

ERP Failure

Failure is usually in terms of projects that are late or over budget, an inability to fully realize the expected benefits or gain the acceptance and enthusiastic support of users and management along with vendors. Failure is a number of events that occur within a project that does not enable it to conform to specification and obtains its mission.

GAP Analysis

This stage helps to identify the gaps that have to be bridged, so that the practice becomes akin to ERP environment. This has been reported as an expensive procedure but it is inevitable. The conglomerate (with the help of CSFs and CFFs) may decide to restructure the business or make any other alterations as suggested by GAP analysis in order to make ERP implementation successful at Indian SMEs.

Chapter Summary

In this chapter, researcher had formulated the conceptual ERP implementation model along with its sub models for successful ERP implementation at Indian

SMEs. Success and failure model has been developed based on theories and knowledge gained from the literature review of the LEs. The conceptual model adapted project management approach as the starting point for the structure of relationships between success factors, and failure factors. The fundamentals of project management were incorporated into the model for analyzing the success and failure of the ERP implementation at Indian SMEs. This chapter also describes critical success and failure factors with their operational definitions and theoretical background. Therefore, the conceptual ERP models have theoretically sound background and can be helpful in providing better understanding about the success and failure of ERP implementation at Indian SMEs. The next chapter gives a presentation of the research design used for this research work that explain complete framework for data collection and analysis in order to answer the research questions of this book.

4 Research Design

"Research is diligent and systematic inquiry or investigation into a subject in order to discover or revise facts, theories, application etc. methodology is the system of methods followed by particular discipline thus research methodology is the way how to conduct the research."
—Kothari, 1991

This chapter discussed the research methodology that has been chosen for this project. Potential research methods are then described and evaluated for usefulness regarding the research project and its nature. Following this, all the data collection techniques used within this research were discussed. The dominant research methodology used was survey method. This chapter gives the detailed and sufficient information in order to make estimates of reliability and validity of the survey instruments (questionnaires) used. It

Table 4.1: Research Design

Research Type	Exploratory Quantitative Survey Based Research
Research Context	Indian SMEs and Indian ERP Consultants
Research Approach	Quantitative Survey Based on the Likert Five Point Scale
Data Type	Nominal and Ordinal Scale (Categorical Variable)
Data Collection Tools	Three Closed Ended Questionnaires (Supported by one open ended question in each of them)
Data Analysis Software	SPSS Version 18.0, MS Excel, MS Word, MS PowerPoint

Source: Author, MS Word

explains and justifies the choice of methodology and approaches that adopted in order to answer the research questions. The purpose of this chapter was to provide information regarding the research contexts, and research strategies with briefly discussion of the statistical techniques that were used.

RESEARCH METHODOLOGY

The primary purpose of this research was to find out the factors that contribute to the success and failure of ERP implementation at Indian SMEs. A two-phased approach was used in constructing the measure:

Phase 1: Develop an initial measure list (survey items for close ended questionnaire)by taking results from the literature review and examining ERP implementation characteristics, then determining whether it was complete and clear by using pilot survey of 15 questionnaires responses from Indian ERP consultants.

Phase 2: Revise the list accordingly and use it in a pilot test with 50 Indian ERP consultants. As a result, the initial survey instrument was extensively revised. For the final data collection new revised survey instruments were then given via a survey to 500+ Indian ERP consultants working with different ERP companies (Top 10 ERP sector companies) in India or abroad. Finally, the tests of reliability for the instruments were conducted from the pilot survey data.

Research Approach

In light of the study's objectives, the quantitative research paradigm was considered the most suitable approach for the study. Statistical techniques like descriptive statistics, reliability test, validity test, exploratory factor analysis and non-parametric tests were used for analysis. The approach for the research was quantitative survey. Quantitative research is the systematic scientific investigation of quantitative properties or phenomena and their relationships. There are number of methods such as surveys, simulation and experiments that are considered to belong to the quantitative tradition the advantage of a quantitative approach is that it is possible to measure the reactions of a great many people to a limited set of questions, thus facilitating comparison and statistical aggregation of the data (Kothari, 1991).

Research Strategy

Research strategy is as a general plan of how to answer the research question(s). The research strategies in this study were carried out in a two phase fashion. After reviewing the relevant literature on study's themes to familiarize with the necessary concepts a preliminary survey was conducted to examine practitioners' views for research themes. This was followed by pilot survey with Indian ERP consultants to increase understanding of the study's themes. Finally, the main survey was conducted, which was hopec would add to the body of knowledge in area of ERP study in future research

The research methodology was illustrated in Figure 4.1 as can be seen quantitative research approaches were used to enhance the validity o findings. This research aims to develop a research model which would justify this book towards the use of ERP for Indian SMEs. This research book adopt "Exploratory Type" of research. The research methodology used for the book was kept very simple. Primary data was collected by questionnaire sent through email and secondary data was collected from the internet, new papers, magazines and journals .Exploratory studies are practical if wish to clarify understating of a problem. It is a method of finding out "what i happing" to seek new insight, to ask questions and to asses' new phenomena in new light (Kothari, 1991). The purpose of this book is exploratory since i wishes to assess ERP implementation in light of critical factors and understand what is happing for an ERP implementation at Indian SMEs. It is necessary to have a picture of phenomena to collect data prior to the collection of dat and clearly structured research purpose. It explores factors or situation or

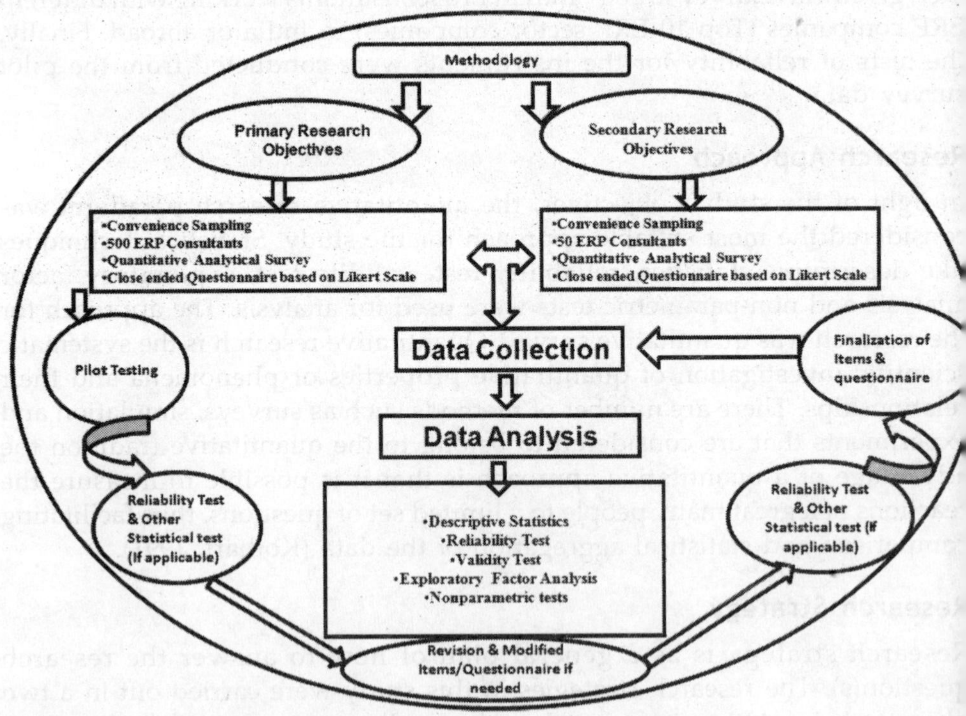

Fig. 4.1: Research Methodology

(**Source**: Author, MS PowerPoint)

problem in order to explain the relationships between variables. The purpose of this study was to find out the information to answer 'what' questions. The study did not require control over behavioral events. Author wanted to collect and analyze new data, comparing it to existing theories and find if there were any differences between book factors and those in literature. This research project was designed to test and validate the hypothetical structural model presented in previous chapter. The study employs a mixed method approach in data collection. The quantitative data gathered through a survey and used to explore the contribution of various factors in all phases of the ERP implementation at Indian SMEs.

Data Collection

In order to collect the data in any research project, such as this book, primary and secondary are the two types in which data were classified. To start with, secondary data were the data that was collected through another source or an existing material, that is; previous knowledge, such as; literature, research articles, magazines, newspapers and internet, while primary data is regarded as own data collected through interview, survey and questionnaire or by any other personal means for a purpose (Kothari,1991). In order to collect the data, this book focused vividly on both secondary and primary data. Secondary data include both quantitative and qualitative data as they were used principally in both pilot and final research. Using secondary data this book, aim at focusing more on the written materials for the documentary. Primary data were collected with the help of exploratory quantitative survey based method.

Data Collection Methods

This book was based on two sources of data. The first source(secondary data) was an academic literature review, the ,articles drawn from the web and respected practitioners, magazines, reports, ERP cases and for the second source of data (primary data) three close ended questionnaires based survey was conducted through e-mails with the help of Indian ERP consultants .

Primary data: The Primary data for this book was collected using close ended questionnaires from about 500 Indian ERP consultants. It was a structured questionnaire which comprised of sequenced questions. An E-mail based questionnaire was used to collect the primary data. This questionnaire was sent to the various Indian ERP consultants to get the opinion and to test the exploratory statements (exploratory hypotheses).

Secondary data: The Secondary data was collected using (*a*) Internet: The Sites of all ERP providing software's were visited (*b*) Journals: research papers from various journals were used to collect data. (*c*) News Papers: daily business news papers were also used as a source for secondary data collection. (*d*) Magazines, On-line database research/Internet or e-mail, Face-to-face, Telephone etc were also used.

Data were collected using questionnaires based survey administered in India. The top ten IT firms that implement ERP systems all over the world were included. This provided a sample of 500 Indian ERP consultants; of these, all 500 received initial email explaining the purpose of project and inquiring whether the individual would be willing to participate in the study. A contact person was identified at each company; this person was asked to distribute the self-administered questionnaires to Indian ERP consultants. Researcher sent out 1000+ questionnaires and approx 600 completed questionnaires were returned. The respondents represented a broad cross-section of management levels and ERP modules.

Table 4.2: Sources Used in Data Collection

People contact methods	Interviews, Brainstorming, Cross-functional groups to customized the survey instrument (three close ended questionnaires were customized) at initial level	Investigative methods	Three close ended questionnaires based on the convenience sampling were used in the survey processes
Written documents	Notes, documents, publications and Web based information were used	Numerical (statistical) techniques were used	Data interpretation was done on the basis of statistical analysis with the help of SPSS

(**Source**: Author, MS Word)

Data Collection Instruments

Invitations were sent to respondents for participating in the survey through a request supported by a cover letter. Respondents were from ERP vendors side (Top 10 ERP implementation vendors were selected) those who were having an Indian nationality along with an experience of minimum one ERP implementation in India, they have been associated with the implementation process for their respective organization (ERP vendor). Questionnaires based survey method was used; it was followed by the previous study to explore the CSFs and CFFs for successful ERP implementation at Indian SMEs that have been found through literature review of the LEs. Questionnaires were used as the research instruments. The questionnaires were focussed on the identification and ranking of critical factors for ERP implementation at Indian

SMEs. It identifies the respondents' perception of the importance for CFs in the ERP implementation process at Indian SMEs. For each of these factors, a statement was formulated through the definition and description of each one in the ERP literature of the LEs. This survey used email containing three questionnaires in order to examine the relationship between the hypothesized CSFs and CFFs of the LEs that were collected from previous research and the successful ERP implementation at Indian SMEs.

Three close ended questionnaires were used. First questionnaire collect data regarding the identification of CSFs for successful ERP implementation at Indian SMEs. Second questionnaire deals with ranking of CSFs for successful ERP implementation at Indian SMEs that identifies the respondents' perception of the importance for the critical success factors in the ERP implementation process at Indian SMEs. Third questionnaire belongs to the identification of critical failure factors for the failure of ERP implementation at Indian SMEs. All the adopted items were modified for the context of this study and, if necessary, paraphrased to suit a five-point Likert-type scale where 1=Strongly Disagree, 2=Disagree, 3=Neutral, 4=Agree, and 5=Strongly Agree. All questions were closed-ended questions. Closed-ended questions are quick to answer, easy to code and there are no differences between articulate and inarticulate respondents (Kothari, 1991). There are two types of scales of measurement used in this survey, namely nominal scale and ordinal scale. All factors shown in the models (See Chapter 3) were being measured through five-point Likert-type scale, which were expected to provide stronger construct validity. Wherever possible, measurement items which have been opeartionalized and tested in previous empirical studies have been re-used, which increased the comparability and reliability of the results. The questionnaire was pilot tested with fifty Indian ERP consultants for content validity and instrument reliability. Based upon the modification the final questionnaires were sent to all respondents. Data were secured by mail questionnaires. The survey instrument was designed based on the conceptual ERP model, and most items in the survey were primarily adapted from the relevant previous research in the ERP contexts. It was tested before conducting the main survey to examine whether or not the proposed model was well developed to analyze ERP implementation success at Indian SMEs. Observations of unordered variables, such as ERP software name, and sector that the consultants works for, are one of the most primitive forms of measurement and were described as constituting a nominal scale.

In nominal scales, numbers may be substituted for the names of the various classes of variable. The numbers serve only to identify the classes and do not indicate anything about the classes other than their difference. This coding allows identification of variables during statistical analysis. In some cases, observations may be ordered in such a way that one observation represents more of a given variable than any other observation (Kothari, 1991). For example, in second questionnaire thirty factors were ranked on one to thirty point scale have the degree of importance of the factors for the ERP consultants. They were scaled from most important (1) to least important (30). Most important were identified by assigning 1 and least important were identified by assigning 30, then this observation would be described as constituting an ordinal scale, a scale that was used in this survey has a special name which is the Likert scale. A Likert scale is a type of ordinal scale. The numbers used in identifying the observations were called ranks. Ranks tell about the degree of the variable within the set of observations at hand these numbers discussed in more detail in the code book where the numbers of codes that were used in this survey were explained. The questionnaires used in this study attempted to measure the theoretical model illustrated and discussed in chapter three. The instrument development methodologies was adopted to generate the pool of items for each construct. Items were drawn from the literature review and based on the interviews with experts. Manual sorting procedure was conducted using experts experienced for the new scale development.

Table 4.3: Data Collection Instruments

Questionnaire One	Identification of CSFs for successful ERP implementation at Indian SMEs
Population	Indian ERP consultants(both certified and non-certified ERP consultants from top 10 ERP vendors) those who were having Indian nationality along with minimum one years of experience in ERP implementation at India
Sample Size and Unit of Analysis	500, Indian ERP Consultants(Individual level or Individuals)
Sampling Procedure	Non-Probabilistic Convenience Sampling
Questionnaire Two	Ranking of CSFs for successful ERP implementation at Indian SMEs
Population	Indian ERP consultants (both certified and non-certified ERP consultants from top 10 ERP vendors) those who were having Indian nationality along with minimum one year's of experience in ERP implementation at India
Sample Size and Unit of Analysis	500, Indian ERP consultants(Individual level or Individuals)
Sampling Procedure	Non-Probabilistic Convenience Sampling

...(Contd.)

Questionnaire Three	Identification of CFFs for failure of ERP implementation at Indian SMEs
Population	Indian ERP consultants(both certified and non-certified ERP consultants from top 10 ERP vendors) those who were having Indian nationality along with minimum one year's of experience in ERP implementation at India
Sample Size and Unit of Analysis	50, Indian ERP Consultants(Individual level or Individuals)
Sampling Procedure	Non-Probabilistic Convenience Sampling

Source: Author, MS Word

Data Types and Coding

Data comes in various sizes and shapes and it is important to know about these so that proper analysis can be conducted on the data. There are usually 4 scales of measurement that must be considered. Nominal Data (Classification of data, e.g. m/f, No ordering, e.g. it makes no sense to state that M > F, Arbitrary labels, e.g., m/f, 0/1, etc), Ordinal Data (ordered but differences between values are not important, e.g., political parties on left to right spectrum given labels 0, 1, 2, e.g., Likert scales, rank on a scale of 1..5 degree of satisfaction, e.g., restaurant ratings) (Kothari,1991). Before the statistical tests take place, the data gathered from the survey converted to a proper form that allows the data to be analyzed. A code book gives information about each variable, such as name and type, along with the units of measurement or categories as in the following example for the survey that takes place in this study. Every variable coded and converted to a proper

Table 4.4: Coding Table

Questionnaire(Q) Type	Variable Type	Codes
(*Q1*) Identification of CSFs for successful ERP implementation at Indian SMEs	Categorical (Nominal and Ordinal Scale)	1= Strongly Disagree 2= Disagree 3= Neutral 4= Agree 5= Strongly Agree
(*Q2*) Ranking of CSFs for successful ERP implementation at Indian SMEs	Categorical (Nominal and Ordinal Scale)	Ranking of 30 CSFs on 1 to 30 point Scale 1 Most Important 30 Least Important
(*Q3*) Identification of CFFs for the failure of ERP implementation at Indian SMEs	Categorical (Nominal and Ordinal Scale)	1= Strongly Disagree 2= Disagree 3= Neutral 4= Agree 5= Strongly Agree

Source: Author, MS Word

form that allows for analysis. After coding the survey, the data was ready to be analyzed for the relationships between variables. So the relationship between ERP implementation at Indian SMEs and factors can be seen. SPSS V 18.0 software takes place in the analysis of this data. The whole codebook is given in the Table 4.4.

As mentioned in the previous section, the data collected in the survey was categorical data. Categorical variables can string (alphanumeric) data or numeric variables that use numeric codes to represent categories (for example, 0 = Unmarried and 1 = Married) (Kothari, 1991). There were two basic types of categorical data: nominal and ordinal data which were both included in the survey. This kind of data has a limited number of distinct values or categories (for example, gender or marital status). It is also referred to as qualitative data.

Sampling

Sampling is a process by which a small part of a population to make judgments about the entire population can be studied. Sampling involves selecting a number of units from a defined population. The thing which sampled can be anything for example, a person, a clinical episode, or a health facility etc (Kothari, 1991).

Population /Universe of the Study

Universe or population is the whole mass under study. The population of study were Indian ERP consultants (both certified and non certified from ERP vendors) those who were having Indian nationality along with minimum one years of experience in ERP implementation at India.

Sample Demography/Sample Profile

A representative sample has all the important characteristics of the study population from which it was drawn. Table 4.5 shows a list of the enterprise

Table 4.5: Sample Characteristics

Organization Name/Enterprise (Dummy name were used in order to maintain the anonymity and confidentiality of information)	Respondents Profile	Condition Check	
		Nationality	Minimum ERP Implementation in India
1	2	3	4
A	Indian ERP Consultants	Indian	One
B	Indian ERP Consultants	Indian	One
C	Indian ERP Consultants	Indian	One

...(Contd.)

1	2	3	4
D	Indian ERP Consultants	Indian	One
E	Indian ERP Consultants	Indian	One
F	Indian ERP Consultants	Indian	One
G	Indian ERP Consultants	Indian	One
H	Indian ERP Consultants	Indian	One
I	Indian ERP Consultants	Indian	One
J	Indian ERP Consultants	Indian	One

Source: Author, MS Word

(ERP vendors) from which the sample were drawn. Most of the Indian ERP consultants use SAP and Oracle.

Sample Plan and Size

It obvious from the definition of the population above that a census was not feasible in this study. Accordingly, the researcher adopted the survey type of research in which a sample from the target population was used for the study. The optimal sample size is often a compromise between what is statistically desirable and what feasible in practice. In general, a minimum sample size is 30 (Kothari, 1991). In order to maintain validity in this research enough conscious efforts has been made while selecting scientific number of sample.

Table 4.6: Sample Size

Questionnaire (Q)	Sample Size
Q1 Identification of CSFs	500 Indian ERP Consultants
Q2 Ranking of CSFs	500 Indian ERP Consultants
Q3 Identification of CFFs	50 Indian ERP Consultants

Source: Author, MS Word

Sampling Techniques

Sometimes it is not possible to get the kind of information about populations required for probability sampling that may complicates and limits statistical analyses in that case non probability sampling often well-suited. Convenience sampling (a type of non probability sampling) relies on available respondents that are most convenient method. It studies the units available at the time of data collection (Kothari, 1991). It won't be reliable to collect the data from the limited sectors therefore for the data collection the respondents were sleeted from different sectors and from different ERP products. In order to make the findings more reliable, validate and diversified information gathered by the respondents through questionnaires based on Likert five point scales so that conscious comparison and analysis can be done. This ensured a fair representation of each group since their operations are significantly different.

Unit of Analysis/Administration and Scoring

The unit of analysis of the study was at the individual level (individual Indian ERP consultants); as such, only Indian ERP consultants (both certified and non-certified) received an email consisting of a cover letter in English languages. Three questionnaires were used as research instruments. Survey instruments manual have been developed in order to standardized the process of administration and scoring.

Survey Methods

The survey instruments were designed based on the conceptual ERP model for this research. Each variable had one questions for reliability purposes. Most of the questions in the survey were primarily adapted from the relevant previous research related to ERP implementation of the LEs All items were measured on a five point Likert scale from strongly disagree to strongly agree. The survey method is one of the most common method in used. A survey is a means of gathering information about the characteristics, actions or opinions of a large group of people, referred to as population. Survey research is usually a quantitative method require standardized information from subjects being studied and is structured in the sense that sampling and questionnaire construction are conducted prior to start of data collection. It is necessary to think through the whole research process before deciding on sample and questionnaire .Survey research can be used for exploration, description, or explanation purposes (Kothari, 1991). The main survey was administered through the email. This tool provided several necessary functions such as tracking responses, managing the list of respondents, exporting data, etc. The survey was e-mailed to the individuals so that they could take the survey at their convenient time. Additional e-mail was sent to no-response individuals and partial-response ones to encourage them to complete the survey several times. Thank you mail was sent to each participant after completing the survey asking them to distribute it to their colleagues or acquaintances that can do the survey. The purpose of survey research is to find out what situations, events, attitudes or opinions are occurring in a population (Kothari, 1991). The first step in the survey was identifying the population's the Indian ERP consultants selection was based on the fact that these large-size companies (ERP vendors) are implementing and relying on ERP systems as their backbone infrastructure for their functionalities. Then the sample was drawn from the identified population.

The sampling covered Indian ERP consultants working in different activities and located in different cities in India or abroad. Thus, it was enough sample size to get the correct results from the research. Because the survey was sent only to companies which implement ERP systems, the expected results were reliable. In other words the sample chosen from a reliable target population so that findings about the sample can be applied (generalized) to the population.

Survey Items

To conduct a broad exploratory study of ERP implementation at Indian SMEs through a quantitative survey based on Likert five point scale questionnaires, following sections were included in the customized survey instruments (questionnaires):

- ERP Consultants Name
- Organization Name (ERP Implementation Vendor Name)
- Consultant's Nationality (Only Indian Citizen)
- ERP Products (SAP, Oracle, Others)
- Consultant's Experience
- Project Characteristics
- Minimum Number of ERP implementation in India
- Critical Success Factors (CSFs) as specified in Conceptual ERP Implementation Success Model
- Critical Failure Factors (CFFs) as specified in Conceptual ERP Implementation Failure Model

Data Analysis Tools

Before exploratory statements (exploratory hypothesis) testing, a normality test was applied to the data in order to find out the most accurate analysis tool to test the exploratory statements (exploratory hypothesis). For this purpose, a non-parametric test, the one-sample Kolmogorov-Smimov test, was used. This test procedure compared the observed cumulative distribution function for a variable with a specified theoretical distribution, which may be normal, uniform, Poisson, or exponential (Kothari, 1991). The Kolmogorov-Smimov was computed from the largest difference (in absolute value) between the observed and theoretical cumulative distribution functions. This goodness-of-fit test tests whether the observations could reasonably have come from the specified distribution. Many parametric tests require normally distributed variables. The one-sample Kolmogorov-Smimov test can be used to test that a variable is normally distributed or not (Kothari, 1991).

Table 4.7: Data Analysis Tools

Data Analysis Tools	SPSS V 18.0MS Excel/Ms Word/ MS PowerPoint
Questionnaire One (Identification of Critical Success Factors for successful ERP implementation at Indian SMEs on Likert five point scale)	Descriptive Statistics (Arithmetic Mean and Standard Deviation)Reliability Test (Cronbach's Alpha)Validity Test Exploratory Factor Analysis
Questionnaire Two(Ranking of Critical Success Factors on 1 to 30 points scale for successful ERP implementation at Indian SMEs)	Descriptive Statistics (Arithmetic Mean and Standard Deviation)One Sample K-S TestNon-Parametric Tests (Friedman Test, Kendall's W Test)
Questionnaire Three(Identification of Critical Failure Factors for the failure of ERP implementation at Indian SMEs on Likert five point scale)	Descriptive Statistics (Arithmetic Mean and Standard Deviation)Reliability Test (Cronbach's Alpha)Validity Test Exploratory Factor Analysis

Source: Author, MS Word

Secondary Data Review

A number of author's list resources such as time, money and effort spent as some of the benefits of using secondary data review as a research data collection technique. The shortcomings of secondary data review are data availability, the lack of possibilities to check data for correctness and the inhibition of creativity (Kothari,1991). Secondary data review was performed to investigate documents, reports and previous research that have been conducted. Secondary data for research was collected from related books, publication, annual reports, and records of organization etc.

Time Scale/Time Frame

The main survey was conducted between May - August 2010, and a total of 600 responses were received. Samples were drawn from top ten ERP implementation company (vendor). A sample consist of 500 Indian ERP consultants were surveyed for present study. 1000 questionnaire were distributed in total out of which 600 questionnaire were returned, comparing the response rate of 60 per cent some responses were eliminated due to excessive missing data. Therefore the same size for the testing exploratory statements (exploratory hypotheses) was 500 (50%).

PILOT SURVEY

Prior to sending the questionnaire to target sample, it was pre-tested. The pre-test revealed that the respondent had no difficulty in understanding the content of the questionnaires. The main round of data collection took place between May and August 2010. A two-phase pilot test of the survey instrument has been conducted, with fifteen academics and ERP practitioners/ professionals. The feedback has been incorporated into the survey instrument and where necessary modifications have been made to suit the context of the present study. The researcher requested that the pilot subjects identify and suggest improvements for any omission, error, or inconsistency in the survey. The pilot test resulted in several small revisions to the primary instrument that included rewording of a few items, the addition of a few demographic questions, and alterations to the instructions to make them easier to understand. No scaled item was dropped or added as a result of the pilot study. The purpose of the pilot test was to confirm the completeness and importance of each item in the instrument and eliminate logically duplicative ones. The 50 Indian ERP consultants were asked to fill out questionnaires. They were also asked to assess the importance of each item. An overall importance ranking was obtained by calculating the mean of the scores for all 50 respondents; scales were given scores of 1 (Strongly Disagree) to 5 (Strongly Agree).The results indicated that each item scored 4 or higher in over 80 per cent of the responses, and suggesting that no wording revision or new items were needed and it establishing instrument completeness.

Data Collection

The population of study was the group of Indian ERP consultants. Study was limited to Indian ERP consultants only. To increase the response rates, a follow-up email were given if did not receive their questionnaires two weeks after sending them out. No consultants received more than two follow-up emails. Answers were then coded and extensively checked for validity. All answers whose validity seemed dubious were discarded. The targeted respondents of the survey were Indian ERP consultants who are currently working for the ERP industry regardless of their company's main business area. The list of targeted respondents was obtained from several sources, i.e., ERP related organizations, trade magazines, ERP vendor websites, and ERP related newsgroups etc.

Data Analysis

Data analyses with the help of pilot survey were conducted in three separate steps:

Step 1—Examining validity and reliability of the items within each questionnaire

Step 2— Calculating descriptive statistics along with exploratory statements (exploratory hypotheses) testing and exploratory factor analysis

Step 3—Testing for nonparametric tests

The first step was examining validity and reliability between items within each variable so that it can identify which variables should be modified. Survey instruments used in research are generally considered reliable if they produce similar results regardless of administrator and forms. Cronbach's alpha is the most widely used as a measure of reliability. It indicates the extent to which a set of test items can be treated as measuring a single variable. Cronbach's alpha generally increases when the correlations between the items increase. For this reason, items in each variable that are highly correlated should have a higher internal consistency of the test (Kothari, 1991). The lower acceptable limit of 0.50–0.60 was suggested by Kaplan and Saccuzzo; however, as a rule of thumb, a reliability of 0.70 or higher is required before an instrument used.

The second step was data analysis with the help of pilot survey. Exploratory factor analysis attempts to identify underlying variables, or factors, that explain the pattern of correlations within a set of observed variables. It is most frequently used to identify a small number of factors representing relationships among sets of interrelated variables. For this reason, factor analysis is considered a statistical data reduction technique that takes a large number of observable instances to measure an unobservable construct. It generally requires four basic steps: 1 calculate a correlation matrix of all variables; 2 extract factors; 3 rotate factors to create a more understandable factor structure; and 4 interpret results For new factors, have to look at variables extracted from factor analyses by examining correlation coefficients and reliability indicators (Kothari,1991). Data analysis including descriptive statistics, correlation, reliability test, factor analysis and non parametric tests was conducted to adjust survey items and extract factors associated with the success of ERP implementation at Indian SMEs. The new survey instrument which has been used in the main survey and the revised ERP success model after adjustment with the pilot survey was proposed in chapter three. The revised model looks much simpler than the conceptual model. The survey that was developed to search for a possible relationship between CFs and ERP implementation was analyzed by using a statistical software package called SPSS V 18. Some of the contacts for this survey were gathered from consulting firms and some of them were found by searching on the web for companies that have implemented ERP system and are already using the package. Statistical test was performed to decide whether this survey was reliable or not. The reliability analysis procedure calculates a number of commonly used measures of scale reliability and also provides information about the relationships between individual items in the scale. There are many models of reliability but the Alpha (Cronbach's) model takes place in this study. This is a model of internal consistency, based on the average inter-item correlation and this fits into this research data properties. Following the reliability analysis, a normality test was applied on the survey data and then according to the results of this analysis parametric and non parametric test were used to test the exploratory statements (exploratory hypothesis). Because survey data was not normal in case of questionnaire two, non parametric test was used to search for relationships between the variables.

Validity Test

Content validity was used to measure the validity of the survey instruments. Content validity refers to the representatives and comprehensiveness of the items used to create an instrument. Evaluating content validity involves judging each item for its presumed relevance (Kothari, 1991). In this study, CFs of the ERP implementation was initially proposed based on a review of studies in the IS/ERP discipline of the LEs. To ensure instrument completeness, items selected were taken from several sources, for example major prior studies, examination of ERP system characteristics and from expert opinions etc were gathered by the researcher. Fifty Indian ERP Consultants were asked to examine the importance and relevance of each item in the instrument for the pilot study of the instruments. This rigorous approach tends to lend credence to the claim of content validity. The content validity of a questionnaire refers to the representativeness of item content domain (Kothari, 1991). It is the manner by which the questionnaire and its items are built to ensure the reasonableness of the claim of content validity. The conceptualization of survey instrument constructs were based on preliminary literature review to form the initial items, the personal interviews with practitioners and experts used for scale purification suggest that the survey instrument has strong content validity.

Construct validity was established by showing that the instrument measures the construct it was intended to measure. Construct validity was evaluated by performing correlation and factor analysis. High correlations considered to indicate construct validity. It was interesting to observe that the relative strength of the correlation between critical factors constructs. The core meaning of validity was explained entirely by accuracy. From this perspective, researcher's data were valid to the extent that the results of the measurement process were accurate. In other words, a measuring instrument was valid to research when it measures what it was supposed to measure. A survey was used for the research topic and for the exploratory statements (exploratory hypothesis) testing. It explained that the questions in the survey were related to the research topic. Surveys are one of the best tools to observe for the relationships between variables. A key part of the survey is the analysis which obtains accurate results for the research. Reliability is one of the basic elements of establishing validity. Reliability is the degree of random variation in the results of the study. An important cause of overall unreliability is a too-small sample size (Kothari, 1991). In this study; the sample size was significant enough to be representative. Reliability is roughly the same as consistency and repeatability. Internal validity in research relates to making proper inferences from the data, considering alternative explanations, use of convergent data and related tactics. This tactic occurred during the data analysis phase, and was done by looking at each specific area across all items and by weighing the views to insure there was consistency. External validity was addressed by multiple respondents to cover all possible responses. Replication of observations across multiple responses means external validity has been met and that results can likely be generalized outside of the studied respondents.

ES10: The customized survey instrument to explore the 30 CSFs for the successful ERP implementation at Indian SMEs can't be used as validate survey tool for current and future research because of the low construct validity of the survey instrument (questionnaire).

For the group of 50 respondents from the top 10 companies of IT(ERP) sector validity was found to be .8865, whereas for a group of 500 respondents from top 10 companies of IT (ERP) sector it was found to be .8508.The validity was found by using Guilford's formula i.e. by applying the square root of the reliability. Construct validity of the instrument was tested with the help of exploratory factor analysis. The factor analysis was valid (See Table 4.12) and the instrument had strong construct validity due to the following reasons:

- The factors were fixed at ten for 50 respondents.
- They together contribute almost 76.415 per cent of total variance.
- The most important factor among these was component 1 which contributes almost 19.356 per cent of the total variance.
- The variables can be divided into different factors based on the values in the rotated component matrix (the higher values were taken). The divisions of variables into different factors can be done for final survey i.e. for 500 respondents.

ES11: The customized survey instrument to rank the 30 CSFs for the successful ERP implementation at Indian SMEs can't be used as validate survey tool for the current and future research because of the low construct validity of the survey instrument (questionnaire).

For the group of 50 respondents from top 10 companies of IT (ERP) sector validity was found to be .9502(By considering W test value as the measure of reliability), whereas for a group of 500 respondents from top 10 companies of IT (ERP) sector it was found to be .9492.The validity was found by using Guilford's formula i.e. by applying the square root of the reliability.

ES12: The customized survey instrument to explore the 20 CFFs for the failure of ERP implementation at Indian SMEs can't be used as validate survey tool for current and future research because of the low construct validity of the survey instrument (questionnaire).

For the group of 50 respondents from the top 10 companies of IT (ERP) sector validity was found to be .8899.The validity was found by using Guilford's formula i.e. by applying the square root of the reliability. Construct validity of the instrument was tested with the help of exploratory factor analysis. The Factor analysis was valid (See Table 4.13) and the instrument had strong construct validity due to the following reasons

- The factors were fixed at seven for 50 respondents.
- They together contribute almost 76.134 per cent of total variance.
- The most important factor among these was Component 1 which contributes almost 15.088 per cent of the total variance.
- The variables can be divided into different factors based on the values in the rotated component matrix (the higher values were taken). The divisions of variables into different factors can be done for final survey.

Reliability Test

Reliability is one of the most critical elements in assessing the quality of the construct measures and it is a necessary condition for scale validity. A statistically reliable scale provides consistent and stable measures of a construct. Composite reliability estimates are used to assess the inter-item reliability of the measures. Estimates greater than .70 are generally considered to meet the criteria for reliability. Some items may be removed from the construct scales if their removal results in increases in the reliability estimate, however, care must be taken to ensure that the content validity of the measures is not threatened by the removal of a key conceptual element (Kothari, 1991). As shown in the table below that reliability of survey instrument was above .75. Table 4.8, list the composite reliability estimates for each of the measurement scales. Testing reliability performance of the surveys was done by measurement in SPSS V 18.0. There are several ways to do this, the most common of which is Cronbach's alpha. Cronbach's alpha is a measure of reliability. More specifically, alpha is a lower bound for the true reliability of

Table 4.8: Reliability Statistics

Questionnaire	Cronbach's Alpha/ Reliability Test	Cronbach's Alpha Based on Standardized Items	N of Items
Questionnaire One (Identification of Critical Success Factors)	**Reliability Statistics** Cronbach's Alpha: .780; Cronbach's Alpha Based on Standardised Items: .786; N of Items: 30	0.785880102925	30
Questionnaire Two (Ranking of Critical Success Factors)	**Test Statistics** N: 50 Kendall's W[3]: 0.903 Chi-square: 1308.708 df: 29 Asymp. Sig.: 0 a. Kendall's Coefficient of Concordance	Kendall's coefficient of concordance (W test) is linearly related to the mean value of the Spearman's rank correlation coefficients between all pairs of the rankings over which it is calculated. If the test statistic W is 1, then all the judges or survey respondents have been unanimous, and each judge or respondent has assigned the same order to the list of objects or concerns. If W is 0, then there is no overall trend of agreement among the respondents, and their responses may be regarded as essentially random. Intermediate values of W indicate a greater or lesser degree of unanimity among the various judges or respondents.	
Questionnaire Three (Identification of Critical Failure Factors)	**Reliability Statistics** Cronbach's Alpha: .792; Cronbach's Alpha Based on Standardised Items: .792; N of Items: 20	0.791998942390	20

Source: Author, SPSS V 18.0

the survey. Mathematically, reliability is defined as the proportion of the variability in the responses to the survey that is the result of differences in the respondents. That is, answers to a reliable survey will differ because respondents have different opinions, not because the survey is confusing or has multiple interpretations. The computation of Cronbach's alpha is based on the number of items on the survey and the ratio of the average inter-item covariance to the average item variance. Prior to conducting formal exploratory factor analysis, internal consistency (a-coefficient) had to be examined to ensure measures were uni-dimensional and to eliminate "garbage items" (Kothari, 1991). The results indicating that the test would correlate well with true scores.

ES07: The customized survey instrument to explore the 30 CSFs for the successful ERP implementation at Indian SMEs can't be used as reliable survey tool for current and future research because of the low construct reliability of the survey instrument (questionnaire).

For the group of 50 respondents from top 10 companies of IT (ERP) sector the Cronbach's alpha was found to be .786, whereas for a group of 500 respondents from top 10 companies of IT (ERP) sector it was found to be .724.

ES08: The customized survey instrument to rank the 30 CSFs for the successful ERP implementation at Indian SMEs can't be used as reliable survey tool for current and future research because of the low construct reliability of the survey instruments (questionnaire).

The rank given to each factors were added and tested with the help of Friedman mean rank test. The lowest the score the highest is the value gain to the concerned factor. Kendall's W (also known as Kendall's coefficient of concordance) is a non-parametric statistic. It is a normalization of the statistic of the Friedman test, and can be used for assessing agreement among raters. Kendall's W ranges from 0 (no agreement) to 1 (complete agreement).Kendall's coefficient of concordance (W test) is linearly related to the mean value of the Spearman's rank correlation coefficients between all pairs of the rankings over which it is calculated. If the test statistic W is 1, then all the judges or survey respondents have been unanimous, and each judge or respondent has assigned the same order to the list of objects or concerns. If W is 0, then there is no overall trend of agreement among the respondents, and their responses may be regarded as essentially random. Intermediate values of W indicate a greater or lesser degree of unanimity among the various judges or respondents.

For the group of 50 respondents from top 10 companies of IT (ERP) sector reliability was found to be .903(By considering W test value as the measure of reliability), whereas for a group of 500 respondents from top 10 companies of IT (ERP) sector it was found to be .901.

ES09: The customized survey instrument to explore the 20 CFFs for the failure of ERP implementation at Indian SMEs can't be used as reliable survey tool for current and future research because of the low construct reliability of the survey instrument (questionnaire).

For the group of 50 respondents from top 10 companies of IT (ERP) sector the Cronbach's alpha was found to be .792.

Descriptive Statistics

Descriptive Statistics (Questionnaire One)

ES01: The perception (response) of Indian ERP consultant's does not support the statement that" all the 30 CSFs of the LEs also contribute in the success of ERP implementation at Indian SMEs"

Table 4.9: Descriptive Statistics (Questionnaire One)

Descriptive Statistics

Identification of Critical Success Factors-CSFs	Mean	Std. Deviation	N
1	2	3	4
Top Management Commitment and Support	4.64	0.48487	50
Change Management Process	4.7	0.46291	50
BPR and Software Configuration	4.7	0.46291	50
Project Champion	4.66	0.47852	50
Business Plan, Vision	4.76	0.43142	50
Effective Communication Plan	4.66	0.47852	50
Post Implementation Evolution	4.68	0.47121	50
Risk Management	4.62	0.49031	50
Focussed performance Measure	4.68	0.47121	50
Quality Improvement Measure	4.68	0.47121	50
Organization/Corporate Culture	4.56	0.50143	50
Implementation Cost	4.64	0.48487	50
Software Development, Testing, Trouble Shooting and Crises Management	4.66	0.47852	50
IT Infrastructure	4.66	0.47852	50
Selection of ERP Package	4.66	0.47852	50
Data Conversion and Integrity	4.66	0.47852	50
Legacy System Consideration	4.76	0.43142	50
Vanilla ERP	4.68	0.47121	50
System Documentation	4.54	0.50346	50
Project Team	4.62	0.49031	50
Implementation Strategy and Timeframe	4.56	0.50143	50
Consultant Selection	4.54	0.50346	50
Vendor/Customer Relationships	4.48	0.50467	50
Project Management	4.56	0.50143	50

...(Contd.)

1	2	3	4
Client Consultations	4.46	0.50346	50
User Involvement	4.6	0.49487	50
User Education and Training	4.42	0.49857	50
Personnel/Staff	4.5	0.50508	50
Employee Attitude and Morale	4.52	0.50467	50
Empowered Decision Makers	4.44	0.50143	50

Source: Author, SPSS V 18.0

The Finding from the Arithmetic Mean values were: Based on Liker 5 point scale (Strongly Agree=5, Agree=4, Neutral=3, Disagree=2, Strongly Disagree=1) all the thirty factors were showing mean value more than 4(Agree). It shows the perception of Indian ERP consultants towards these thirty factors, that means these factors are critical for the successful ERP implementation at Indian SMEs and can be names as Critical Success Factors (CSFs).

Descriptive Statistics (Questionnaire Two)

ES03: There are no KCSFs for the successful ERP implementation at Indian SMEs because all the 30 CSFs have same ranks (and hence importance/mean values) given by the Indian ERP consultants.

Table 4.10 Descriptive Statistics (Questionnaire Two)

Descriptive Statistics

Ranking of Critical Success Factors-RCSFs	Mean	Std. Deviation	N
1	2	3	4
Top Management Commitment and Support	4.58	2.21396	50
Change Management Process	4.96	2.82814	50
BPR and Software Configuration	6.88	2.84741	50
Project Champion	4.78	2.81606	50
Business Plan, Vision	4.26	2.64042	50
Effective Communication Plan	5.44	3.13089	50
Post Implementation Evolution	6.18	2.92554	50
Risk Management	5.74	2.59363	50
Focussed performance Measure	4.86	3.09054	50

...(Contd.)

1	2	3	4
Quality Improvement Measure	7.32	2.02474	50
Organization/Corporate Culture	14.58	2.21396	50
Implementation Cost	14.96	2.82814	50
Software Development, Testing, Trouble Shooting and Crises Management	16.88	2.84741	50
IT Infrastructure	14.78	2.81606	50
Selection of ERP Package	14.26	2.64042	50
Data Conversion and Integrity	15.38	3.06987	50
Legacy System Consideration	16.18	2.92554	50
Vanilla ERP	15.74	2.59363	50
System Documentation	14.86	3.09054	50
Project Team	17.38	2.05923	50
Implementation Strategy and Timeframe	24.58	2.21396	50
Consultant Selection	24.96	2.82814	50
Vendor/Customer Relationships	26.88	2.84741	50
Project Management	24.78	2.81606	50
Client Consultations	24.26	2.64042	50
User Involvement	25.38	3.06987	50
User Education and Training	26.18	2.92554	50
Personnel/Staff	25.74	2.59363	50
Employee Attitude and Morale	24.86	3.09054	50
Empowered Decision Makers	27.38	2.05923	50

Source: Author, SPSS V 18.0

The Findings from the Arithmetic Mean were: Based on 1 to 30 point scale (Most Important =1, Least Important=30) all the thirty factors were showing different mean value. It shows the perception of Indian ERP consultants towards the ranking of these thirty factors that means, these factors were not equally important for the successful ERP implementation at Indian SMEs and can be names as Key Critical Success Factors (KCSFs) according to their importance.

Descriptive Statistics (Questionnaire Three)

ES02: The perception (response) of Indian ERP consultant's does not support the statement that" all the 20 CFFs of the LEs also contribute in the failure of ERP implementation at Indian SMEs".

ES04: There are no KCFFs for the failure of ERP implementation at Indian SMEs because all the 20 CFFs have same mean value (and hence importance) given by the Indian ERP consultants.

Table 4.11: Descriptive Statistics (Questionnaire Three)

Descriptive Statistics

Critical Failure Factors-RCSFs	Mean	Std. Deviation	N
Poor Consultant Effectiveness	4.6	0.49487	50
Poor Quality of BPR	4.48	0.50467	50
Poor Project Management Effectiveness	4.54	0.50346	50
ERP Software Misfit	4.56	0.50143	50
High Turnover Rate of Project Team Members	4.46	0.50346	50
Over-Reliance on Heavy Customization	4.56	0.50143	50
Poor IT Infrastructure	4.48	0.50467	50
Poor Knowledge Transfer	4.52	0.50467	50
Unclear Concept of the Nature and Use of the ERP System from the Users Perspective	4.5	0.50508	50
Unrealistic Expectations from Top Management Concerning the ERP Systems	4.62	0.49031	50
Too Tight Project Schedule	4.6	0.49487	50
Users' Resistance to Change	4.6	0.49487	50
Poor Top Management Support	4.62	0.49031	50
Poor Quality of Testing	4.68	0.47121	50
Lack of Formal Communication	4.56	0.50143	50
Software Modification	4.6	0.49487	50
Informal Strategy	4.42	0.49857	50
Part-Time Dedication	4.52	0.50467	50
Functionality Problems with the System	4.6	0.49487	50
Cost Over Runs	4.5	0.50508	50

Source: Author, SPSS V 18.0

CFF*- Item related to Identification of Critical Failure Factors, Questionnaire Three.

N*-Number of respondents in questionnaire

The Findings from the Arithmetic Mean were: Based on Liker 5 point scale (Strongly Agree=5, Agree=4, Neutral=3, Disagree=2, Strongly Disagree=1) all the twenty factors were showing mean value more than 4(Agree). It shows the perception of Indian ERP consultants towards these twenty factors that means, these factors are critical for the failure of ERP implementation at Indian SMEs and can be names as Critical Failure Factors (CFFs) and KCFFS according to their importance(mean value).

Factor Analysis

Exploratory Factor Analysis (EFA) was used to identify the various dimensions underlying the data set. 50 responses were examined using principal-components factor analysis as the extraction technique and varimax as the rotation method.

Questionnaire One (Identification of Critical Success Factors)

- *ES05:* All the 30 CSFs can't be categorized to form a unified structure for the successful ERP implementation at Indian SMEs because of their independent nature from each other and hence the exploratory factor analysis was not valid
- *ES13:* No dimensions can be identified for the customized survey instrument (questionnaires) related to the identification (exploring) of CSFs for the successful ERP implementation at Indian SMEs in order to facilitate the standardization process of the survey instrument in the future research.

H0: The factor analysis was not valid

H1: The factor analysis was valid

Table 4.12: KMO and Bartlett's Test,

Kaiser-Meyer-Olkin Measure of Sampling Adequacy		0.511
Bartlett's Test of Sphericity	Approx. Chi-Square	893.007
	df	435
	Sig.	0

Source: SPSS V 18.0

The significance value (0.000) was less than assumed value (.05) so researcher reject the Null Hypothesis *H0*. This means that factor analysis was valid. Next look at the KMO coefficient (0.511). The value was more than .5. So this implies that the factor analysis for data reduction was effective.

Questionnaire Three (Identification of Critical Failure Factors)

- *ES06:* All the 20 CFFs can't be categorized to form a unified structure for the failure of ERP implementation at Indian SMEs because of their independent nature from each other and hence the exploratory factor analysis was not valid
- *ES14:* No dimensions can be identified for the customized survey instrument (questionnaires) related to the identification (exploring) of the CFFs for the failure of ERP implementation at Indian SMEs in order to facilitate the standardization process of the survey instrument (instrument) in future research.

H0: The factor analysis was not valid

H1: The factor analysis was valid

Table 4.13 :KMO and Bartlett's Test for Questionnaire Three

KMO and Bartiett's Test

Kaiser-Meyer-Olkin Measure of Sampling Adequacy		.529
Barleft's Test of Sphericity	Approx. Chi-Square	541.610
	df	190
	Sig.	.000

Source: SPSS V 18.0

The significance value (0.000) was less than assumed value (.05) so researcher reject the Null Hypothesis *H0*. This means that factor analysis was valid. Next look at the KMO coefficient (.529). The value was more than .5. So this implies that the factor analysis for data reduction was effective.

Non-Parametric Tests

From the results of the normality test (one-sample Kolmogorov-Smimov test) it was derived that all of the asymptotic significance levels were below 0.05 and this value was an alpha value for the Kolmogrov Smimov test. So, the null hypothesis was rejected. Thus, these variables were not belonging to a normal distributed sample. Especially, it was really important to find out if the ordinal data is normal or not. In this case (second questionnaire), the ordinal data gathered from the survey was not normal so, as a result, non-parametric tests were applied to search for a possible relationship. In order to choose the most appropriate statistical test for this research, it was very important to know the type of data that was going to be analyzed. In the previous chapter, it was mentioned that the data from the survey was categorical data with nominal and ordinal scales. Following K-related sample tests (non-parametric test) were used for questionnaire two (ranking of critical success factors):

- Friedman Test
- Kendall's W Test

Friedman Test

Non-parametric (distribution-free) tests used to compare observations repeated on the same subjects. Unlike the parametric repeated measures ANOVA or paired t-test, this non-parametric makes no assumptions about the distribution of the data (e.g., normality). This test is an alternative to the repeated measures ANOVA, when the assumption of normality or equality of variance is not met. Many non-parametric tests use the ranks of the data rather than their raw values to calculate the statistics. The hypothesis makes no assumptions about the distribution of the populations. These hypotheses could also be expressed as comparing mean ranks across measures. The null hypothesis for the Friedman test is that there are no differences between the ranks. The test statistic for the Friedman's test is a Chi-square with a-1 degrees of freedom, When the p-value for this test is small (usually <0.05) that have evidence to reject the null hypothesis (Kotahri, 1991)

ES03: There are no KCSFs for successful ERP implementation at Indian SMEs because all the 30 CSFs have same ranks (and hence importance) given by the Indian ERP consultants.

- All the critical success factors have same ranking (and hence importance) for the successful ERP implementation at Indian SMEs

Or

- All the critical success factors do not have same ranking (and hence importance) for the successful ERP implementation at Indian SMEs

Table 4.14 *a* : Friedman Test-Questionnaire Two

Test Statistics[a]	
N	50
Chi-square	1308.708
df	29
Asymp. Sig.	0
a. Friedman Test	

Source: SPSS V 18.0

The significance value (.000) was less than a .05 and the chi-square value being higher, this means reject the *H0*. The rank given to all critical success factors are not same. The order of importance was understood from the descriptive statistics table. The most important factor was Top management commitment and support (mean rank was 4.58), (See Table 1.14*a*, *b*).

Table 4.14*b*: Friedman Test-Questionnaire Two

Mean Ranks

*RCSF (Ranking of Critical Success Factors)	Mean Rank
Top Management Commitment and Support	4.58
Change Management Process	4.96
BPR and Software Configuration	6.88
Project Champion	4.78
Business Plan, Vision	4.26
Effective Communication Plan	5.44
Post Implementation Evolution	6.18
Risk Management	5.74
Focussed performance Measure	4.86
Quality Improvement Measure	7.32
Organization/Corporate Culture	14.58
Implementation Cost	14.96
Software Development, Testing, Trouble Shooting and Crises Management	16.88
IT Infrastructure	14.78
Selection of ERP Package	14.26
Data Conversion and Integrity	15.38
Legacy System Consideration	16.18
Vanilla ERP	15.74
System Documentation	14.86
Project Team	17.38
Implementation Strategy and Timeframe	24.58
Consultant Selection	24.96
Vendor/Customer Relationships	26.88
Project Management	24.78
Client Consultations	24.26
User Involvement	25.38
User Education and Training	26.18
Personnel/Staff	25.74
Employee Attitude and Morale	24.86
Empowered Decision Makers	27.38

ource: Author,SPSS V 18.0

Kendall's W Test

Kendall's W (also known as Kendall's coefficient of concordance) is a non parametric statistic. It is a normalization of the statistic of the Friedman test and can be used for assessing agreement among raters. Kendall's W range from 0 (no agreement) to 1 (complete agreement).Kendall's coefficient o concordance (W test) is linearly related to the mean value of the Spearman' rank correlation coefficients between all pairs of the rankings over which i is calculated. If the test statistic W is 1, then all the judges or survey respondents have been unanimous, and each judge or respondent ha assigned the same order to the list of objects or concerns. If W is 0, ther there is no overall trend of agreement among the respondents and thei responses may be regarded as essentially random. Intermediate values of W indicate a greater or lesser degree of unanimity among the various judges o respondents (Kothari, 1991).

ES08: The customized survey instrument to rank the 30 CSFs for th successful ERP implementation at Indian SMEs can't be used as reliabl survey tool for the current and future research because of the low construc reliability of the survey instrument(questionnaire)

- There was no overall trend of agreement among the response fron the Indian ERP consultants and their responses may be regarde as essentially random for the successful ERP implementation a Indian SMEs

Or

- There was overall trend of agreement among the response fron the Indian ERP consultants and their responses may not b regarded as essentially random for the successful ERP implementation at Indian SMEs

Kendall's W ranges between 0 (no agreement) to 1 (100% agreement) The test statistic W was near to 1, i.e. .903. There was overall trend o agreement among the response from the Indian ERP consultants and thei responses may not be regarded as essentially random for the successful ERP implementation at Indian SMEs. All the judges or respondents have almos assigned the same order to the list of objects or concerns (CSFs). It wa basically an overall descriptive statistic indicating the strength of th agreement among responses, and for the most part, can be interpreted muc like a correlation coefficient, so W = .903, it was statistically significant an it was in the strong form. Although different ranks were given to differen factors (all the factors were not given the same rank) but there was a tren of agreement among the responses while ranking them (See Table 4.15 a, b)

Table 4.15 a: Kendall's W Test-Questionnaire Two

Test Statistics	
N	50
Kendall's Wa	0.903
Chi-square	1308.708
df	29
Asymp. Sig.	0
a. Kendall's Coefficient of Concordance	

(**Source**: SPSS V 18.0)

Table 4.15 b:Kendall's W Test-Questionnaire Two

Mean Ranks

*RCSF (Ranking of Critical Success Factors)	Mean Rank
1	2
Top Management Commitment and Support	4.58
Change Management Process	4.96
BPR and Software Configuration	6.88
Project Champion	4.78
Business Plan, Vision	4.26
Effective Communication Plan	5.44
Post Implementation Evolution	6.18
Risk Management	5.74
Focussed Performance Measure	4.86
Quality Improvement Measure	7.32
Organization/Corporate Culture	14.58
Implementation Cost	14.96
Software Development, Testing, Trouble Shooting and Crises Management	16.88
IT Infrastructure	14.78
Selection of ERP Package	14.26
Data Conversion and Integrity	15.38
Legacy System Consideration	16.18
Vanilla ERP	15.74
System Documentation	14.86
Project Team	17.38

...(Contd.)

1	2
Implementation Strategy and Timeframe	24.58
Consultant Selection	24.96
Vendor/Customer Relationships	26.88
Project Management	24.78
Client Consultations	24.26
User Involvement	25.38
User Education and Training	26.18
Personnel/Staff	25.74
Employee Attitude and Morale	24.86
Empowered Decision Makers	27.38

Source: Author, SPSS V 18.0

RESEARCH ETHICS

The ethics of research concern the responsibility of the researchers for the consequences of their research and its results (Kothari, 1991). The main ethical issues related to this research was to adhere to the privacy and protection for the survey respondents. It was addressed by allowing them to choose the level of confidentiality and the respondent was also free to choose the level of anonymity. The participants name was not mentioned. Even if they had disclosed their identity in questionnaire, their identity was kept confidential. Proper consideration was made, that there will be no harm or risk to any participants' in future .All professional, human ethics was followed. All the ethical and welfare aspects were carefully considered by following norms and using scientific research methodology.

Chapter Summary

This chapter outlined the research approach that was adopted for this research project. The research approach was naturally influenced by the nature of the research questions. ERP systems research is part of the IS research field. A number of different research approaches and methods have been used within the IS research community. This chapter reflects the research method and the approach of the research project. A quantitative survey based approach has been selected as the most appropriate research method for this research problem. Main data collection techniques were primary data collection through three close ended questionnaires along with the review of secondary data. This chapter placed this research work along and amongst the growing number of ERP research due to the careful consideration of all the related aspects by following norms and using scientific research methodology. The next chapter gives a presentation of data analysis for the actual (final) survey of the research project.

5 Analysis of ERP Implementation Success and Failure Models

" After analysis, when you find that anything agrees with reason and is conducive to the good and benefit of one and all, then accept it and apply it"

– Herzog, 1996

This chapter applies the theoretical framework, as described in chapter three and presents the findings from the research project. The findings in this chapter focus on critical success and failure factors for the ERP implementation at Indian SMEs. The factors identified apply to the whole Indian SMEs and are listed as CSFs and CFFs. Each of the CSFs and CFFs were summarized in a table with a short description that was derived from the Indian ERP consultants' perceptions. This study was exploratory in nature which identifies thirty critical success and twenty critical failure factors for the successful ERP implementation at Indian SMEs along with the list of KCSFs and KCFFs by ranking of those CSFs and CFFs. It identified factors that appeared to explain variation between successful and unsuccessful ERP implementations at Indian SMEs, besides this, these factors that appeared to be innovative or counterintuitive in light of the established literature in terms of ERP implementation success and failure at Indian SMEs.

DESCRIPTIVE STATISTICS

Table 5.1 presents the mean and standard deviations for the 30 CSFs in descending order (5=Strong Agree, 4=Agree, 3= Neutral, Disagree, 2=Disagree and 1=Strong Disagree). Second part of the descriptive statistics (See Table 5.2) presents the mean and standard deviations for the 30 KCSFs in order of importance (1=Most Important and 30= Least Important). Table

5.3 presents the mean and standard deviations for the 20 CFFs in descending order (5=Strong Agree, 4=Agree, 3= Neutral, Disagree, 2=Disagree and 1=Strong Disagree). The items used in constructing the survey for this study were adapted from several relevant prior research studies of the large enterprise. To understand mean ranks, order of importance was also calculated with the help of Friedman's Test for the questionnaire two (see Table 5.14a, 14b). Table 5.16 presents mean ranking for the questionnaire two. Order of importance was also presented with the help of mean ranking for the questionnaire three's response (identification of CFFs) (see Table 5.17).

Descriptive Statistics of Response from Questionnaire One

ES01: The perception (response) of Indian ERP consultant's does not support the statement that" all the 30 CSFs of the LEs also contribute in the successful ERP implementation at Indian SMEs"

Table 5.1: Descriptive Statistics of Response from Questionnaire One

Identification of Critical Success Factors-CSFs	Mean	Std. Deviation	N
1	2	3	4
Top Management Commitment and Support	4.4740	.49982	500
Change Management Process	4.4500	.49799	500
BPR and Software Configuration	4.4420	.49712	500
Project Champion	4.4420	.50114	500
Business Plan, Vision	4.4560	.50256	500
Effective Communication Plan	4.4900	.50040	500
Post Implementation Evolution	4.4640	.49920	500
Risk Management	4.4640	.51501	500
Focussed Performance Measure	4.4860	.50030	500
Quality Improvement Measure	4.4760	.50392	500
Organization/Corporate Culture	4.5040	.50048	500
Implementation Cost	4.4280	.49528	500
Software Development, Testing, Trouble Shooting and Crises Management	4.4760	.49992	500
IT Infrastructure	4.4660	.49934	500
Selection of ERP Package	4.4380	.49664	500

...(Contd.)

1	2	3	4
Data Conversion and Integrity	4.4460	.51343	500
Legacy System Consideration	4.4240	.49469	500
Vanilla ERP	4.4420	.50907	500
System Documentation	4.4360	.50040	500
Project Team	4.4620	.49905	500
Implementation Strategy and Timeframe	4.4580	.49873	500
Consultant Selection	4.4460	.50158	500
Vendor/Customer Relationships	4.4560	.49856	500
Project Management	4.4540	.49838	500
Client Consultations	4.4320	.49988	500
User Involvement	4.4420	.54335	500
User Education and Training	4.4380	.50066	500
Personnel/Staff	4.4320	.49988	500
Employee Attitude and Morale	4.5060	.50046	500
Empowered Decision Makers	4.4420	.50907	500

Source: SPSS V 18.0

The Findings from the Arithmetic Mean were as below: Based on Liker 5 point scale (Strongly Agree=5, Agree=4, Neutral=3, Disagree=2, Strongly Disagree=1) all the thirty factors were showing mean value more than 4(Agree). It shows the perception of Indian ERP consultants towards these thirty factors that means, these factors were critical for the successful ERP implementation at Indian SMEs and can be names as Critical Success Factors (CSFs).

Descriptive Statistics of Response from Questionnaire Two

ES03: There are no KCSFs for the successful ERP implementation at Indian SMEs because all the 30 CSFs have same ranks (and hence importance) given by the Indian ERP consultants.

Table 5.2: Descriptive Statistics of Response from Questionnaire Two

Ranking of Critical Success Factors-RCSFs	Mean	Std. Deviation	N
1	2	3	4
Top Management Commitment and Support	4.7060	2.02281	500
Change Management Process	4.8860	2.91513	500

...(Contd.)

1	2	3	4
BPR and Software Configuration	6.5740	3.06844	500
Project Champion	5.1940	2.56076	500
Business Plan, Vision	4.0100	2.62596	500
Effective Communication Plan	5.1160	3.05569	500
Post Implementation Evolution	6.2500	2.58008	500
Risk Management	6.0500	2.89279	500
Focussed Performance Measure	5.0960	3.20364	500
Quality Improvement Measure	7.1180	2.07284	500
Organization/Corporate Culture	14.7060	2.02281	500
Implementation Cost	14.8860	2.91513	500
Software Development, Testing, Trouble Shooting and Crises Management	16.5740	3.06844	500
IT Infrastructure	15.1940	2.56076	500
Selection of ERP Package	14.0100	2.62596	500
Data Conversion and Integrity	15.1040	3.04232	500
Legacy System Consideration	16.2500	2.58008	500
Vanilla ERP	16.0500	2.89279	500
System Documentation	15.0960	3.20364	500
Project Team	17.1300	2.08081	500
Implementation Strategy and Timeframe	24.7060	2.02281	500
Consultant Selection	24.8860	2.91513	500
Vendor/Customer Relationships	26.5740	3.06844	500
Project Management	25.1940	2.56076	500
Client Consultations	24.0100	2.62596	500
User Involvement	25.1040	3.04232	500
User Education and Training	26.2500	2.58008	500
Personnel/Staff	26.0500	2.89279	500
Employee Attitude and Morale	25.0960	3.20364	500
Empowered Decision Makers	27.1300	2.08081	500

Source: SPSS V 18.0

The Findings from the Arithmetic Mean were as below: Based on 1 to 30 point scale (Most Important=1, Least Important=30) all the thirty factors were showing different mean value. It shows the perception of Indian ERP consultants towards the ranking of these thirty factors. These factors were critical for the successful ERP implementation at Indian SMEs and can be names as Key Critical Success Factors (KCSFs) based on their importance.

Descriptive Statistics of Response from Questionnaire Three

ES02: The perception (response) of Indian ERP consultant's does not support the statement that" all the 20 CFFs of the LEs also contribute in the failure of ERP implementation at Indian SMEs".

Table 5.3: Descriptive Statistics of Response from Questionnaire Three

Identification of Critical Failure Factors-CFFs	Mean	Std. Deviation	N
1	2	3	4
Poor Consultant Effectiveness	4.6000	.49487	50
Poor Quality of BPR.	4.4800	.50467	50
Poor Project Management Effectiveness	4.5400	.50346	50
ERP Software Misfit	4.5600	.50143	50
High Turnover Rate of Project Team Members	4.4600	.50346	50
Over-Reliance on Heavy Customization	4.5600	.50143	50
Poor IT Infrastructure	4.4800	.50467	50
Poor Knowledge Transfer	4.5200	.50467	50
Unclear Concept of the Nature and Use of the ERP System from the Users Perspective	4.5000	.50508	50
Unrealistic Expectations from Top Management Concerning the ERP Systems	4.6200	.49031	50
Too Tight Project Schedule	4.6000	.49487	50
Users' Resistance to Change	4.6000	.49487	50
Poor Top Management Support	4.6200	.49031	50
Poor Quality of Testing	4.6800	.47121	50
Lack of Formal Communication	4.5600	.50143	50
Software Modification	4.6000	.49487	50

...(Contd.)

1	2	3	4
Informal Strategy	4.4200	.49857	50
Part-Time Dedication	4.5200	.50467	50
Functionality Problems with the System	4.6000	.49487	50
Cost Over Runs	4.5000	.50508	50

Source: SPSS V 18.0

The Findings from the Arithmetic Mean were as below: Based on Liker 5 point scale (Strongly Agree=5, Agree=4, Neutral=3, Disagree=2, Strongly Disagree=1) all the twenty factors were showing mean value more than 4(Agree). It shows the perception of Indian ERP consultants towards these twenty factors that means, these factors were critical in the failure of ERP implementation at Indian SMEs and can be names as Critical Failure Factors (CFFs).

FACTOR ANALYSIS

Factor analysis is an *m* by *n* matrix of correlations between the original variables and their factors. Where n is number of variables and m is the number of retained factors. A rule of thumb frequently used is that factors loading greater than .45 in absolute value were considered to be significant. Using SPSS statistical package and the scree plot of the Eigen values from the principal component analysis, components were revealed. The goal in labelling each of these components was to come up with a term that best describes the content domain of the attributes that load highly on each factor.

Analysis of Responses from Questionnaire One

The data collected on the critical success factors were first perused to check whether the data could be analyzed using factor analysis or not. The results of this analysis indicate that the correlations among the factors were greater than .50 *(See Table 5.7 on page 124)*, the measure of sampling adequacy ranged from mediocre to meritorious, and the Bartlett's test of sphericity was significant *(See Table 5.4 on next page)*. The data were hence found suitable for the conduct of factor analysis. An exploratory factor analysis was conducted on the different measures to purify the instrument. Factor analysis was also used to identify underlying factors or the dimensional composition of instrument. Exploratory factor analysis (EFA) was used to validate the various dimensions underlying the data set. The 500 responses were examined using principal-components factor analysis as the extraction technique and Varimax as the rotation method (See Table 5.7). Only factors with Eigen value (Total variance explained) more than 1 were included in final solutions *(See Table*

5.6 on page 123). Factor loading is simple correlation between the factors and all the variables. It can be used to decide which variable belongs to which factors .this judgment best done in raoted factor matrix (See table 5.7). Each variables belongs to the factors with which it has the highest loading (neglect the negative sign).This process was used to find out all the constituent variables of each factors *(See Table 5.8 on page 126)*.

KMO and Bartlett's Test with Exploratory Factor Analysis

- *ES05:* All the 30 CSFs can't be categorized to form a unified structure for the successful ERP implementation at Indian SMEs because of their independent nature from each other and hence the exploratory factor analysis was not valid
- *ES10:* The customized survey instrument to explore the 30 CSFs for the successful ERP implementation at Indian SMEs can't be used as validate survey tool for current and future research because of the low construct validity of the survey instrument (questionnaire).
- *ES13:* No dimensions can be identified for the survey instrument (questionnaires) related to the identification (exploring) of CSFs for the successful ERP implementation at Indian SMEs in order to facilitated the standardization process of the survey instrument (questionnaire) for future research.

H0: The factor analysis was not valid

H1: The factor analysis was valid

Table 5.4: KMO and Bartlett's Test for Questionnaire One

KMO and Bartlett's Test		
Kaiser-Meyer-Olkin Measure of Sampling Adequacy		0.658
Bartlett's Test of Sphericity	Approx. Chi-Square	3016.483
	df	435
	Sig.	0

(**Source:** Author, SPSS V 18.0)

The significance value (0.000) is less than assumed value (.05) so reject the Null Hypothesis H0.This means that factor analysis was valid. Next look at the KMO coefficient (0.658).The value was more than .5.So this implies that the factor analysis for data reduction was effective.

Critical Success Factors Identification and Exploratory Hypotheses (Statements) Testing

The conceptualization of survey instrument constructs was based on preliminary literature review to form the initial items. The personal interviews with ERP practitioners and experts views for scale purification suggest that the survey instrument has strong content validity. Construct validity was evaluated by performing factor analysis (See Table 5.8). High correlations among the CSFs were considered to indicate construct validity. Estimates greater than .70 were generally considered to meet the criteria for reliability. In Table 5.5 the composite reliability estimates for the measurement scales were listed .As shown in the table below that reliability was above .7 thus sufficient internal consistency has been judged for the reliable measure of the customized instrument. It was observed from the reliability analysis that alpha value for the questionnaire one was as below.

ES07: The customized survey instrument to explore the 30 CSFs for the successful ERP implementation at Indian SMEs can't be used as reliable survey tool for current and future research because of the low construct reliability of the survey instrument (questionnaire).

ES10: The customized survey instrument to explore the 30 CSFs for the successful ERP implementation at Indian SMEs can't be used as validate survey tool for current and future research because of the low construct validity of the survey instrument (questionnaire).

Table 5.5: The Composite Reliability for Questionnaire One

Reliability Statistics		
Cronbach's Alpha	**Cronbach's Alpha Based on Standardized Items**	**N of Items**
0.723	0.724	30

(**Source**: Author, SPSS V 18.0).

For the group of 50 respondents from the top 10 companies of IT(ERP) sector validity was found to be .8865, whereas for a group of 500 respondents from top 10 companies of IT(ERP) sector it was found to be .8508.The validity was found by using Guilford's formula i.e. by applying the square root of the reliability. Construct validity of the instrument was tested with the help of factor analysis. The Factor analysis was valid and the instrument had strong construct validity. It can be seen from the total variance explained in the Table that 11 factors have Eigen value over 1 (See Table 5.6).It shows cumulative variance of 63.681 per cent which means a good factor analysis has been done. The factor analysis performed on 30 items resulted into the extraction of 11 components (See Table 5.6). Based on the content of each component they were suitably named. Factor analysis was used to identify the critical success factors that contribute in the successful ERP implementation at Indian SMEs.

- The factors were fixed at eleven. See Table 5.6.

- They together contribute almost 63.681 per cent of total variance. See table 5.6
- The most important factor among these was component 1: Risk related CSFs, which contribute almost 11.845 per cent of the total variance. See Table 5.8.
- The variables were divided into different factors based on the values in the rotated component matrix (the higher values were taken) see Table 5.7. The divisions of variables into different factors were given in Table 5.8.

Table 5.6: Total Variance Explained for Questionnaire One-Identification of CSFs

Component	Initial Eigenvalues			Extraction sums of Squared Loadings		
	Total	% of Variance	Comulative %	Total	% of Variance	Comulative %
1	2	3	4	5	6	7
1	3.554	11.845	11.845	3.554	11.845	11.845
2	2.426	8.086	19.931	2.426	8.086	19.931
3	2.007	6.690	26.622	2.007	6.690	26.622
4	1.872	6.240	32.862	1.872	6.240	32.862
5	1.743	5.808	38.670	1.743	5.808	38.670
6	1.550	5.166	43.836	1.550	5.166	43.836
7	1.364	4.548	48.384	1.364	4.548	48.384
8	1.270	4.233	52.617	1.270	4.233	52.617
9	1.169	3.896	56.513	1.169	3.896	56.513
10	1.117	3.722	60.235	1.117	3.722	60.235
11	1.034	3.446	63.681	1.034	3.446	63.681
12	983	3.278	66.959			
13	.844	2.815	69.773			
14	.809	2.696	72.470			
15	.728	2.427	74.897			
16	.714	2.381	77.278			
17	.704	2.346	79.624			
18	6.48	2.160	81.783			
19	6.30	2.102	83.885			
20	.550	1.833	85.718			
21	.546	1.818	87.536			
22	.516	1.720	89.256			

...(Contd.)

1	2	3	4	5	6	7
23	.485	1.615	90.872			
24	.469	1.564	92.436			
25	.425	1.417	93.853			
26	.400	1.334	95.187			
27	.391	1.304	96.491			
28	.367	1.222	97.713			
29	.357	1.190	98.903			
30	.329	1.097	100.000			

Extraction Method: Principal Component Analysis.
(**Source**: Author, SPSS V 18.0)

Table 5.7: Rotated Components Matrix for Questionnaire One-Identification of CSFs

Rotated Component Matrixa

Critical Success Factors	Component										
	1	2	3	4	5	6	7	8	9	10	11
CSF30 Empowred Decision Makers	0.777	0.124	-0.06	0.016	-0.012	0.055	0.073	0.051	0.0022	-0.016	-0.029
C9F25 Client Consultations	0.765	0.054	0.065	-0.033	-0.056	0.072	0.052	0.129	0.025	0.036	0.11
CSF8 risk Management	0.596	-0.204	0.029	0.114	0.249	0.092	-0.048	-0.045	0.172	0.091	-0.098
CSF16 DATA Conversion & Integrity	0.539	0.116	0.23	0.073	-0.111	-0.028	0.099	0.35	-0.06	0.184	-0.034
CSF 13 Software Development, Testing, Trouble Shoo	0.013	0.768	0.02	0.118	0.131	0.037	-0.031	-0.034	0.079	0.089	-0.086
CSF18 Vanilla ERP	-0.047	0.695	-0.026	-0.065	0.368	-0.001	-0.027	-0.026	-0.04	-0.019	-0.071
CSF29 Employee Attitude & Morale	0.188	0.686	-0.026	0.212	-0.131	0.02	0.013	-0.043	-0.034	-0.096	0.226

...(*Contd.*)

Critical Success Factors	Component										
	1	2	3	4	5	6	7	8	9	10	11
CSP3 BPR & Software Configuration	0.085	-0.063	09.746	-0.06	-0.07	-0.014	0.2	-0.009	0.133	-0.043	0.075
CSPF6 Effective Communication Plan	0.071	-0.029	0.683	0.019	0.053	0.224	-0.181	0.097	0.006	-0.135	-0.061
CSF10 Quality Improvement Measure	-0.041	0.078	0.587	0.113	-0.119	-0.137	0.068	0.055	0.47	0.202	0.019
CSF1 Top Management Commitment & Support	-0.059	0.061	0.533	0.055	0.174	0.51	-0.122	0.07	-0.098	0.032	-0.005
CSF4 Project Champion	-0.045	0.077	0.017	0.811	0.029	0.111	0.002	-0.026	0.107	-0.078	0.037
CSF21 Implementation Strategy & Timeframe	0.008	0.25	-0.075	0.728	-0.042	-0.21	-0.024	0.088	0.022	0.042	0.025
CSF11 Organization Corporate Culture	0.16	-0.093	0.107	0.657	0.075	0.001	0.293	-0.057	0.01	-0.039	0.007
CSF17 Legacy System Consideration	0.021	0.031	0.061	0.066	0.803	0.006	0.091	-0.002	0.051	0.048	0.178
CSF15 Selection of ERP Package	0.005	0.387	-0.29	0.002	0.744	0.026	0.004	0.025	-0.017	0.027	-0.071
CSF20 Project Team	0.03	0.078	-0.051	0.9029	-0.045	0.79	0.164	0.012	-0.013	0.131	0.048
CSF5 Business Plan, Vision	0.163	-0.073	0.18	0.023	0.062	-0.08	0.616	0.048	-0.198	-0.01	-0.107
CSF2 Change Management Process	0.087	-0.001	0.008	-0.01	0.035	0.099	0.826	0.044	0.091	-0.05	-0.054
CSF9 Focused performance Measure	0.03	-0.121	0.012	0.323	0.162	-0.08	0.616	0.048	-0.198	-0.001	-0.107
CSF7 Post Implementation Evolution	0.037	0.088	-0.009	0.05	-0.113	0.513	0.594	-0.007	0.078	0.06	0.083

...(Contd.)

Critical Success Factors	Component										
	1	2	3	4	5	6	7	8	9	10	11
CSF28 Personnel Staff	0.062	-0.131	0.071	-0.017	0.052	0.049	0.018	0.763	0.09	-0.02	0.068
CSF27 User Education & Training	0.124	-0.013	-0.1	0.025	0.015	0.045	-0.11	0.688	0.388	-0.151	-0.1
CSF22 Consultant Selection	0.173	0.092	0.175	0.009	-0.05	-0.008	0.209	0.611	-0.48	0.354	0.095
CSF24 Project Management	0.099	-0.009	0.25	0.053	0.022	-0.037	-0.031	0.028	0.778	-0.028	0.057
CSF14 IT Infrastructure	0.027	0.015	-0.045	0.051	0.062	0.118	0.042	0.22	0.694	0.116	-0.036
CSF12 Implementation Cost	-0.012	0.075	-0.034	0.002	-0.059	0.083	-0.074	0.088	-0.008	0.805	-0.09
CSF19 System Documentation	0.244	-0.134	-0.068	-0.115	0.218	0.029	0.044	-0.089	0.189	0.611	0.54
CSF26 User Involvement	0	0.02	-0.007	0.067	-0.43	0.013	-0.075	0.009	-0.039	-0.011	0.821
CSF23 Vendor Customer Relationships	-0.008	-0.03	0.049	-0.032	0.457	0.026	0.001	0.073	0.092	-0.054	0.66
Extraction Method: Principal Component Analysis											
Rotation Method: Varimax with Kaiser Normalization											

[a]Rotation converged in 13 literations.
(**Source**: Author, SPSS V 18.0)

Table 5.8: Interpretation of Output from the Factor Analysis for Questionnaire One

Categorization of CSFs in terms of Component	TVE	List of CSFs for Indian SMEs	RCMV
1	2	3	4
Component 1 This component was named as Risk related CSFs, it consist of the following items:	11.845%	Empowered Decision Makers Client Consultations Risk Management Data Conversion and Integrity	.777 .765 .596 .539

...(*Contd.*)

1	2	3	4
Component 2 This component was named as Process related CSFs, it consist of the following items:	8.806%	Software Development, Testing, Trouble Shooting and Crises Management Vanilla ERP Employee Attitude and Morale	.768 .695 .686
Component 3 This component was named as Quality related CSFs, it consist of the following items:	6.690%	BPR and Software Configuration Effective Communication Plan Quality Improvement Measure Top Management Commitment and Support	.746 .683 .587 .533
Component 4 This component was named as Enterprise related CSFs, it consist of the following items:	6.240%	Project Champion Implementation Strategy and Timeframe Organization/Corporate Culture	.811 .728 .657
Component 5 This component was named as Technology Related CSFs, it consist of the following items:	5.5808%	Legacy System Consideration Selection of ERP Package	.803 .744
Component 6 This component was named as Project related CSFs, it consist of the following items:	5.166%	Project Team Business Plan, Vision	.790 .706
Component 7 This component was named as Performance related CSFs, it consist of the following items:	4.548%	Change Management Process Focussed Performance Measure Post Implementation Evolution	.826 .616 .594
Component 8 This component was named as Employee/ HR related CSFs, it consist of the following items:	4.233%	Personnel/Staff User Education and Training Consultant Selection	.763 .688 .611
Component 9 This component was named as Strategy related CSFs, it consist of the following items:	3.896%	Project Management IT Infrastructure	.778 .694
Component 10 This component was named as Vendor related CSFs, it consist of the following items:	3.722%	Implementation Cost System Documentation	.805 .611
Component 11 This component was named as End-user related CSFs, it consist of the following items:	3.446%	User Involvement Vendor/Customer Relationships	.821 .660

(**Source**: SPSS V 18)

Final Adjusted ERP Implementation Success Model

These study consuls that all these thirty critical success factors contribute in the success of ERP implementation at Indian SMEs and they have different priorities (ranking) during all the phases of ERP implementation at Indian SMEs *(see Table 5.16 on page 142)*. This study also makes group of important factors for the successful ERP implementation at Indian SMEs by identifying KCSFs. ERP consultants, ERP vendors and Indian SMEs may consider all these CSFs for the successful ERP implementation. Since the groping of variables were done on basis of data collected from the Indian ERP consultants the results of the study may be acceptable for the Indian ERP vendors and may be acknowledged by the Indian ERP consultants. Based on the results obtained from the above analysis following model can be proposed for the successful ERP implementation at Indian SMEs.

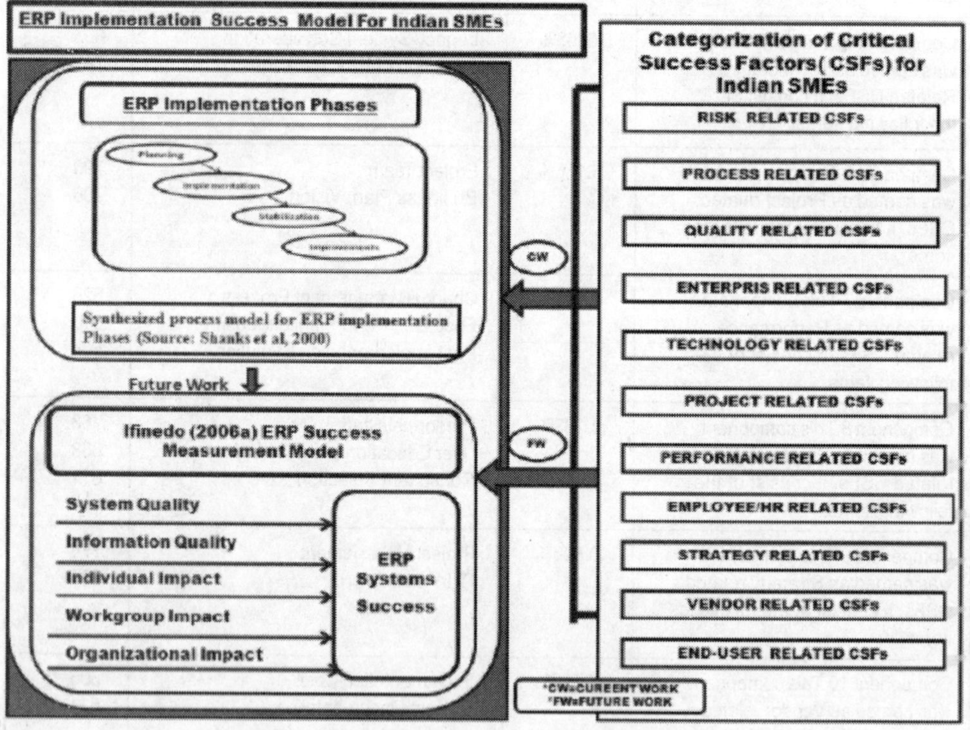

(**Source**: Author, MS-PowerPoint)

Fig. 5.1 : ERP Implementation Success Model for Indian SMEs

The Conceptual ERP Implementation Success Model (See Figure 5.1) for the Successful ERP implementation at Indian SMEs along with the list of KCSFs (see Table 5.16) may be used during all the phases of ERP implementation at Indian SMEs to make ERP implementation successful because the boundaries between planning, implementation, stabilization and improvements are not rigid. The conceptual ERP implementation success model simplifies the functionality of ERP implementation at Indian SMEs.

The simplification of system makes easier to understand the ERP requirements. Commonly, a better system is easier to understand, implement and maintain for the ERP users and the implementers. By using this model for small and medium-size companies ERP implementation, especially in India, ERP consultants and vendors may helps to Indian SMEs to achieve global business process by implementing ERP systems efficiently and effectively. The Findings of the research were as below:

- Significant relationships were found between CSFs of the LEs and the successful ERP implementation at Indian SMEs;
- Thirty critical success factors were identified (See Figure5.1, ERP implementation success model) and ranked (Key Critical Success Factors, see Table 5.16) according to their priority (mean ranks) for the successful ERP implementation at Indian SMEs.

Analysis of Responses from Questionnaire Three

The data collected on the critical failure factors were first perused to check whether the data could be analyzed using factor analysis or not. The results of this analysis indicate that the correlations among the factors were greater than .45 and the Bartlett's test of sphericity was significant *(See Table 5.9 on next page)*. The measure of sampling adequacy ranged from mediocre to meritorious. The data were hence found suitable for the conduct of factor analysis. An exploratory factor analysis was conducted on the different measures to purify the instrument. Factor analysis was also used to identify underlying factors or the dimensional composition of instrument. Exploratory Factor Analysis (EFA) was used to validate the various dimensions underlying the data set *(See Table 5.13 on page 134)*. The 50 responses were examined using principal-components factor analysis as the extraction technique and Varimax as the rotation method *(See Table 5.12 on page 132-133)*. Only factors with Eigen value (Total variance explained) more than 1 were included in final solutions *(See Table 5.11 on page 132)*. Factor loading is simple correlation between the factors and all the variables. It can be used to decide which variable belongs to which factors. This judgment best done in rotated factor matrix *(See Table 5.12)*. Each variables belongs to the factors with which it has the highest loading (neglect the negative sign).This process was used to find out all the constituent variables of each factors *(See Table 5.13 on page 134)*.

KMO and Bartlett's Test with Exploratory Factor Analysis

- *ES06:* All the 20 CFFs can't be categorized to form a unified structure for the failure of ERP implementation at Indian SMEs because of their independent nature from each other and hence the exploratory factor analysis was not valid
- *ES12:* The customized survey instrument to explore the 20 CFFs for the failure of ERP implementation at Indian SMEs can't be used as validate survey tool for current and future research because of the low construct validity of the survey instrument (questionnaire).
- *ES14:* No dimensions can be identified for the survey instrument (questionnaire) related to the identification (exploring) of the CFFs for the failure of ERP implementation at Indian SMEs in order to facilitate the standardization process of the survey instrument(questionnaire) for future research.

H0: The factor analysis was not valid

H1: The factor analysis was valid

Table 5.9: KMO and Bartlett's Test for Questionnaire Three

Kaiser-Meyer-Olkin Measure of Sampling Adequacy	.529
Bartiett's Test of Sphericity Approx. Chi-Square	541.610
df	190
Sig.	.000

(**Source**: Author, SPSS V 18.0)

The significance value (0.000) was less than assumed value (.05) so reject the Null Hypothesis H0.This means that factor analysis was valid. Next look at the KMO coefficient (.529).The value was more than .5.So this implies that the factor analysis for data reduction was effective.

Critical Failure Factors Identification and Exploratory Hypotheses (Statements) Testing

The conceptualization of survey instrument constructs was based on preliminary literature review to form the initial items. The personal interviews with ERP practitioners and experts views for scale purification suggest that the survey instrument has strong content validity. Construct validity was evaluated by performing factor analysis *(See Table 5.13 on page 134)*. High correlations among the CFFs were considered to indicate construct validity. Estimates greater than .70 were generally considered to meet the criteria for reliability. In table 5.10 the composite reliability estimates for the measurement scales were listed. As shown in the table below that reliability was above .75 thus sufficient internal consistency has been judged for the reliable measure of the customized survey instrument. It was observed from the reliability analysis that alpha value of the questionnaire was as below.

ES09: The customized survey instrument to explore the 20 CFFs for the failure of ERP implementation at Indian SMEs can't be used as reliable survey tool for current and future research because of the low construct reliability of the survey instrument (questionnaire).

ES12: The customized survey instrument to explore the 20 CFFs for the failure of ERP implementation at Indian SMEs can't be used as validate survey tool for current and future research because of the low construct validity of the survey instrument (questionnaire).

Table 5.10: The Composite Reliability for Questionnaire Three

Reliability Statistics		
Cronbach's Alpha	**Cronbach's Alpha Based on Standardized Items**	**N of Items**
.792	.792	20

(**Source**: Author, SPSS V 18.0)

For the group of 50 respondents from the top 10 companies of IT (ERP) sector validity was found to be .8899.The validity was found by using Guilford's formula i.e. by applying the square root of the reliability. Construct validity of the instrument was tested with the help of factor analysis. The Factor analysis was valid and the instrument had strong construct validity. It was seen from the total variance explained table that only 7 factors have Eigen value over 1(See Table 5.11).It shows cumulative variance of 76.134 % which means a good factor analysis has been done *(See Table 5.11)*. The factor analysis performed on 20 items resulted into the extraction of 7 components *(See Table 5.13 on page 134)*. Based on the content of each component they were suitably named. Factor analysis was used to identify the critical failure factors that contribute in the failure of ERP implementation at Indian SMEs.

- The factors were fixed at seven. See Table 5.11.
- They together contribute almost 76.134 % of total variance. See Table 5.11
- The most important factor among these was Component 1: Technology and Vendor related CFFs, which contribute almost 15.088% of the total variance. See Table 5.13.
- The variables were divided into different factors based on the values in the rotated component matrix (the higher values were taken), See Table 5.12. The divisions of variables into different factors were given in Table 5.13

Table 5.11: Total Variance Explained for Questionnaire Three—Identification of CFFs

Total Variance Explained									
Component	Initial Eigen values			Extraction Sums of Squared Loadings			Rotation Sums of Squared Loadings		
	Total	% of Variance	Cumulative %	Total	% of Variance	Cumulative %	Total	% of Variance	Cumulative %
1	4.824	24.118	24.118	4.824	24.118	24.118	3.018	15.088	15.088
2	2.957	14.786	38.905	2.957	14.786	38.905	2.869	14.344	29.432
3	2.35	11.748	50.653	2.35	11.748	50.653	2.691	13.454	42.886
4	1.587	7.934	58.587	1.587	7.934	58.587	2.025	10.127	53.013
5	1.38	6.901	65.488	1.38	6.901	65.488	1.56	7.799	60.813
6	1.115	5.575	71.063	1.115	5.575	71.063	1.538	7.69	68.503
7	1.014	5.071	76.134	1.014	5.071	76.134	1.526	7.632	76.134
8	0.906	4.531	80.665						
9	0.785	3.927	84.592						
10	0.569	2.843	87.435						
11	0.553	2.766	90.201						
12	0.431	2.157	92.358						
13	0.397	1.983	94.341						
14	0.312	1.559	95.9						
15	0.263	1.315	97.215						
16	0.199	0.996	98.212						
17	0.134	0.668	98.879						
18	0.124	0.619	99.498						
19	0.055	0.273	99.771						
20	0.046	0.229	100						

(**Source**: Author, SPSS V 18.0)
Extraction Method: Principal Component Analysis.

Table 5.12: Rotated Components Matrix for Questionnaire Three—Identification of CFFs

Rotated Component Matrix							
Critical Failure Factors	**Component**						
	1	**2**	**3**	**4**	**5**	**6**	**7**
Poor Consultant Effectiveness	0.828	0.268	0.067	0.058	-0.145	0.102	0.085
ERP Software Misfit	0.796	0.296	-0.058	0.28	0.089	0.195	0.085

...(Contd.)

Critical Failure Factors	Component						
	1	2	3	4	5	6	7
Unrealistic Expectations from Top Management	0.771	0.116	0.311	-0.055	0.329	-0.179	-0.075
Over-Reliance on Heavy Customization	0.668	0.255	-0.126	0.258	0.305	0.325	0.159
Poor Quality of BPR	0.144	0.874	-0.095	-0.044	-0.088	0.092	-0.122
High Turnover Rate of Project Team Members	0.236	0.873	0.074	-0.072	-0.104	-0.124	0.017
Poor IT Infrastructure	0.179	0.831	0.019	-0.022	0.121	0.041	0.155
Functionality Problems with the System	-0.371	0.049	0.834	-0.018	0.022	0.124	0.059
Unclear Concept	0.118	0.141	0.734	-0.003	0.053	-0.287	-0.13
Too Tight Project Schedule	0.202	0.003	0.601	0.324	0.208	-0.221	0.246
Lack of Formal Communication	0.206	-0.175	0.581	0.143	0.396	0.174	0.234
Part-Time Dedication	0.386	-0.238	0.548	0.08	-0.157	0.08	-0.144
Poor Project Management Effectiveness	0.143	-0.091	0.097	0.903	0.012	0.003	-0.139
Poor Knowledge Transfer	0.13	-0.023	0.112	0.777	0.158	0.097	0.28
Poor Quality of Testing	0.073	-0.104	0.085	0.057	0.867	0.162	-0.181
Users' Resistance to Change	0.135	0.263	0.125	0.332	0.462	-0.233	0.38
Poor Top Management Support	-0.035	0.165	0.34	-0.005	-0.143	-0.762	0.107
Software Modification	0.295	0.263	0.267	0.045	0.015	0.653	0.01
Cost Over Runs	-0.038	0.037	0.039	-0.078	0.148	0.078	-0.875
Informal Strategy	0.118	0.343	0.298	-0.441	0.191	0.2	0.484
Extraction Method: Principal Component Analysis.							
Rotation Method: Varimax with Kaiser Normalization.							
a. Rotation converged in 10 iterations.							

(**Source**: Author, SPSS V 18.0)

Table 5.13: Interpretation of Output from the Factor Analysis for Questionnaire Three

Categorization of CFFs in terms of Component	TVE*	List of CFFs for Indian SMEs	RCMV**
Component 1 this component was named as Technology and Vendor related CFFs. It Consist following items:	15.088%	Poor consultant effectiveness ERP software misfit Unrealistic expectations from top management concerning the ERP systems Over-reliance on heavy customization	.828 .796 .771 .668
Component 2 this component was named as Employee/ Personnel/HR and Process related CFFs. It Consist following items:	14.344%	Poor quality of BPR High turnover rate of project team members Poor IT Infrastructure	.874 .873 .831
Component 3 This component was named as Performance related CFFs. It Consist following items:	13.454%	Functionality problems with the system Unclear concept of the nature and use of the ERP system from the users perspective Too tight project schedule Lack of formal communication Part-time dedication	.834 .734 .601 .581 .548
Component 4 This component was named as Project related CFFs. It Consist following items:	10.127%	Poor project management effectiveness Poor knowledge transfer	.903 .777
Component 5 This component was named as Quality and End-user Related CFFs. It Consist following items:	.799%	Poor quality of testing Users' resistance to change	.867 .462
Component 6 This component was named as Enterprise related CFFs. It Consist following items:	7.690%	Poor top management support Software modification	(-.762) .653
Component 7 This component was named as Strategy related CFFs. It Consist following items:	7.632 %	Cost over runs Informal strategy	(-.875) .484

(**Source**: Author, SPSS V 18.0)

Final Adjusted ERP Implementation Failure Model

This study show that all these twenty critical failure factors contribute in the failure of ERP implementation at Indian SMEs and they have different priorities (ranking) during all the phases of ERP implementation at Indian SMEs. The study also makes group of important factors responsible for the failure of ERP implementation at Indian SMEs by identifying KCFFs *(See Table 5.17 on page 143)*. ERP consultants, ERP vendors and Indian SMEs may consider all these CFFs to determine the failure of ERP implementation. Since the groping of variables were done on the basis of data collected from the Indian ERP consultants the results of the study may be acceptable for the Indian ERP vendors and may be acknowledged by the Indian ERP consultants. Based on the results obtained from the above analysis following model can be proposed for the failure of ERP implementation at Indian SMEs.

The Conceptual ERP Implementation failure model (See Figure 5.2) for the failure of ERP implementation at Indian SMEs along with the list of KCFFs (See Table 5.17) may be used during all the phases of ERP implementation at Indian SMEs in order to avoid the failure of ERP because the boundaries

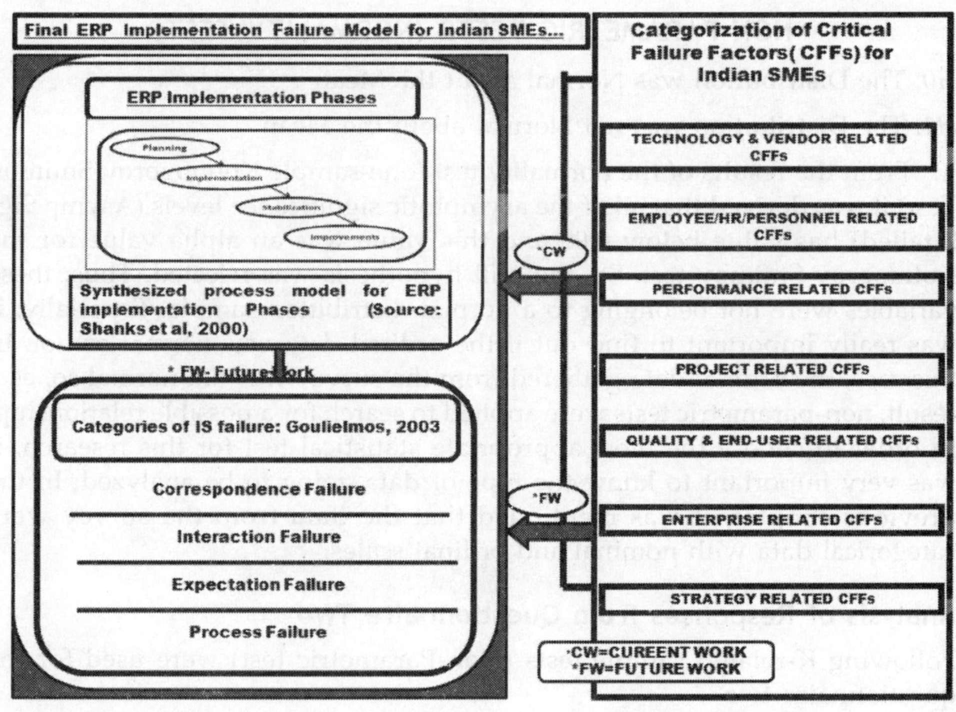

(**Source**: Author, MS-PowerPoint)

Fig. 5.2: ERP Implementation Failure Model for Indian SMEs

between planning, implementation, stabilization and improvements are not rigid.

The conceptual ERP implementation failure model simplifies the functionality of ERP implementation at Indian SMEs. The simplification of system makes easier to understand the ERP requirements. Commonly, a better system is easier to understand, implement and maintain for the ERP users and the implementers. By using this model for small and medium-size companies ERP implementation, especially in India, ERP consultants and vendor may help to Indian SMEs to achieve global business process by implementing ERP package efficiently and effectively. The Findings of the research were as below:

- Significant relationships were found between CFFs of the LEs and the failure of ERP implementation at Indian SMEs *(See Table 5.13 on page 134)*.
- Twenty critical failure factors were identified (See Figure 5.2, ERP implementation failure model) and ranked (Key Critical Failure Factors, *(see Table 5.17 on page 143)* according to their mean values.

NON-PARAMETRIC TESTS (NORMALITY TEST)

H0: The Distribution was Normal about the Mean

H1: The Distribution was not Normal about the Mean

From the results of the normality test (one-sample Kolmogorov-Smimov Test) it was derived that all of the asymptotic significance levels (Asymp Sig-2 tailed) has value below 0.05 and this value was an alpha value for the Kolmogrov Smimov test. So, the null hypothesis was rejected. Thus, these variables were not belonging to a normal distributed sample. Especially, it was really important to find out if the ordinal data was normal or not. In this case, the ordinal data gathered from the survey was not normal so, as a result, non-parametric tests were applied to search for a possible relationship. In order to choose the most appropriate statistical test for this research, it was very important to know the type of data going to be analyzed. In the previous chapter, it was mentioned that the data from the survey were categorical data with nominal and ordinal scales.

Analysis of Responses from Questionnaire Two

Following K-related sample tests (Non-Parametric test) were used for the questionnaire two

- Friedman Test
- Kendall's W Test

Friedman Test

A non-parametric (distribution-free) test used to compare observations repeated on the same subjects. Unlike the parametric repeated measures ANOVA or paired t-test, this non-parametric makes no assumptions about the distribution of the data (e.g., normality). This test is an alternative to the repeated measures ANOVA, when the assumption of normality or equality of variance is not met. Many non-parametric tests use the ranks of the data rather than their raw values to calculate the statistic. The hypothesis makes no assumptions about the distribution of the populations. These hypotheses could also be expressed as comparing mean ranks across measures. The null hypothesis for the Friedman test is that there are no differences between the ranks. The test statistic for the Friedman's test is a Chi-square with a-1 degrees of freedom, When the p-value for this test is small (usually <0.05) that have evidence to reject the null hypothesis. It is used in the situations in which the same subjects /variables are observed by more than once, a form of rank order (Kothari, 1991). So here Friedman test was used.

ES03: There are no KCSFs for the successful ERP implementation at Indian SMEs because all the 30 CSFs have same ranks (and hence importance) given by the Indian ERP consultants.

- All the 30 critical success factors have same ranking (and hence importance) for the successful ERP implementation at Indian SMEs

Or

- All the 30 critical success factors do not have same ranking (and hence importance) for the successful ERP implementation at Indian SMEs

Table 5.14a: Friedman Test for Questionnaire Two Test Statistics[a]

N	500
Chi-square	13063.880
df	29
A Symp. Sig.	.000

a. Friedman Test

Source: Author, SPSS V 18.0)

The significance value (.000) was less than a .05. While comparing degree of freedom and chi-square value, calculated value being higher this means *H0* was rejected. The rank given to all 30 critical success factors were not same. The order of importance was understood from the descriptive statistics, See Table 5.2. The most important factor was business plan, vision (mean rank was 4.01), top management commitment and support (mean rank was 4.71) and so on, See Table 5.16 on page 142.

Table 5.14b: Friedman Test for Questionnaire Two Ranks

*RCSF (Ranking of Critical Success Factors)	Mean Rank
Top Management Commitment and Support	4.71
Change Management Process	4.89
BPR and Software Configuration	6.57
Project Champion	5.19
Business Plan, Vision	4.01
Effective Communication Plan	5.12
Post Implementation Evolution	6.25
Risk Management	6.05
Focussed Performance Measure	5.1
Quality Improvement Measure	7.12
Organization/Corporate Culture	14.71
Implementation Cost	14.89
Software Development, Testing, Trouble Shooting and Crises Management	16.57
IT Infrastructure	15.19
Selection of ERP Package	14.01
Data Conversion and Integrity	15.1
Legacy System Consideration	16.25
Vanilla ERP	16.05
System Documentation	15.1
Project Team	17.13
Implementation Strategy and Timeframe	24.71
Consultant Selection	24.89
Vendor/Customer Relationships	26.57
Project Management	25.19
Client Consultations	24.01
User Involvement	25.1
User Education and Training	26.25
Personnel/Staff	26.05
Employee Attitude and Morale	25.1
Empowered Decision Makers	27.13

(**Source**: Author, SPSS V 18.0)

Kendall's W Test

Kendall's W (also known as Kendall's coefficient of concordance) is a non-parametric statistic. It is a normalization of the statistic of the Friedman test, and can be used for assessing agreement among raters. Kendall's W ranges from 0 (no agreement) to 1 (complete agreement).Kendall's coefficient of concordance (W test) is linearly related to the mean value of the Spearman's rank correlation coefficients between all pairs of the rankings over which it is calculated. If the test statistic W is 1, then all the judges or survey respondents have been unanimous, and each judge or respondent has assigned the same order to the list of objects or concerns. If W is 0, then there is no overall trend of agreement among the respondents and their responses may be regarded as essentially random. Intermediate values of W indicate a greater or lesser degree of unanimity among the various judges or respondents (Kothari, 1991).

ES08: The customized survey instrument to rank the 30 CSFs for the successful ERP implementation at Indian SMEs can't be used as reliable survey tool for the current and future research because of the low construct reliability of the survey instrument (questionnaire)

ES11: The customized survey instrument to rank the 30 CSFs for the successful ERP implementation at Indian SMEs can't be used as validate survey tool for current and future research because of the low construct validity of the survey instrument (questionnaire).

- There was no overall trend of agreement among the response from the Indian ERP consultants and their responses may be regarded as essentially random for the successful ERP implementation at Indian SMEs

Or

- There was overall trend of agreement among the response from the Indian ERP consultants and their responses may not be regarded as essentially random for the successful ERP implementation at Indian SMEs

For the group of 50 respondents from top 10 companies of IT (ERP) sector reliability was found to be .903(By considering W test value as the measure of reliability), whereas for a group of 500 respondents from top 10 companies of IT (ERP) sector it was found to be .901. For the group of 50 respondents from the top 10 companies of IT (ERP) sector validity was found to be .9502 whereas for a group of 500 respondents from top 10 companies of IT (ERP) sector it was found to be .9492.The validity was found by using Guilford's formula i.e. by applying the square root of the reliability. The instrument had strong construct validity due to the following reasons, Kendall's W ranges between 0 (no agreement) to 1 (100% agreement).' The test statistic W was near to 1, i.e. .901. There was overall trend of agreement among the response from the Indian ERP consultants and their responses may not be regarded as essentially random for the successful ERP implementation at Indian SMEs. All the judges or respondents have almost assigned the same order to the list of objects or concerns (CSFs). It was basically an overall descriptive statistic indicating the strength of the agreement among responses, and for the most part, can be interpreted much like a correlation coefficient, so W = .901, it was statistically significant and it was in the strong range. Although different ranks were given to different factors (all the factors were not given the same rank) but there was a trend of agreement among the responses while ranking them (See Table 5.15 a, b).

Table 5.15a: Kendall's W Test for Questionnaire Two

Test Statistics	
N	500
Kendall's W[a]	0.901
Chi-square	13063.88
df	29
Asymp. Sig.	0

a. Kendall's Coefficient of Concordance
(**Source**: Author, SPSS V 18.0)

Table 5.15b: Kendall's W Test for Questionnaire Two

*RCSF (Ranking of Critical Success Factors)	Mean Rank
1	2
Top Management Commitment and Support	4.71
Change Management Process	4.89
BPR and Software Configuration	6.57
Project Champion	5.19
Business Plan, Vision	4.01
Effective Communication Plan	5.12
Post Implementation Evolution	6.25
Risk Management	6.05
Focussed Performance Measure	5.1
Quality Improvement Measure	7.12
Organization/Corporate Culture	14.71
Implementation Cost	14.89

...(Contd.)

1	2
Software Development, Testing, Trouble Shooting and Crises Management	16.57
IT Infrastructure	15.19
Selection of ERP Package	14.01
Data Conversion and Integrity	15.1
Legacy System Consideration	16.25
Vanilla ERP	16.05
System Documentation	15.1
Project Team	17.13
Implementation Strategy and Timeframe	24.71
Consultant Selection	24.89
Vendor/Customer Relationships	26.57
Client Consultations	24.01
User Involvement	25.1
User Education and Training	26.25
Personnel/Staff	26.05
Employee Attitude and Morale	25.1
Empowered Decision Makers	27.13

ource: Author, SPSS V 18.0)

dentification of Key Critical Success Factors

S03: There were no KCSFs for the successful ERP implementation at Indian MEs because all the 30 CSFs have same ranks (and hence importance) given y the Indian ERP consultant.

Order of importance was also presented with the help of Friedman test or questionnaire two (ranking of CSFs), See Table 14a, b. Table 5.16 presents anking from the questionnaire two. In case of second questionnaire the riedman test has the significance value (.000) which was less than the ssumed value of this test (.05) and the chi square value being higher this neans that mean ranks given to the 30 CSFs were not same, See Table 5.16. he order of importance can also be understood from the descriptive statistics ee Table 5.2. As shown in the Table 5.16 the most important factor was usiness plan, vision (mean rank was 4.01) followed by top management ommitment and support (mean rank was 4.71) and so on, See Table 5.16. hey were rank on 1 to 30 points scale where 1 = Most Important and 0 = Least Important.

Table 5.16: List of Key Critical Success Factors for Indian SMEs

Sl. No.	Key Critical Success Factors-KCSFs	Mean	Ranking
1.	Business Plan, Vision	4.01	1
2.	Top Management Commitment and Support	4.71	2
3.	Change Management Process	4.89	3
4.	Focussed Performance Measure	5.1	4
5.	Effective Communication Plan	5.12	5
6.	Project Champion	5.19	6
7.	Risk Management	6.05	7
8.	Post Implementation Evolution	6.25	8
9.	BPR and Software Configuration	6.57	9
10.	Quality Improvement Measure	7.12	10
11.	Selection of ERP Package	14.01	11
12.	Organization/Corporate Culture	14.71	12
13.	Implementation Cost	14.89	13
14.	Data Conversion and Integrity	15.1	14
15.	System Documentation	15.1	15
16.	IT Infrastructure	15.19	16
17.	Vanilla ERP	16.05	17
18.	Legacy System Consideration	16.25	18
19.	Software Development, Testing, Trouble Shooting and Crises Management	16.57	19
20.	Project Team	17.13	20
21.	Client Consultations	24.01	21
22.	Implementation Strategy and Timeframe	24.71	22
23.	Consultant Selection	24.89	23
24.	User Involvement	25.1	24
25.	Employee Attitude and Morale	25.1	25
26.	Project Management	25.19	26
27.	Personnel/Staff	26.05	27
28.	User Education and Training	26.25	28
29.	Vendor/Customer Relationships	26.57	29
30.	Empowered Decision Makers	27.13	30

(**Source**: Author, SPSS V 18)

Table 5.16 presents interpretation of output from the Friedman test analysis based on questionnaire two that is ranking of critical success factors. All the CSFs were rank on 1 to 30 point scale in order to identify which factors were most important for successful ERP implementation at Indian SMEs and that should be given high priory. Table 5.16 presents the list of Key Critical Success Factors (KCSFs) for the successful ERP Implementation at Indian SMEs. The conceptual CSFs model for successful ERP implementation at Indian SMEs (See Figure 5.1) along with list of KCSFs (See Table 5.16) can be used during all the phases of ERP implementation at Indian SMEs because the boundaries between planning, implementation, stabilization and improvements are not rigid.

IDENTIFICATION OF KEY CRITICAL FAILURE FACTORS

ES04: There are no KCFFs for the failure of ERP implementation at Indian SMEs because all the 20 CFFs have same mean value (and hence importance) given by the Indian ERP consultants.

The list of Key Critical Failure Factors (KCFFs, See Table 5.17) for the failure of ERP implementation at Indian SMEs shows the ranking of all the

Table 5.17: List of Key Critical Failure Factors for Indian SMEs

Sl.No.	Key Critical Failure Factors-KCFFs	Mean	Ranking
1.	Poor quality of testing	4.6800	1
2.	Unrealistic expectations from top management concerning the ERP systems, Poor top management support	4.6200	2
3.	Poor consultant effectiveness, Too tight project schedule, Users' resistance to change, Software modification, Functionality problems with the system	4.6000	3
4.	ERP software misfit, Over-reliance on heavy customization, Lack of formal communication	4.5600	4
5.	Poor project management effectiveness,	4.5400	5
6.	Poor knowledge transfer, Part-time dedication	4.5200	6
7.	Unclear concept of the nature and use of the ERP system from the users perspective, Cost over runs	4.5000	7
8.	Poor quality of BPR, Poor IT infrastructure	4.4800	8
9.	High turnover rate of project team members	4.4600	9
10.	Informal strategy	4.4200	10

(**Source**: Authors, SPSS V 18)

CFFs in terms of their mean ranks on 1 to 10 points rank scale. Same rank was given for all the factors which have equal mean value in order to identify which factors are most important in the failure of ERP implementation at Indian SMEs and should get high priority. Following is the list of Key Critical failure factors (KCFFs) responsible for the failure of ERP Implementation at Indian SMEs (see Table 5.17).Few CFFs have got the same ranking that means they were equally critical(important) and play equal important role in the failure of ERP implementation at Indian SMEs.

The conceptual CFFs model for the failure of ERP implementation at Indian SMEs (See Figure 5.2) along with list of KCFFs (See Table 5.17) can be considered during all the phases of ERP implementation at Indian SMEs because the boundaries between planning, implementation, stabilization and improvements are not rigid. The conceptual ERP implementation failure model simplifies the functionality of ERP implementation and may reduces the probability of ERP failure at Indian SMEs. The simplification of system makes easier to understand the ERP requirements. Commonly, a better system is easier to understand, implement and maintain for the ERP users and the implementers. By using this model for small and medium-size companies ERP implementation, especially in India, ERP consultants and vendors may help Indian SMEs to achieve global business process by acquiring ERP systems efficiently and effectively.

- Significant relationships were found between CFs of the LEs and the ERP implementation at Indian SMEs.
- Exploratory hypotheses (statements) have been tested with the help of descriptive statistics, reliability test, validity test, exploratory factor analysis and non parametric test.
- Few more categories (dimensions) were also identified for the successful ERP implementation at Indian SMEs.
- Thirty critical success factors were identified with the help of ERP implementation success model (See Figure 5.1) along with the list of Key Critical Success Factors (see Table 5.16) to facilitate successful ERP implementation at Indian SMEs.
- Twenty critical failure factors were identified with the help of ERP implementation failure model (See Figure 5.2) along with the list of Key Critical Failure Factors (see Table 5.17) to avoid the failure of ERP implementation at Indian SMEs.
- Three customized survey instruments(close ended questionnaires) were developed.
- Three user manuals were developed to facilitated the instrument standardization process for current and future research.

- Analysis concludes that all these thirty critical success factors and twenty critical failure factors of the LEs also contribute in the , the ERP implementation at Indian SMEs and they have different priorities (ranking/importance) during all the phases of ERP implementation at Indian SMEs

Chapter Summary

The main survey was conducted between May and August 2010, and a total of 500 responses were analyzed .With extensive data analysis, the proposed models were revised, and factors were fixed by reflecting a series of exploratory factor analyses along with the non parametric test to rank these factors. Two revised models were presented with the help of factor analysis by exploring CSFs and CFFs for the ERP implementation at Indian SMEs. This analysis concluded with the list of KCSFs and KCFFs to examine the priority of the proposed CSFs and CFFs as a complementary analysis. The results were adjusted with proposed research model using SPSS V 18.0. The next chapter gives an interpretation of the analysis along with the gap identification to formulate strategies for successful ERP implementation at Indian SMEs.

6 Research Findings and Discussions

"Good judgement comes from experience, and experience comes from bad judgement, the only possible interpretation of any research whatever in the 'social sciences' is: some do, some don't"

—Herzog, 1996

This chapter presents the research output by comparing the key findings of the work along with an evaluation of the research project. Key findings of the works were presented in terms of gap analysis (e.g., planning gap, knowledge gap) and guidelines for the successful ERP implementation at Indian SMEs. Most of the research questions and the sub-research questions were addressed in previous chapter. With the help of strategic ERP model, final theoretical framework was presented as an end result of the research along with its usefulness. It includes guidelines and checklist that have been drawn from the previous chapter analysis. It includes a through evolution of the investigation carried out and brings out the contribution from the study. This leads to logical inferences, conclusions as well as the scope for possible future research in area of ERP implementation at Indian SMEs.

Comparison of Factor Analysis Results of the Critical Success and Failure Factors for the Successful ERP Implementation at Indian SMEs

An ERP system may allow Indian SMEs to integrate their business functions. It may provide a transactional system, which provides for a disciplined way of doing business. Thus Indian SMEs may be able to increase their efficiency and productivity by implementing a suitable ERP system. according to International Data Corporation (IDC), a market research and analysis firm, over the next five years the ERP market in India is expected to reach more than Rs. 1,550 crore ($341 million). The SME potential in India for the enterprise class was projected to be more than Rs. 728 crore ($160 million) 47 per cent of the overall market (Munjal, 2006). ERP vendors like SAP, Oracle, Microsoft, QAD etc. are all trying to increase their customer base in the Indian SME segment and have products specifically designed to cater to the needs of Indian SMEs. The important regret in ERP implementations seems to be that there was not enough time and attention devoted to the internal readiness factor and their changes during the ERP implementation process at Indian SMEs. This was true for all Indian SMEs that have had implemented an ERP system. Management support and commitment is a strategy, necessary to create the environment for a successful introduction of the changes brought about by an ERP system at Indian SMEs. As noted, user resistance and readiness for change were the reasons for implementation failure at Indian SMEs. It is absolutely imperative for Indian SMEs to be responsive to their 'internal customers' while they are creating systems that will help them deal more efficiently with 'external customers'. Implementing an ERP system may be the one of the most challenging projects for any Indian SMEs, regardless of size, can undertake. Success does not come easily, and those who implement only for an immediate return on investment are in for a rude and expensive awakening. It is clear that most Indian SMEs implement ERP systems just to stay competitive. The process has to be part of the business objective, and it has to be clear that a successful 'go-live' is not the brass ring. This fateful date, set early on in project planning, cannot be viewed as the end goal or even the end of the project, but rather only a milestone along road to the true goal that is realizing the benefits for Indian SMEs .

One important factor for the failure of the ERP systems at Indian SMEs is the misleading information given by the ERP vendors and consultants about the ERP system. Sometimes budgeting becomes a factor of failure when ERP vendors/consultants could not give proper information about the installation charges and also investing on other third party tools. Lack of training to the employees leads to confusions and slow working which also causes failures. In short ERP consultants, vendors and Indian SMEs have to have proper knowledge about the product, should have a proper budget planning and appropriate training to the staffs to avoid the failure of ERP implementation for each and every Indian SMEs.ERP applications are well equipped of delivering industry specific solutions but still large number of Indian SMEs fails to implement them. There are some simple and basic rules to follow, to avoid failures at Indian SMEs. The common reason of Indian SMEs failing to utilize ERP for benefits may be the wrong selection of ERP software.

Table 6.1: Comparison of Factor Analysis Results for Critical Success and Failure Factors

CSFs for the Successful ERP Implementation at Indian SMEs	CFFs for the failure of ERP Implementation at Indian SMEs
• Business Plan, Vision • Top Management Commitment and Support • Change Management Process • Focussed Performance Measure • Effective Communication Plan • Project Champion • Risk Management • Post Implementation Evolution • BPR and Software Configuration • Quality Improvement Measures • Selection of ERP Package • Organizational/Corporate Cultures • Implementation Cost • Data Conversion and integrity • System Documentation • IT Infrastructures • Vanilla ERP • Legacy System Consideration • Software Developments, Testing, Trouble Shooting and Crises Management • Project Team • Client Consultations • Implementation Strategy and Timeframe • Consultant Selections • User Involvements • Employee Attitude and Morale • Project Management • User Education and Training • Personnel/Staff • Vendor/Customer Relationship • Empowered Decision Makers	• Poor quality of testing • Unrealistic expectations from top management concerning the ERP systems • Poor top management support • Poor consultant effectiveness • Too tight project schedule • Users' resistance to change • Software modification • Functionality problems with the system • ERP software misfit • Over-reliance on heavy customization • Lack of formal communication • Poor project management effectiveness • Poor knowledge transfer • Part-time dedication • Unclear concept of the nature and use of the ERP system from the users perspective • Cost over runs • Poor quality of BPR • Poor IT infrastructure • High turnover rate of project team members • Informal strategy (**Source**: Author, MS Word)

COMPARISON OF CRITICAL SUCCESS AND FAILURE FACTORS RANKS

Key Critical Success Factors—KCSFs	Ranking
Business Plan, Vision	1
Top Management Commitment & Support	2
Change Management Process	3
Focussed Performance Measure	4
Effective Communication Plan	5
Project Champion	6
Risk Management	7
Post Implementation Evolution	8
BPR & Software Configuration	9
Quality Improvement Measure	10
Selection of ERP Package	11
Organization/Corporate Culture	12
Implementation Cost	13
Data Conversion & Integrity	14
System Documentation	15
IT Infrastruture	16
Vanilla ERP	17
Legacy System Consideration	18
Software Development, Testing, Trouble Shooting & Crises Management	19
Project Team	20
Client Consultations	21
Implementation Strategy & Timeframe	22
Consultant Selection	23
User Involvement	24
Employee Attitude & Morale	25
Project Management	26
Personnel/Staff	27
User Education & training	28
Vendor/Customer Relationships	29
Empowered Decision Makers	30

...(Contd.)

Key Critical Success Factors—KCSFs	Ranking
Poor quality of testing	1
Unrealistic expectations from top management concerning the ERP systems	2
Poor top mangement support	
Poor consultant effectiveness	
Too tight project schedule	3
Users' resistance to change	
Software modification	
Functionality problems with the system	
ERP Software misfit	
Over-reliance on heavy customization	4
Lack of formal communication	
Poor Project management effectiveness	5
Poor knowledge transfer	
Part-time dedication	6
Unclear concept of the nature and use of the FRP system from the users perspective	7
Cost over runs	
Poor uality of BPR	
Poor IT Infrastructue	8
High turnover rate of project team members	9
Information strategy	10

(**Source**: Author, MS PowerPoint)

Fig. 6.1: Comparison of Critical Success and Failure Factors Ranks

Basically every Indian SMEs has its typical work process and business flow and ERP consultants and vendors have to first identify the process and the business flow and they need to choose their right ERP package for successful ERP implementation at Indian SMEs, but in most cases the functional requirements are not being checked properly. Also there is a need of detailed study of the ERP product and its characteristics else lack of the study will lead to a bad selection of the ERP system and which in turn makes most of the Indian SMEs fail in implementing ERP. There is one simple way to avoid this, before implementing any ERP system everyone from top management to the end users of the Indian SMEs should be involved in detailed research of the ERP product. If needed always take expert advices and services to plan the functional requirements of the Indian SMEs and an exclusive cross checking of the product need to be done with the requirements, for an appropriate selection of the ERP package.

GAP ANALYSIS

(*Note:* Gap analysis was based on through literature review, Operationalization and analysis of survey items. concepts were discussed with special reference to Indian SMEs without changing the language of ERP literature, in order to maintain the meaning of standard terms used in the ERP literature of the LEs. Although due credit were already given to all respective authors in chapter two -literature review). Gap analysis is a tool that can helps ERP consultants/vendors/Indian SMEs to compare actual and potential performance drivers with performance reducer factors for a successful ERP implementation at Indian SMEs. At its core there are two questions: "Where are we (Indian SMEs/ ERP consultants/vendors)?" and "Where do we (Indian SMEs/ ERP consultants/vendors) want to be?" If an Indian SMEs is not making the best use of its current resources or is forgoing investment in capital or technology, then it may be producing or performing at a level below its potential. The goal of gap analysis was to identify the gap between the optimized allocation and integration of the inputs in terms of standards, and the current level of misallocation in terms of deficiency for an successful ERP implementation at Indian SMEs. This gap provides insight to the ERP consultants/ vendors/Indian SMEs into the areas which could be improved for the successful ERP implementation at Indian SMEs. The gap analysis process involves determining, documenting and approving the variance between ERP requirements and current capabilities of Indian SMEs. Gap analysis naturally flows from benchmarking and other assessments. Once the general expectation and standards of the performance were understood, it was possible to compare those expectation and standards with the deficiency for a successful ERP implementation at Indian SMEs. Such analysis can be performed at the strategic or operational level or at the both level for an Indian SMEs. Gap analysis is a formal study of what contribute in success and what results in the failure to guide a successful ERP implementation at India SMEs. Based on the CSFs and CFFs it was conducted, in different perspectives, as follows:

- Indian SMEs (e.g., human resources, finance, marketing, production, systems)
- Business policies
- Business processes
- Information technology etc

This gap analysis can provides a foundation for measuring investment of time, money and human resources etc required to achieve a successful ERP implementation at Indian SMEs .Note that 'GAP Analysis' has also been used as a means for classification of how well a ERP product or solution meets a targeted need or set of requirements for an Indian SMEs. In this research, 'GAP' can be used/identified as a ranking of 'Success' and 'Failure'. That gap has to be filled if the Indian SMEs has to survive and grow with the help of successful ERP implementation at Indian SMEs. Thus an examination of what factors are forecasted for the ERP implementation success at Indian SMEs as a whole compared with what factors resulted in failure of the ERP implementation at Indian SMEs to be represents what was called the Planning Gap'. For guidance one can look to the guidelines derived from the gap analysis. This was an important comparison to make successful ERP implementation at Indian SMEs. These gaps, therefore, relate to comparative activity. Indian SMEs could profitably address, the worth of the theoretical gap analysis described here by getting answer for their questions. Instead, they would immediately start proactively to pursue a search for a competitive advantage. What is meant by 'Gap Analysis', is understands the surrounding environment, taking a wholistic approach to understanding the environment, determining a framework for analysis and compiling supportive data that can help to obtain important information about key areas to focus on in Indian SMEs process or ERP project improvement.

STEP 1: Identify Strategic Objectives

STEP 2: Identify Current Standards and Deficiency to Develop Action Plan

STEP 3: Create a Plan of Action to Achieve Strategic Objectives

STEP 1: Identify Strategic Objectives

While many methods for undertaking a gap analysis start with looking at performance but it is helpful to first have a goal, or end in mind before undertaking the analysis process by looking to benchmarking and best practices to perform gap analysis. This research use CSFs approach as standards to determine the success of ERP implementation at India SMEs. Let's say that Indian SMEs wants successful ERP implementation from ERP consultants/vendors. In this research the process of conducting gap analysis moved between what are the critical success factors that results in the successful ERP implementation and what are the critical failure factors that results in the failure of ERP implementation at Indian SMEs. Critical success factors for successful ERP implementation at Indian SMEs were identified as standards and critical failure factors for the failure of ERP implementation at Indian SMEs were identified as deficiency .standards can be compared with deficiency to develop action plan or to fill the planning gap. This research use MS Word and Ms Excel for gap analysis template along with the SPSS ackage. These were the standards and deficiency identified for the strategic bjectives that was successful ERP implementation at Indian SMEs.

TEP 2: Identify Current Standards and Deficiency

)nce strategic objectives were identified, it needs to observe and collect the ata on identification for standards with regards to the strategic objectives. ı this gap analysis scenario, the 30 survey items (CSFs) were identified as tandards and 20 survey items (CFFs) were identified as deficiency for the uccessful ERP implementation at Indian SMEs (strategic objectives).

TEP 3: Create a Plan of Action

.t this point, it was clear that 20 CFFs were the areas of deficiency and need plan for improvement. An complete action plan in terms of guidelines and ıecklist presented below may be used to avoid the future failure of ERP nplementation at Indian SMEs so that strategic objective can be achieved ıat is successful ERP implementation at Indian SMEs. Finally, to do this, ıdian SMEs/ERP consultants and vendors may use gap analysis template. his report includes things like the background of the Indian SMEs, an ıalysis along with the problems that have occurred, and even reasons for ndertaking the analysis. For unacceptable situation this report presents a ›urse of action for improvement. Finally, all of the finding can be backed up ith the data gathered during the analysis.

Table 6.2: Gap Analysis for Successful ERP Implementation at Indian SMEs

Strategic Objectives	Identification of Standards	Identification of Deficiency	Action Plan
Successful ERP mplementation at Indian SMEs	30 Critical Success Factors(CSFs) for the successful ERP implementation at Indian SMEs.	20 Critical Failure Factors (CFFs) that results in the failure of ERP implementation at Indian SMEs.	30 Critical Success and 20 Critical Failure Factors of the ERP implementation at Indian SMEs may results in the successful ERP implementation at Indian SMEs if all are managed efficiently and effectively otherwise it may results in the failure of ERP.

urce: Author, MS Word)

ERP implementations at Indian SMEs are, in fact, projects without an d. Implementing ERP at Indian SMEs can become a mind-altering experience for those involved (ERP consultants, vendors and Indian SMEs). Following a sound methodology will greatly increase likelihood of success. Yet, it wil not guarantee success. Only one can do that some things (CSFs and CFFs which must be taken care before the start of ERP implementation at Indiar SMEs. Study the structure, needs of the users and the causes of potentia resistance among them. Deal with the situation by using the appropriat strategies and techniques in order to introduce ERP implementatior successfully at Indian SMEs. Evaluate the status of change management efforts ERP consultants, vendors and Indian SMEs should look towards implementing the ERP packages in step wise manner, if possible evaluating the success rat of each stage. ERP information system implementation is a complex task anc hence complex ERP environments present several challenges. Indian SME may have complex ERP environments consisting of customized packages fron multiple vendors, as well as an array of internally developed software tha must integrate with the ERP packages. And there is also a perpetual ga between package functionality and business needs of the Indian SMEs. Indiar SMEs address the gap by customizing the software, building extensions o buying specialized, best of- breed packages. These remedies limit flexibilit as business needs evolve and increase implementation and integration costs Customization is compounded by an unwillingness to change busines processes. Alignment of business processes to ERP software, rather thai modifying the software may proved to be a success factor for many ER implementations at Indian SMEs. However, took advantage of vendor provided tools to implement the software to the nuances of Indian SME business needs. This often raised implementation and support costs we beyond the business value of the software changes.ERP environments ar costly to maintain. Escalating vendor maintenance fees along with mandator upgrades contribute to higher costs of ownership .Customization increase ownership costs, as the applications become more difficult to upgrade. Th findings holds significance for any Indian SMEs which wishes to leverag the benefits of integration of business processes by implementing an ER system. Literature shows many instances of ERP implementation which faile to deliver the business returns and in some cases the entire proje implementation cost may be a sunk cost for the Indian SMEs getting n return on their investment. These outcomes may be acute in case of India SMEs because of their inherent peculiarities. A significant amount experience must have been accumulated. By adopting a structured and a integrated approach, it is believed that the shortcomings of traditional studi could be overcome. The following questions do not cover every possib contingency, but should be helpful to stimulate thought and discussion f successful ERP implementation at Indian SMEs:

- How do Indian SMEs want to run their business?
- What business problems of Indian SMEs need to be solved?
- Do Indian SMEs know and understand their priorities?
- Do Indian SMEs fully understand their as-is condition versus there should be processes?
- Have Indian SMEs carefully defined an action plan for pre-implementation preparation activities?
- What tasks will be accomplished and when?
- What are the missing links in the current systems of Indian SMEs and their software of choice?
- What are the real costs, benefits and timetable going to be after the ERP implementation?
- Do Indian SMEs have an executive-level ERP champion to provide the necessary link to top management and other involves parties of ERP implementation?
- Who will implement ERP and make it work for Indian SMEs? Etc...

Gap analysis may helps to offer evidence in advance that something important may happen to the fundamentals or the psychology of the crowd for the ERP implementation movement at Indian SMEs. There is an old saying that the time abhors a vacuum and all gaps will be filled. While this may have some merit for common and exhaustion gaps, holding positions waiting for breakout or runaway gaps to be filled can be devastating to ERP implementation at Indian SMEs. Likewise, waiting to get a right trend by waiting for right time to fill a gap can cause to miss the big move for successful ERP implementation at Indian SMEs. Gaps are a significant technical development in action and analysis, and should not be ignored. There is a need to strengthen Indian SMEs. There is a need to provide capacity building for improved environmental management and monitoring for successful ERP implementation at Indian SMEs. There is a need for direct training capacity building specific best practices. There is a need to improve access to finance. There is a need for a better integration. There is a need for information on the costs and benefits of such practices over the long term (micro and macro level). There is a need for assessing experiences from ongoing project work for further developing tools, instruments and approaches (efficiency and outreach) for the successful ERP implementation at Indian SMEs. There is a need for specifying roles of key stakeholders. There is a need for upgrading support structures in countries. There is need for supporting the work of prominent initiatives for facilitating know-how transfer to/in/amongst all departments. Another reason of failing is the shortage of time and manpower required for ERP implementation at Indian SMEs. Most of the time the employees are over burden with their regular work and when they give an additional responsibilities of ERP implementation, they could not do it properly as they are already exhausted with their regular work. This may leads to the failure of the ERP implementation at Indian SMEs. In order to get maximum output from the existing staffs, proper time schedule, working hours of the employees and other managerial, strategic issues shall be worked out for the successful ERP implementation process at Indian SMEs.

Final Adjusted Gap Analysis Model

The Gap Analysis/Strategic ERP Model presented here is a conceptual and analytical tool that can be readily used by ERP project practitioners/ consultants/vendors for successful ERP implementation at Indian SMEs. It is demonstrably a tool that ERP project managers or consultants may use for post hoc risk identification. This can be use as a means for understanding why an ERP application wholly or partially failed at Indian SMEs and how it can be successful. The recommendations made in the next chapter can be equally applied as a 'per hoc' tool. Once these factors identified may be, easily usable at the time of initial feasibility study. For both pre hoc and per hoc application it may not only identify factors but also by using gap analysis approaches outlined in Table 6.2 offer some prediction of likely ERP project outcome for successful ERP Implementation at Indian SMEs. Risk identification has an important value in ERP project management at Indian SMEs. However, risk mitigation is arguably more important. The Gap Analysis/Strategic ERP Model helps identify risk mitigation actions for challenged ERP projects at Indian SMEs through its general prescription that risks can be reduced by changing Indian SMEs reality to more closely match ERP design, or by changing ERP design to more closely match Indian SMEs reality. But there are also more generic actions that can be identified on the basis of their gap-closing potential. Examples would include, mapping Indian SMEs realities, finding ways to expose the true situation within the organization, and integrate that into ERP implementation processes at Indian SMEs.

One example would be the use of hybrid ERP professionals those who combine an understanding of information systems with an understanding of the main business of the client organization. Such individuals could therefore act as a bridge between the ERP system design and Indian SMEs reality, helping to recognize and reduce planning gaps. There is need to be incremental to the extent possible with an ERP system, by breaking the overall change down into smaller steps and therefore reducing the extent of gap between design and reality that is undergone at any one time. Having said this, the caveats outlined above must be recognized. Despite the practical value of the Gap Analysis/Strategic ERP Model for managing success and mitigation of failure, ERP implementations at Indian SMEs are likely to remain highly challenging. Analyzing ERP implementation in terms of the fit between dimensions i.e. investigating whether mismatches between factors such as processes, staffing, structures and technology are the cause of problems or analyzing any mismatch between the assumptions and expectations of different stakeholders groups. The Gap Analysis/Strategic ERP Model could be interpreted as a simple form of this, encompassing and comparing the views of ERP consultants/vendors. However, stakeholders groups in practice are more numerous, and so further research would be needed to investigate this properly. Gap Analysis/Strategic ERP Model will form the basis for future research. Such work could seek to broaden the current study by applying the model to other ERP cases or by using the model in longitudinally during the implementation process. The work could seek to deepen, by utilizing the ideas to understand how assumptions come to be built into both ERP system project management and Indian SMEs, and how if at all can be modified.

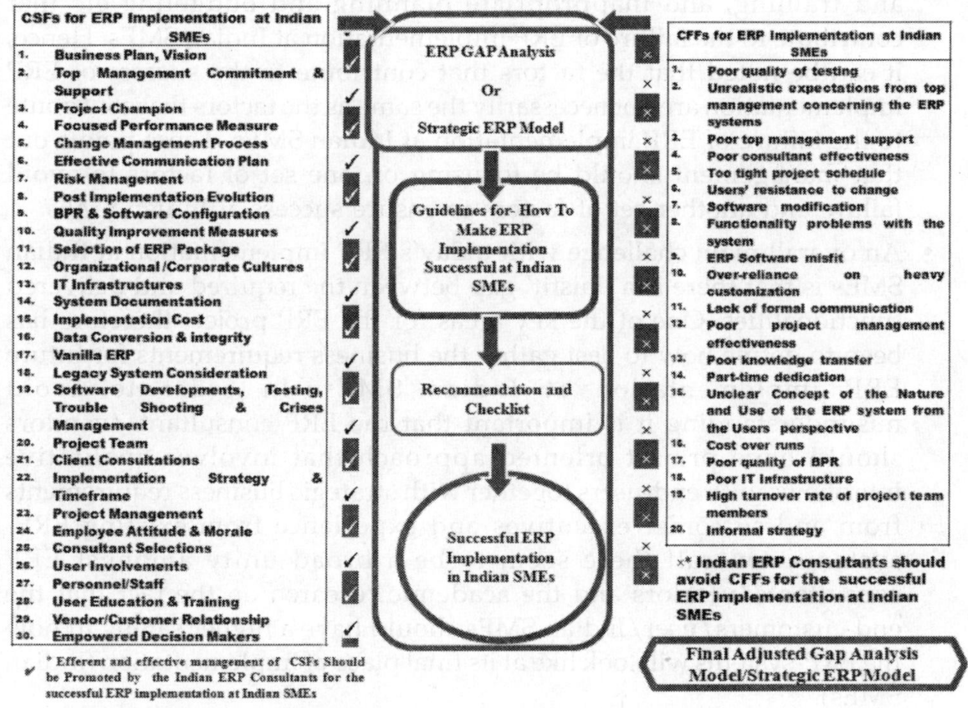

(**Source**: Author, MS PowerPoint)

Fig. 6.2: Final Adjusted ERP Gap Analysis/Strategic ERP Model

Guidelines for the Successful ERP Implementation at Indian SMEs

(*Note:* guidelines were prepared based on through literature review, Operationalization and gap analysis of survey items . concepts were discussed with special reference to Indian SMEs without changing the language of ERP literature, in order to maintain the meaning of standard terms used in the ERP literature of the LEs. Although due credit were already given to all respective authors in chapter two (Literature Review). Guidelines should be considered as the interpretations of the literature related to the ERP implementation in LEs with special reference to the survey items and ERP implementation at Indian SMEs)

- At the central level, the strong promotion from the top executives and the close following of performance evaluation mechanism are the important guarantee for the successful ERP implementation at Indian SMEs. It has been noted that the success factors like the working with ERP functionality and maintained scope, and project team/management support/consultants for successful ERP implementation at Indian SMEs are different from the failure factors like inadequate internal readiness and training, and inappropriate planning and budgeting etc that contribute to the failure of ERP implementation at Indian SMEs. Hence, it can be noted that the factors that contribute to the success of ERP implementation are not necessarily the same as the factors that contribute to the failure of ERP implementation at Indian SMEs. These points out that management should be focusing on one set of factors to avoid failure and another set of factors to ensure success at Indian SMEs.
- An overall main challenge with today's ERP implementation at Indian SMEs is that there is a 'misfit' gap between the required and delivered functionalities. One of the key areas for the ERP project therefore has been to define how to best gather the business requirements for future ERP implementation at Indian SMEs. In order to avoid misunderstanding it is important that the ERP consultants/vendors should have project oriented approach that involves qualitative interviews with end-users together with strategic business requirements from end-customer executives and experience from existing ERP-systems. Overall there seem to be a broad unity amongst ERP consultants/vendors and the academic research on the fact that the end-customers/user/Indian SMEs should have a higher saying in how the ERP-systems will look like at its final place of implementation (Indian SMEs).
- When talking about the end-customers, it has also been suggested that ERP-systems should focus more on them in the sense, that the ERP-system should be oriented towards the user instead of the only business

processes of the Indian SMEs. This role-based approach is argued to decrease the need for training and be more intuitive for the end-user and thereby ensure higher the ERP implementation success rate and value realization at Indian SMEs. Also vanilla systems seem to have earned an increasing interest, but the obvious benefits still seem missed out, since the savings from vanilla ERP approach, both the community based as well as the commercial based approach, are converted into other types of extra expenses related to the implications of ERP-systems at Indian SMEs.

- ERP products, particularly maintenance costs and upgrades, are very expensive. In many cases, they are therefore not viable. The so-called 'best' practices and very high level of integration embodied in ERP software clash with business practices and culture. Lack of knowledge of how to configure, customize, and use the software further reduces the benefits obtainable from the ERP implementation at Indian SMEs.
- To avoid any resistance staff reduction facilitated by ERP implementation should not clashes with the cultural norms of the labor market/Indian SMEs. If ERP software is to become more widely used at Indian SMEs both ERP consultants/vendors and potential customers' (Indian SMEs) needs to change their current practices.ERP consultants/vendors must consider different pricing strategies that can be attractive to Indian SMEs. It would help Indian SMEs if ERP products were designed with multiple integration levels, so that Indian SMEs can select the level of integration they desire. ERP consultants/vendors could consider developing different versions of their software for different sectors with similar cultural and business practices of Indian SMEs.
- ERP consultants/vendors considering ERP implementation at Indian SMEs should be even more wary of the likely scale of social upheaval. There are two things they can do to reduce the shock. First, they should seek to improve their business processes prior to embarking on an ERP project through adoption of international standard practices such as ISO quality certifications etc. Second, they should seek to raise staff skill levels and change work practices to align more closely with the global practices currently embodied in ERP software it may facilitated the successful ERP implementation at Indian SMEs.
- Indian SMEs need to be made 'ERP aware'. ERP consultants/vendors need to provide the ERP solution to better meet the requirements of Indian SMEs. Since the financial resources of Indian SMEs are limited, the cost of ERP system needs to be further reduced. Indian SMEs on their part need to carefully evaluate their current IT systems, document and its shortcomings while creating a wish list of what they want to achieve from ERP package.

- There is a low level of awareness amongst Indian SMEs for ERP vendors, applications etc. Most of the time they do not even know what ERP systems are and what they can do. They consider ERP systems to be a magic wand, which will help solve all their business problems, be it in terms of quality, or process defects. ERP brings in a more disciplined execution of business process giving more transparency and visibility to the working of the Indian SMEs.
- Indian SMEs may have the perception that ERP is meant only for large firms mainly owing to the high costs of acquisition, implementation and maintenance as also the complexity. Some of the Indian SMEs may even feel they do not need ERP. Indian SMEs may have heard of the much-publicized failures in ERP which have led firms to bankruptcy. Some SMEs who have implemented ERP earlier have failed. This may led Indian SMEs to believe that ERP implementations are a waste of time and effort and can even lead to the demise of Indian SMEs, that perception needs to be corrected.
- ERP consultants/ vendor may advice Indian SMEs to mould the business to ERP's way of working, considering that ERP systems bring with it best business practices. This is the plain vanilla approach that was mentioned earlier, which would bring down the cost of implementation. But generally Indian SMEs may have processes that they have evolved over time and hold very dear to their hearts. As a result, Indian SMEs are having the entire ERP system customized to meet their requirements. This would increase the overall cost of implementation. A good approach would be to keep the customization to a minimum level for successful ERP implementation at Indian SMEs.
- Indian SMEs may have less of capital than their larger counterparts. In these situations, approach should be to go in and first document the pain points and requirements. If Indian SMEs will go into an ERP implementation without a clear definition of what are trying to achieve they are going to fail. It is important to setup a baseline for what want to achieve. However, ensure don't go overboard with requirements.
- Indian SMEs should not use ERP implementation as an opportunity to ask for everything ever wanted. Just be shooting in foot. Keep requirements focused to what will solve the pain and then as they come up with list to haves but ensure the nice to haves are clearly marked.
- Ensure requirements list meets a) Key pain points that Indian SMEs have today and b) Core functionality that Indian SMEs have today and want to ensure that it retain even after ERP implementation. While

many ERP teams do their requirements they only focus on pain points and what they need to change but often forget to document what may works for Indian SMEs.

- To make ERP implementation successful at Indian SMEs, ERP consultants and vendors needs a robust solution design done upfront. It may seems obvious but it is surprising how many ERP disasters walk into that have no or very little design documentation. ERP consultants/vendors need not to document every scenario because consultants can improve implementation as it goes. However, consultants need to document key scenarios especially those that Indian SMEs consider key to business. Every business is a little different and consultants need to ensure implementation cover those nuances in document design. Other businesses may do this differently and to ensure implementation is successful document both scenarios as well as use cases with an appropriate solution to each use case. Validate the documented solution design back with Indian SMEs requirements. Consultants need to verify that implementation addressed Indian SMEs key pain points well and with a solution that is significantly better than what Indian SMEs have today.
- Most customers/client/Indian SMEs spent a lot of time evaluating a variety of ERP solutions and picking up the right solution. Sometimes this period is over 6-9 months. However, not putting the right internal people on the project can make a project fail or break it. Key to this is the Indian SMEs should put project management team around be able to manage scope. Scope has a direct tie to budget, project timeline and risk. Software modification increase scope and budget, project timeline which means the increase their risk of failure exponentially. If the project management team doesn't have the teeth and ability to manage scope and change then Indian SMEs will end up with a project that never ends and an ERP that is over-customized irrespective of the solution choose. It is important that consultants manage scope well and be able to clearly mark out what needs to go in a first phase versus what can go in later phases and are nice to haves for successful ERP implementation at Indian SMEs.
- Begin testing early and test often. ERP consultants must test every day once system starts getting even close to final shape. And test with best users. Don't put in sideline folks to test. Consultants need to put best users there and set expectations with them that they will find holes, gaps, and since consultants are in 'lab mode' they will not find a perfect system. In fact set expectations that they should expect to find an imperfect system and it is their goal to work with consultant's

implementation partner to get it ready in time for go-live. Make users, key owners of the system and not just passive bystanders for the successful ERP implementation at Indian SMEs.

- The best approach to training is to do it several times. Once is not enough. Three recommend points of training at India n SMEs can be applied, which are: On Design: When consultants have a high level design complete in the form of conference room pilot .Before test: Before detailed user testing so that users are familiar with the system and can test for scenarios specific to Indian SMEs business. Post go-live: After Consultants have been live for 2-3 weeks go back and re-train the uses of Indian SMEs if needed.
- ERP consultants/vendors will find the most questions at testing stage and update training documents to answer questions that come up that were not addressed in the training documentation. Then repeat this every time. To know how much training is enough?
- ERP consultants/vendors should ensure user have minimum level class room/trainer lead training. Hands-on testing to the user with post go live training per user per module. Ensure internal team gets self-reliant to the point that they can own training documents and become a first level support. Ideally ERP consultants/vendors want post go-live support to be done by internal team members.
- If possible test training also at least in little part by internal team members. Training others will be the best way for users to learn the system for successful ERP implementation at Indian SMEs.
- ERP consultants/vendors should formalize their relationship with Indian SMEs. The knowledge gain on the project can be share with others, which could bring in additional satisfaction. A series of meeting should be arranged for the client's consideration to provide the benefits with formal relationship. If possible ERP consultants/vendors should have monthly issues review of the system in each area and quarterly issues reviews of how the system is working between the different areas for the successful ERP implementation at Indian SMEs.
- Indian SMEs should begin working on renewing their existing contract with the hardware vendor. If possible, Indian SMEs should try to extend the current contract. At the same time, a small team should be form to research possible alternatives. Indian SMEs should form a small team to monitor growth and how it relates to the current system. The team should work closely with the hardware team to determine immediate and future needs for the successful ERP implementation at Indian SMEs.

- Consultants should work to determine a better integration method of sharing data from one area to another for the successful ERP implementation at Indian SMEs. The need to have a more concurrent and integrated data among areas is necessary in the future to stay competitive and profitable.
- ERP consultants/vendors should work on converting and porting legacy data into the new ERP system. The data could be vital for analysis purposes as it may results in the successful ERP implementation at Indian SMEs.
- All the involve parties of ERP implementation at Indian SMEs like ERP consultants/vendors suppliers and customers etc should have access to information and perform processes for the successful ERP implementation at Indian SMEs. By allowing suppliers and customers this ability, consultants may improve their ERP implementation efficiency. ERP consultants/vendors are available to review these findings with Indian SMEs systems, and can get answer to questions regarding analysis and recommendations. ERP consultants/vendors should also prepare to assist Indian SMEs systems, which have been considered appropriate for future success of the ERP system at Indian SMEs.
- One of the major reasons why ERP implementations nationwide have been known to fail may be due to the ERP implementation at Indian SMEs being considered as an automation project instead of one that involves change management. This results in the system being put in place but not being used effectively due to the people not ready to accept the change.
- Generally Indian SMEs do not have an in-house IT team. Due to this they have to rely on external agencies to help them and this adds to the ERP implementation costs. Before embarking on an ERP system journey, Indian SMEs have to ask themselves whether they are ERP ready. Some of the factors to be considered before starting an ERP system for the successful ERP implementation at Indian SMEs.
- These critical factors may help ERP consultants/vendors as well as to Indian SMES to understand their level of preparedness for an ERP implementation.
- Though it is assumed that all Indian SMEs desire growth, only few survive beyond 10 years. Majority of the Indian SMEs do not think of long-term business strategy but focus only on survival that may create issues for successful ERP implementation at Indian SMEs. There is need for clear business plan and vision.

- Indian SMEs think of change only when the business begins to fail as a result of not keeping track of the changing market scenario. Indian SMEs who survive and grow are the ones who have the ability to take risks and respond to the changing circumstances that is also applicable for successful ERP implementation at Indian SMEs.
- Problem faced by Indian SMEs were lack of good information on ERP, less maximum workers' performance, disintegrated systems among departments, and obsolete systems and computer device. Those problems results on other crucial problems occurred. Successful ERP implementation at Indian SMEs could integrate data and even business process that previously disintegrated. Therefore, it would solve problems occurred such as time consumes to get work done.
- There are several choices to implement ERP system within the Indian SMEs whether it is in-house development, or acquire existing system offered on the market. The ERP system that fits to Indian SMEs is that could minimize the failure of ERP implementation since it has several steps to analyze problems and implementation process. The failure of ERP systems implementation could be minimized by studying the possible problems that might occurs from the previous research.
- The important thing is the power of ERP should be tasted by every type of Indian SMEs, between countless software vendors, systems integrators, and consultants, ERP selection can take on many forms. However, the advice and steps described in this guide will help to increase awareness regarding the realities of ERP selection for Indian SMEs. If Indian SMEs are actively looking at ERP solutions or is planning to begin the selection process, their business will be best served by a system that is chosen based upon particular needs. If these guidelines will be implemented ERP consultants/vendors and Indian SMEs can get full benefits or it can get answer of several questions regarding the successful ERP implementation at Indian SMEs.

Though Indian SMEs may be risk averse, they are keen on implementing ERP systems for several reasons. Some of them are:

- Due to globalization, Indian SMEs today operate in a wider arena. Majority of them have MNCs as their clients. These MNCs require Indian SMEs to implement the same ERP system as them to allow for tighter integration in their supply chain, which permits them to design and plan the production and delivery so as to reduce the turnaround time.
- Considering the growth in ERP implementation at Indian SME segment, several Indian SMEs are adopting ERP systems as their peers have done so.

- To gain competitive advantage and respond quickly to the dynamic market scenario.
- This benefit will accrue from the close integration between large enterprises and Indian SMEs.
- Easier access to internet reduces the costs further.
- With the advances in technology, the costs of both hardware in the form of servers, cables, switches etc. and software like databases have come down. There also appears to be an optimal level of functional integration in ERP with benefits declining at some level for Indian SMEs.

Checklist for the Successful ERP Implementation at Indian SMEs

Table 6.3: A - Z Checklist for Successful ERP Implementation at Indian SMEs

A - Z	CSFs –Results in successful ERP implementation and CFFs—Results in the failure of ERP implementation at Indian SMEs	Success	Failure
1	2	3	4
A	Analysis of ERP Package/Selection of ERP	S	
B	BPR and Minimum Software Configuration	S	
C	Change Management Process	S	
	Consultant Selection	S	
	Cost Over Runs		F
D	Data Conversion and Integrity	S	
E	Effective Communication Plan	S	
	Empowered Decision Makers	S	
	ERP Software Misfit		F
F	Focussed Performance Measure	S	
	Functionality Problems with the System		F
G	Goals, Plan, Vision, Mission Clarity	S	
H	Human Resource/Personnel/Staff	S	
	High Turnover Rate of Project Team Members		F
I	Implementation Cost Consideration	S	
	Informal Strategy		F
J	Joint Return Policy by Vendor/Customer Relationships	S	

...(Contd.)

1	2	3	4
K	Knowledge Transfer by User Education and Training	S	
L	Legacy System Consideration	S	
	Lack of Formal Communication		F
M	Morale and Attitude of Employee	S	
N	Need Analysis by Client Consultations	S	
O	Organizational/Corporate Culture	S	
	Over-Reliance on Heavy Customization		F
P	Project Champion	S	
	Post Implementation Evolution	S	
	Project Team	S	
	Poor Consultant Effectiveness		F
	Poor Quality of BPR		F
	Poor Project Management Effectiveness		F
	Poor IT Infrastructure		F
	Poor Knowledge Transfer		F
	Poor Top Management Support		F
	Poor Quality of Testing		F
	Part-Time Dedication		F
Q	Quality Improvement Measure	S	
R	Risk Management	S	
S	System Readiness or IT Infrastructure	S	
	Software Modification		F
T	Top Management Commitment and Support	S	
	Too Tight Project Schedule		F
U	User Involvement	S	
	Unclear Concept of the Nature and Use of the ERP System from the Users Perspective		F
	Unrealistic Expectations from Top Management Concerning the ERP Systems		F
	Users' Resistance to Change		F
V	Vanilla ERP	S	
W	Wholistic Approach in Project Management	S	
X	Xerox Copy of Work by System Documentation	S	
Y	Yes Man Ship Implementation by Right Strategy and Timeframe	S	
Z	Zero error systems by right Software Development, Testing, Trouble Shooting and Crises Management	S	

(**Source**: Author, MS Word)

Chapter Summary

This chapter presented the findings of the research project in terms of gap analysis (e.g., planning gap, knowledge gap), guidelines and checklist. The findings were derived from feeding the research questions into the developed theoretical framework. The critical success and failure factors for ERP implementation at Indian SMEs were identified and ranked according to their importance. With the help of gap analysis it was found that ERP consultants ' perceptions also supports that a number of the CSFs and CFFs identified from the literature reviews of the LEs also existed within the ERP implementation at the Indian SMEs. The next chapter concludes this research project.

7 Summary and Conclusions

"ERP-systems ends where it began: the ambition of ERP-systems has been to: 1) integrate all transaction systems within the same system; 2) share common data and practices across entire enterprises, and 3) produce relevant information for decision-making purposes in real-time."

—Akkermans, 2002

This chapter completes the research work by summarizing the key findings of the project along with the contributions of this study to the existing body of knowledge in the area of ERP implementation at Indian SMEs. The research question and the sub-research questions were addressed in previous chapters. This research used and discussed a theoretical framework as a research tool along with its usefulness and limitations for the research. It includes recommendations that have been drawn from the research project. Finally, this book proposes possible future research areas and recommendations for advanced studies.

NEED AND RATIONAL BEHIND THE STUDY

Technology has had a major impact on every organization. Whether it is a small or large organization, being competitive is the key to success. Issue in dealing with a new ERP system is not solely technology, but it involves high degree of planning and commitment too. SME's face many of the same competitive problems as larger organizations, but have limited resources, experience and staffing skills (Nelson and Millet, 2001). As with the larger enterprises, ERP implementation is becoming critically important to SMEs in streamlining business processes, improving operational performance, and integrating data. Understanding the CSFs for the success of ERP implementation is more critical to SMEs than larger organizations due to their more limited resources. SMEs may not be able to withstand the financial impact of the partial failures and project abandonments that have impacted on many of their larger counterparts (Muscatello *et al.*, 2003). Most of the existing studies that investigate the success factors for ERP implementations focus on the projects that have been carried out in North America and Western Europe. In recent years, researchers such as (Martinsons, 2004), have examined ERP implementations in other countries. Considering that most ERP systems are designed by western information technology (IT) professionals, the structure and processes embedded in these systems reflect western culture. As a result, fundamental misalignments are likely to exist between foreign ERP systems and Indian companies requirements. These factors can result in design with undesirable reality gaps, which tend to lead to underperforming systems (Walden and Browne, 2002). Over the past years, the global economic crisis has put the spotlight on many business organizations of any size. With India not being spared of the impact, large establishments have attempted to tackle this crisis in their own ways. SME's are increasingly being brought into focus on account of their huge growth potential. Various researchers have recommended research into the implementation and use of ERP at SMEs (Huin, 2004; Jacobs and Bendoly, 2003; Muscatello *et al.*, 2003). Huin,(2004) argues that" unless differences between small and large firms are understood, managing ERP projects in SMEs will continue to be slow, painful and at times even unfruitful". Thus, it appears from previous studies that organizational conditions at SMEs differ from that of large organizations. This suggests that the relative importance of CSFs in ERP implementation at Indian SMEs may also differ.

Since literature on ERP implementation at Indian SMEs is relatively sparse, this research helps to narrow this knowledge gap by investigating ERP implementation at Indian SMEs. This research study conducted to assess the Indian ERP consultant's perception for the critical success and failure factors for ERP implementation at Indian SMEs. It is done in order to know how to make successful ERP implementation at Indian SMEs by exploring 30 CSFs and 20 CFFs so that CSFs can be promoted and CFFs can be avoided to increase the probability of ERP success at Indian SMEs due to the efficient and effective management of these factors. This research may help to ERP consultants/vendors and Indian SMEs for successful ERP implementation at Indian SMEs. They will get insight of various strength and weakness related to ERP implementation at Indian SMEs. With the help of ERP implementation success model, ERP implementation failure model and ERP implementation gap analysis they may chalk out the strategies to overcome from the failure of ERP implementation at Indian SMEs. Guidelines supported by checklist and recommendations may helps to ERP consultants/vendors and Indian SMEs for managing ERP project in better way for Indian SMEs as it simplifies the process of ERP implementation at Indian SMEs.

OPERATIONAL DEFINITIONS

The operational definitions for the thirty critical success factors, twenty critical factors along with the terms used in this research have been given in chapter four (research design).

STATEMENT OF THE PROBLEM

"A study on Critical Success Factors for Successful ERP Implementation at Indian SMEs"

OBJECTIVE OF THE STUDY

Primary (Specific) Objectives of this Research were as below:

- To explore the 30 CSFs for successful ERP implementation at Indian SMEs
- To identify KCSFs(Key Critical Success Factors) by ranking the CSFs based on their importance for the successful ERP implementation at Indian SMEs
- To explore the 20 CFFs for the failure of ERP implementation at Indian SMEs
- To identify the KCFFs (Key Critical Failure Factors) by ranking the CFFs based on their importance in the failure of ERP implementation at Indian SMEs
- To categorize the CSFs in order to form a unified structure for the successful ERP implementation at Indian SMEs
- To categorize the CFFs in order to form a unified structure for the failure of ERP implementation at Indian SMEs
- To find out the reliability of customized survey instrument (questionnaire) in totality for exploring and defining the CSFs for the successful ERP implementation at Indian SMEs
- To find out the reliability of customized survey instrument (questionnaire) in totality for ranking the CSFs for the successful ERP implementation at Indian SMEs
- To find out the reliability of customized survey instrument (questionnaire) in totality for exploring and defining the CFFs for the failure of ERP implementation at Indian SMEs

- To find out the validity of customized survey instrument(questionnaire) in totality for exploring and defining the CSFs for the successful ERP implementation at Indian SMEs
- To find out the validity of customized survey instrument(questionnaire) in totality for ranking the CSFs for the successful ERP implementation at Indian SMEs
- To find out the validity of customized survey instrument(questionnaire) in totality for exploring and defining the CFFs for the failure of ERP implementation at Indian SMEs
- To develop a strategic ERP model for the successful ERP implementation at Indian SMEs.
- To provide a checklist for the successful ERP implementation at Indian SMEs.
- To provide the guidelines and recommendations for the successful ERP implementation at Indian SMEs.
- To develop a theoretical framework for future research in the area of successful ERP implementation and adoption at India SMEs
- To find out the possible dimensions for the customized survey instruments (questionnaires) in order to facilitate the standardization process of survey instruments (questionnaires) in future research.

Secondary (General) Objectives of this Research were as below:

- To develop ERP implementation success model for Indian SMEs
- To develop ERP implementation failure model for Indian SMEs
- To develop Strategic ERP Model /ERP Gap Analysis Model by conducting a gap analysis (planning gap) between 30 CSFs and 20 CFFs that may facilitated the process of strategy formulation for the successful ERP implementation at Indian SMEs
- To develop the user manual for the customized survey instruments for current and future research
- To validate 30 CSFs of the LEs for the successful ERP implementation at Indian SMEs
- To validate 20 CFFs of the LEs for the failure of ERP implementation at Indian SMEs

REVIEW OF RELATED LITERATURE

Within ERP implementation context, CSFs were defined as "factors needed to ensure a successful ERP implementation". Implementing successful ERP systems was investigated by many researchers. Their general focus was on identifying CSFs that need to exist in large organization to have successful ERP implementation. These factors include, but not limited to, clear objectives, user involvement, effective communications, change management, project team, project champion, consultants, architecture choices, minimal customization, excellent project management, top management support, data analysis and conversion, business process reengineering ,user training and education etc. It has to be noted that much of the attention was focused on the critical success factors for the successful ERP implementation in the large enterprise. Within ERP implementation context, CFFs were defined as "as the key aspects (areas) where 'things must go wrong' in order for the ERP implementation process to achieve a high level of failure". These factors have been tested in different organizations in many developed and developing countries by many researchers. These factors include, but not limited to, poor consultant effectiveness, ERP software misfit, unrealistic expectations from top management concerning the ERP systems, over-reliance on heavy customization, poor quality of BPR, high turnover rate of project team members, poor IT infrastructure, functionality problems, unclear concept of the nature and use of the ERP system, too tight project schedule, lack of formal communication, part-time dedication etc. It has to be noted that much of the attention focused on the critical failure factors for the failure of ERP implementation in the large enterprise.

The success and failure of ERP implementation in both SMEs and LEs are equally important. The definition of Indian SMEs, according to MSME Development Act, 2006 is based on the ceilings on investment for an enterprise (micro, small and medium size) was adopted in the current study. There seems to be insufficient research investigation on the critical success factors for the successful ERP implementation at Indian SMEs for all the phases of ERP implementation from planning to post ERP implementation. This study aims at achieving these objectives by considering ERP implementation process based on "Synthesized process model for ERP implementation phases" (Shanks *et al.,* 2000) to identify and rank the critical success and failure factors for the ERP implementation at Indian SMEs.

VARIABLES OF THE STUDY

- Thirty critical success factors for the successful ERP implementation in the Large Enterprise (LEs) were indentified. All these were further tested and ranked for the successful ERP implementation at Indian SMEs *(See Table 7.1 on next page).*
- Twenty critical failure factors for the failure of ERP implementation in the Large Enterprise (LEs) were indentified. All these were further tested and ranked for the failure of ERP implementation at Indian SMEs *(See Table 7.1 on next page).*

Table 7.1: Variables of the Study

• Business Plan, Vision • Top Management Commitment and Support • Change Management Process • Focussed Performance Measure • Effective Communication Plan • Project Champion • Risk Management • Post Implementation Evolution • BPR and Software Configuration • Quality Improvement Measures • Selection of ERP Package • Organizational /Corporate Cultures • Implementation Cost • Data Conversion and integrity • System Documentation • IT Infrastructures • Vanilla ERP • Legacy System Consideration • Software Developments, Testing, Trouble Shooting and Crises Management • Project Team • Client Consultations • Implementation Strategy and Timeframe • Consultant Selections • User Involvements • Employee Attitude and Morale • Project Management • User Education and Training	• Personnel/Staff • Vendor/Customer Relationship • Empowered Decision Makers • Poor quality of testing • Unrealistic expectations from top management concerning the ERP systems • Poor top management support • Poor consultant effectiveness • Too tight project schedule • Users' resistance to change • Software modification • Functionality problems with the system • ERP Software misfit • Over-reliance on heavy customization • Lack of formal communication • Poor project management effectiveness • Poor knowledge transfer • Part-time dedication • Unclear Concept of the Nature and Use of the ERP system from the Users perspective • Cost over runs • Poor quality of BPR • Poor IT Infrastructure • High turnover rate of project team members • Informal strategy

Source: Author, MS Word

EXPLORATORY HYPOTHESES (EXPLORATORY STATEMENTS)

- *ES01:* The perception (response) of Indian ERP consultant's does not support the statement that" all the 30 CSFs of the LEs also contribute in the success of ERP implementation at Indian SMEs"
- *ES02:* The perception (response) of Indian ERP consultant's does not

support the statement that" all the 20 CFFs of the LEs also contribute in the failure of ERP implementation at Indian SMEs".

- *ES03:* There are no KCSFs for the successful ERP implementation at Indian SMEs because all the 30 CSFs have same ranks (and hence importance) given by the Indian ERP consultants.
- *ES04:* There are no KCFFs for the failure of ERP implementation at Indian SMEs because all the 20 CFFs have same mean value (and hence importance) given by the Indian ERP consultants.
- *ES05:* All the 30 CSFs can't be categorized to form a unified structure for the successful ERP implementation at Indian SMEs because of their independent nature from each other and hence the exploratory factor analysis is not valid
- *ES06:* All the 20 CFFs can't be categorized to form a unified structure for the failure of ERP implementation at Indian SMEs because of their independent nature from each other and hence the exploratory factor analysis is not valid
- *ES07:* The customized survey instrument to explore the 30 CSFs for the successful ERP implementation at Indian SMEs can't be used as reliable survey tool for current and future research because of the low construct reliability of the survey instrument (questionnaire).
- *ES08:* The customized survey instrument to rank the 30 CSFs for the successful ERP implementation at Indian SMEs can't be used as reliable survey tool for current and future research because of the low construct reliability of the survey instrument (questionnaire).
- *ES09:* The customized survey instrument to explore the 20 CFFs for the failure of ERP implementation at Indian SMEs can't be used as reliable survey tool for current and future research because of the low construct reliability of the survey instrument (questionnaire).
- *ES10:* The customized survey instrument to explore the 30 CSFs for the successful ERP implementation at Indian SMEs can't be used as validate survey tool for current and future research because of the low construct validity of the survey instrument (questionnaire).
- *ES11:* The customized survey instrument to rank the 30 CSFs for the successful ERP implementation at Indian SMEs can't be used as validate survey tool for the current and future research because of the low construct validity of the survey instrument (questionnaire).
- *ES12:* The customized survey instrument to explore the 20 CFFs for the failure of ERP implementation at Indian SMEs can't be used as validate survey tool for current and future research because of the low construct validity of the survey instrument (questionnaire).

- *ES13:* No dimensions can be identified for the customized survey instrument (questionnaires) related to the identification (exploring) of the 30 CSFs for the successful ERP implementation at Indian SMEs, in order to facilitate the standardization process of the customized survey instrument in future research.
- *ES14:* No dimensions can be identified for the customized survey instrument (questionnaires) related to the identification (exploring) of the 20 CFFs for the failure of ERP implementation at Indian SMEs, in order to facilitate the standardization process of the customized survey instrument in future research.

RESEARCH DESIGN

Table 7.2: Research Design

Research Type	Exploratory Research
Research Context	Indian SMEs and Indian ERP Consultants (Specific to India Only)
Research Approach	Quantitative Survey based on the Likert Five Point Scale Approach
Sampling	500 Indian ERP Consultants, Non-Probabilistic Sampling
Data Type	Nominal and Ordinal Scale (Categorical Variable)
Variables of the Study	30 CSFs and 20 CFFs of the LEs ERP implementation
Data Collection Tools	Three Customized Survey Instruments(Three Closed Ended Questionnaires, Supported by one open ended question in each of them)
Data Analysis Tools	Descriptive Statistics, Reliability Test, Validity Test, Exploratory Factor Analysis, Non Parametric Test
Data Analysis Software	SPSS Version 18.0 ,MS Word, MS Excel, MS PowerPoint

(**Source**: Author, MS Word)

Reliability: Reliability was one of the most critical elements in assessing the quality of the construct measures and it was a necessary condition for scale validity. A statistically reliable scale provides consistent and stable measures of a construct. Composite reliability estimates were used to assess the inter-item reliability of the measures. Estimates greater than .70 were considered to meet the criteria for reliability. In general some items may be removed from the construct scales if their removal results in increases in the reliability estimate, however, care must be taken to ensure that the content validity of the measures is not threatened by the removal of a key conceptual element (Kothari, 1991). As shown in the table below that reliability of each survey instrument was above .7. Table 7.2 listed the composite reliability estimates for each of the measurement scales.

Validity: It was established by selecting the item which had significant alpha on instrument in total reliability. Favorable results from Guilford's formula along with the exploratory factor analysis had also supported the strong construct validity of the instrument.

- *Content validity:* The choice of an item depend in the first instance upon the judgment of competent person as to its suitability for the purpose of the research. This constructs the content validity. The content validity is non-statistical type of validity its strength depends on the rigorous theoretical exercise employed in its application (Kothari, 1991), therefore the tools were content validated by experts in the specialized field.
- *Cross Validity:* The scales was said to possess cross validity since the sample selected for tryout was not included in the establishment of final reliability and validity of the scale. This avoids the chance error of increasing the reliability coefficient.
- *Item validity:* This was established by selecting the item which had significant alpha value on instrument total reliability.

Table 7.3: Research Summary

Survey Instruments-Questionnaire	Survey Items	Sample Size	Reliability	Validity	Total Variance Explained in EFA	No. of Dimensions Identified for the Questionnaires	Categorizations of Dimensions for the Standardization Process of Questionnaires
1	2	3	4	5	6	7	8
Questionnaire One-30 CSFs were Explored for Indian SMEs	30	50 -Pilot Survey	.786	.8865	76.415%	10	1. Process 2. Enterprise 3. Technology 4. Vendor 5. Employee (Personnel HR) 6. End-user 7. Performance 8. Quality 9. Starategy 10. Project
Questionnaire One-30 CSFs were Explored for Indian SMEs	30	500 -Final Survey	.724	.8508	63.681%	11	1. Risk 2. Process 3. Quality 4. Enterprises 5. Techology 6. Project 7. Performance

...(Contd.)

1	2	3	4	5	6	7	8
							8. Employee (Personnel/HR) 9. Starategy 10. Vendor 11. End-user
Questionnaire Two-30 KCSFs were Explored	30	50 -Pilot Survey	W test Value .903	Kendall's coefficient of concordance (W test) is linearly related to the mean value of the Spearman's rank correlation coefficients between all pairs of the rankings over which it is calculated. If the test statistic W is 1, then all the judges or survey respondents have been unanimous, and each judge or respondent has assigned the same order to the list of objects or concerns. If W is 0, then there is no overall trend of agreement among the respondents, and their responses may be regarded as essentially random. Intermediate values of W indicate a greater or lesser degree of unanimity among the various judges or respondents. For the group of 50 respondents from the top 10 companies of IT (ERP) sector validity was found to be .9502(While considering W test value as a measure of reliability) whereas for a group of 500 respondents from top 10 companies of IT (ERP) sector it was found to be .9492			
Questionnaire Two-30 KCSFs were Explored	30	500 -Final Survey	W test Value .901				
30 KCSFs (Key Critical Success Factors) were identified with the help of Friedman Mean Rank test based on the Descriptive Statistics(Arithmetic Mean and Standard Deviations) of the response from 500 Indian ERP Consultants							
Questionnaire Three-20 CFFs were Explored for Indian SMEs	20	50 -Pilot Survey	.792	.8899	76.134%	7	1. Technology and Vendor 2. Employee (Personnel/ HR), 3.Performance, 4.Project, 5.Quality and End user, 6.Enterprise, 7.Strategy
Questionnaire Three-20 CFFs were Explored for Indian SMEs	20	50-Final Survey	.792	.8899	76.134%	7	1. Technology and Vendor 2. Employee (Personnel/ HR) 3. Performance 4. Project 5. Quality and End user 6. Enterprise 7. Strategy
30 KCFFs (Key Critical Failure Factors) were identified with the help of Descriptive Statistics (Arithmetic Mean and Standard Deviations) of the response from 50 Indian ERP Consultants							

(**Source:** SPSS V 18.0)

SAMPLING TECHNIQUES

Sampling is the process of selecting number of individuals for a study in such a way that the individual represent the larger group from which they were selected. The purpose of a sampling was to use a sample to gain information about a population.

- *Population of the Study:* The population for the study consists of all Indian ERP consultants either certified or not those who are having Indian nationality along with an experience of minimum one ERP implementation at India.
- *Sample of the Study (Sample Characteristics):* A sample consists of 500 Indian ERP consultants were surveyed for the present study.1000 questionnaires were distributed in total out of which 600 questionnaires were returned, comparing the response rate of 60%. Some responses were eliminated due to excessive missing data. Therefore the sample size for the testing exploratory hypotheses (statements) was 500 (50 %)
- *Sampling Techniques:* The non-probabilistic sampling techniques (convenience sampling) were adopted. Sample was drawn from top 10 companies of IT (ERP) sectors those are involved in worldwide ERP implementation including India.

TOOLS ADOPTED FOR THE STUDY (ADMINISTRATION AND SCORING)

The questionnaires (three close-ended) were designed in such way that it was explaining full purpose of the research along with the proper guidance to fill it. Each questionnaire was attached with a cover letter and thanks letter. It was distributed with the help of email and intranet of top 10 IT (ERP) sectors companies. The investigator had collected data from 500 Indian ERP consultants from top 10 companies of IT (ERP) sector. Clear cut guidance was given to fill up the responses to the items in the tools (three close-ended questionnaires). Filled questionnaires were collected back. The confidentiality of the responses was assured. After collection of the questionnaire scores were assigned and systematically pooled for further analysis. It took 15-20 minutes to complete the each questionnaire. The scoring of the items were done according to the instructions received in manual. The scoring was done on a Likert five point scale ranging from strongly disagree (1) to strongly agree(5).Scale range was analyzed between 30 to 150 for Likert Five Point Scale.

STATISTICAL TECHNIQUES USED FOR THE STUDY

The following statistical techniques were used for analyzing the data as per the objectives of this research project:

- Cronbach's Alpha to find out the reliability of the survey instruments(questionnaires)
- Guilford's Formula to check validity of the customized survey instruments(questionnaires)
- Descriptive Statistics(arithmetic mean and standard deviation) to map the perception of respondents(Indian ERP consultants)
- Friedman mean rank test to rank the CSFs for ERP implementation at Indian SMEs
- Kendall W test to check the reliability and validity of the rank given by Indian ERP consultants
- Exploratory Factor analysis was used to explore the CSFs, CFFs and to validate the survey instruments (questionnaires). It was also used to identify the damnations for the customized survey instruments in order to facilitate its standardization process in future research.

MAJOR AND GENERAL FINDINGS

Major Findings-Exploratory Hypothesis (Exploratory Statements) related Findings

- There are 30 CSFs for the successful ERP implementation at Indian SMEs
- There are 20 CFFs for the failure of ERP implementation at Indian SMEs
- The 30 CSFs have different ranks (and hence different importance) given by the Indian ERP consultants. There are KCSFs also for the successful ERP implementation at Indian SMEs
- Most of the 20 CFFs have different mean value (and hence different importance) given by the Indian ERP consultants. Only few CFFs have same mean value (and hence same importance). there are KCFFs also for the failure of ERP implementation at Indian SMEs
- All the 30 CSFs can be categorized into 11 categories to form a unified structure for successful ERP implementation at Indian SMEs because all the 30 CSFs are not fully independent from each others. Few of them had strong factor loading (correlation) among each other and exploration factor analysis was valid.
- All the 20 CFFs can be categorized into 7 categories to form a unified structure for failure of ERP implementation at Indian SMEs because all the 20 CFFs are not fully independent from each others. Few of them had strong factor loading (correlation) among each other and exploration factor analysis was valid.

- The customized survey instrument to explore the CSFs for the successful ERP implementation at Indian SMEs can be used as reliable survey tool for current and future research because of the high construct reliability of the survey instrument (questionnaire).
- The customized survey instrument to rank the CSFs for the successful ERP implementation at Indian SMEs can be used as reliable survey tool for current and future research because of the high construct reliability of the survey instrument (questionnaire).
- The customized survey instrument to explore the CFFs for the failure of ERP implementation at Indian SMEs can be used as reliable survey tool for current and future research because of the high construct reliability of the survey instrument (questionnaire).
- The customized survey instrument to explore the CSFs for the successful ERP implementation at Indian SMEs can be used as validate survey tool for current and future research because of the high construct validity of the survey instrument(questionnaire).
- The customized survey instrument to rank the CSFs for the successful ERP implementation at Indian SMEs can be used as validate survey tool for current and future research because of the high construct validity of the survey instrument(questionnaire).
- the customized survey instrument to explore the CFFs for the failure of ERP implementation at Indian SMEs can be used as validate survey tool for current and future research because of the high construct validity of the survey instrument(questionnaire).
- Eleven dimensions were identified for the customized survey instrument (questionnaires) related to identification (exploring) of the CSFs for the successful ERP implementation at Indian SMEs, in order to facilitate the standardization process of the customized survey instrument (questionnaire) in future research.
- Seven dimensions were identified for the customized survey instrument (questionnaires) related to identification (exploring) of the CFFs for the failure of ERP implementation at Indian SMEs, in order to facilitate the standardization process of the customized survey instrument (questionnaire) in future research.

General Finding

- A strategic ERP model has been developed for the successful ERP implementation at Indian SMEs (See Chapter 6, strategic ERP model part).

- Checklist has been provided for the successful ERP implementation at Indian SMEs (See Chapter 6, checklist part).
- Guidelines were provided along with the fifty recommendations for the successful ERP implementation at Indian SMEs (See Chapter 6, guidelines part and Chapter 7, recommendations part).
- A theoretical framework has been developed and tested for future research in the area of ERP implementation at India SMEs (See Chapter 5 and Chapter 6).
- A theoretical framework has been developed for the future research in the area of ERP adoption at India SMEs (See Chapter 5 and Chapter 6).
- Based on pilot survey results user manuals have been developed for all three customized survey instruments(three close ended questionnaire) in order to facilitate present and future research related to ERP implementation at Indian SMEs.
- A common ERP model has been developed for the successful ERP implementation at Indian SMEs (See Chapter 5)
- ERP implementation at Indian SMEs(See Chapter 5)
- ERP implementation failure model has been developed to understand the failure of ERP implementation at Indian SMEs (See Chapter 5)
- 30 CSFs of the LEs were also validated for the successful ERP implementation at Indian SMEs (See Chapter 5)
- 20 CFFs of the LEs were also validated for the failure of ERP implementation at Indian SMEs(See Chapter 5)
- Gap analysis had been conducted by comparing CSFs and CFFs for the successful ERP implementation at Indian SMEs(See Chapter 6)

CONTRIBUTIONS

The results of this exploratory study contribute to the understanding of CSFs and CFFs for the successful ERP implementation at Indian SMEs. It provide models that can serve as both a framework for practitioners to understand contribution of CFs in ERP implementation at Indian SMEs and a avenues to identify and manage ERP customizations for Indian SMEs. It can also be used as a reference point for future research on ERP implementation at Indian SMEs. Subsequent studies could, for instance, extend the findings to a different context or can examine the issue at a more detailed level. The exploratory survey identified ERP implementation specific success and failure factors for Indian SMEs with justification of their inclusion in the survey instruments. The exploratory survey (supported by a comprehensive literature review of the large enterprise) identified thirty critical success factors and twenty critical failure factors for the ERP implementation at Indian SMEs. The 50 critical factors constitute perhaps the most comprehensive ERP implementation factors identification survey instruments validated yet. While a limited number of ERP implementation evaluation studies have employed for Indian SMEs. Most ERP related research in the area of Indian SMEs generally proposes research models without theories. Furthermore, since this type of research is still relatively new to ERP research. Many surveys have been developed without sound theoretical background. This study identifies the important factors by comparing the mean values of factors, and rank factors in accordance with their importance.

This research was the first study that has been identified the thirty critical success and twenty critical failure factors contributing in the ERP implementation at Indian SMEs with strong theoretical background in ERP implementation related research. The proposed models adapted were theoretically validated with the help of ERP implementation phases, ERP success measurement model, IS failure categories, and the fundamentals of project management in ERP implementation. Therefore, the academic contribution of the research can be found in a deliberate attempt to formulate the ERP models for Indian SMEs. The factors identified in literature were mostly based on the experiences of organizations or senior managers involved in ERP implementation projects. For these reasons, this research focused on identifying the factors for the ERP implementation at Indian SMEs from ERP consultant's/vendors perspectives. Furthermore, this research suggested recommendations for the successful ERP implementation at Indian SMEs, showing how to approach successfully for ERP implementation at Indian SMEs in order to avoid failure and what factors should be considered as the significant based on the findings of this study. These recommendations can provide helpful information to ERP consultants and vendors when they are going to consider ERP implementation or even up gradation for Indian SMEs. This information may help to ERP consultants and Indian SMEs to reduce tremendous ERP implementation risks so that they may have more chances to improve their business value with the success of EPR implementation. Such practical implications can be applied to the most of the Indian SMEs for a better understanding about the factors that may lead to the success of ERP implementation.

This approach should be valuable information for decision makers of Indian SMEs before or during their ERP implementation. The sample sizes of the responses were large enough to verify the proposed ERP models statistically. This research focused on critical success and failure factors for implementing an ERP system at Indian SMEs. Key findings of this study were derived from ERP consultant's perceptions with the help of three close ended questionnaires based on literature review and secondary data review. This framework was developed based on existing knowledge in the IS development and project implementation literature as well as literature on ERP systems. The theoretical model was useful in that it has given the researcher a possibility to group research that had been done previously in the IS implementation and ERP development areas and link it with existing knowledge from the ERP research field .The models relates all the identified CSFs and CFFs from the research findings to the author's developed theoretical framework for Indian SMEs. As shown in the models, the ERP implementation project has several CSFs and CFFs related to all the phases of ERP implementation at Indian SMEs. Where appropriate, some of the CSFs and CFFs found in the literature were also found to be evident for Indian SMEs from the tested theoretical framework. Based on the Indian ERP consultants' perceptions all of the identified CSFs and CFFs were linked to the theoretical framework. The fact that some of the CSFs and CFFs were found in more than one concept of the theoretical framework might be identification to the fact that the theoretical framework needed more detail. However, the researcher feel that the theoretical model guided the research and made it easier to clearly identify a structured approach to conducting survey for successful ERP implementation at Indian SMEs. It also relying on previous research conducted in the IS and ERP research field. The research method and the data collection techniques were chosen due to their practicality and because the researcher believed that they were the most appropriate methods available in order to answer the research questions. Various research topics and research methods exist in the ERP field, as identified by (Esteves and Pastor, 2001) where a major focus has been on implementation phase.

This researcher however has shown the link between the IS implementation school of thought and an ERP implementation environment, specifically focusing on CSFs and CFFs for ERP implementation at Indian SMEs. The researcher has attempted to link the ERP consultant's perceptions with actual theoretical general concepts in the literature. To some extent, this generalization was limited to the given time frame of the research project and could have gone over a longer period of time. Arguably, criticism can be raised in relation to the lack of follow-up in order to clarify issues. The author regarded this as to be outside the scope of the project due to time constraints.

- What are the critical success factors for the successful ERP implementation at Indian SMEs?

  This question relates to the primary findings of the study. Indian ERP consultant's responses on thirty different factors those were relevant to be addressed to ensure the success of an ERP implementation at Indian SMEs. From these findings, it was clear that there are 30 CSFs that may contribute in the successful ERP implementation at Indian SME and can be ranked according to their importance.

- What are the critical failure factors for the failure of ERP implementation at Indian SMEs?

  This question relates to the secondary findings of the study. Indian ERP consultant's responses on twenty different factors those were relevant to be addressed to the failure of an ERP implementation at Indian SMEs. From these findings, it was clear that there are 20 CFFs that may contribute in the failure of ERP implementation at Indian SME and can be ranked according to their importance.

- Does the CFs (both CSFs as well as CFFs) of the LEs for ERP implementation can also be considered for the ERP implementation at Indian SMEs?

  Based on the Indian ERP consultant's perceptions, literature review, and secondary data review it was found that an ERP implementation at Indian SMEs is not exactly same as the ERP implementations in LEs. When discussing the CSFs and CFFs for an ERP implementation at Indian SMEs, it was found that although the factors are more or less same but the importance of factors in term of their priority were defiantly different from the ERP implementation of the LEs.

The contributions of this research work are the definition of new constructs (CFs) associated with the ERP implementation at Indian SMEs and the development of new multi-item measurement scales for exploring these constructs (CFs). Unlike much prior ERP implementation research, this study takes a Critical Factors (CFs),ERP project management and implementation phases based approach using Indian ERP consultants' perceptions. A secondary contribution of this work is the demonstration of a rigorous empirical scale and item development process for the successful ERP implementation at Indian SMEs.

RECOMMENDATIONS

(Davenport, 2000) argues that companies are doing more than installing a computer system with ERP projects, but are in fact, changing the way the company is organized across national boundaries and often acting against the prevailing company culture. Awareness of cultural differences and preferences will certainly improve the assessment of ERP suitability and any subsequent implementation for Indian SMEs. This may implies that a one-size-fits all or one-business-model-fits-all approach is unlikely to be successful for Indian SMEs. ERP developers, consultants and SMEs need to adapt their products and services for different cultural markets. Ineffective communication is the important obstacle to successful ERP implementation at Indian SMEs.

More than anything ERP packages may takes time to comprehend different languages and cultures. Sometimes it is not at all about technology it is about change. Overcoming these natural instincts and getting people to work together for a common goal is a primary challenge for any Indian SMEs and ERP consultant. In order to minimize the communication obstacles cultural awareness classes or cultural training meeting/seminars may be very helpful. There is a need to convince, employees about the important of information technology for the Indian SMEs to minimize the resistance to change effect. The rapid changing of information and communication technology and its penetration should considered by the Indian SMEs as its tool in order to increase its performance as a whole. Specifically, the author would recommend that an emphasis should be placed on informing the users of changes, getting user participation in the development for the successful implementation of the ERP system at Indian SMEs, thus ensuring that users will get and share technical and business knowledge through business process reengineering activities. If new processes are derived, it is important that all affected users of the system must be made aware of these changes. Successfully implementing ERP at Indian SMEs requires a structured methodology that is strategy, people and process-focused. This is the important way to manage the risk effectively for Indian SMEs. A good methodology covers all the bases, but when the unexpected pops up, as it usually does, Indian SMEs should be prepared to handle these exceptions without severe negative consequences. One very common mistake may be, not having employees prepared to use the new processes and support system while implementation ERP system at Indian SMEs. The consequence here can range all the way to total failure, but they are avoidable.ERP consultants, vendor and Indian SMEs should evaluate business strategy and ERP plan before commit to software acquisition and installation. Doing it right the first time is the important cost effective way to go for successful ERP implementation at Indian SMEs. It may set the standards and epitomize the best business practices. In order for this is to happen, ERP consultants, vendor and Indian SMEs need to choose an option that may not only suffice for the time being, but which may have the potential to accommodate the various growth paths an Indian SMEs has as it evolves. Choosing an option that works for now, but does not allow for growth may seem cheaper, but when one factor in the amount Indian SMEs may eventually spend to extend the system and make changes to functionality; an Indian SMEs may end up paying more for this temporary solution than for a system that can grow. It is a real challenge for an ERP consultant, vendor and Indian SMEs to plan and execute a long term implementation strategy as both the internal business scenario and the software from the vendors are evolving continuously.

ERP consultants, ERP vendors and Indian SMEs are suggested to follow these recommendations for the successful ERP implementation at India SMEs:

- *Top Management Commitment and Support:* The commitment and support of the top management (from both the side vendor as well as the client side) should be continuous throughout the process, for the successful ERP implementation at Indian SMEs.
- *Change Management Process:* The change management approach will ensure the acceptance and readiness of the ERP consultants, ERP vendor and Indian SMEs for the successful ERP implementation as it allows the Indian SMEs to get the benefits from using ERP. It will also help to reduce the customization by facilitating best software fit process for Indian SMEs.
- *BPR and Software Configuration:* Modifications in ERP package should be avoided to reduce the amount of errors and to take the full advantage of newer versions of the ERP systems at Indian SMEs. Aligning the Indian SMEs business process to the ERP implementation package is important.
- *Project Champion:* The presence of an effective project champion for the successful ERP implementation at Indian SMEs is must, who can perform the crucial functions of transformational leadership, facilitation, and marketing of the ERP implementation to the ERP users at Indian SMEs.
- *Business Plan, Vision:* Indian SMEs must carefully define why the ERP is being implemented and what critical business need the ERP system will address, that will helps to ERP consultants, ERP vendor and Indian SMEs for better customization at Indian SMEs.
- *Effective Communication Plan:* For successful ERP implementation at Indian SMEs it is necessary that ERP consultants, ERP vendor and Indian SMEs should pay particular attention to communicate expectation, changes, future plans etc to the entire team as it tends to have much better chance of achieving implementation correctly at the Indian SMEs.
- *Post Implementation Evolution:* There should be some allowance for some kind of post-evaluation for successful ERP implementation at Indian SMEs, there is a need for an allowance for a feedback network from both the side ERP consultants (ERP vendors) as well as from Indian SMEs side.

- *Risk Management:* ERP consultants, ERP vendor and Indian SMEs should have proper risk management strategy to minimize the impact of unplanned incidents by identifying and addressing potential risks before significant consequences occur for the successful ERP implementation at Indian SMEs.
- *Focussed Performance Measures:* It is needed to ensure expected outcomes are achieved by the ERP implementation for Indian SMEs. ERP consultants, ERP vendor and Indian SMEs should enable effective measurement for the SMEs business process improvement provided by the ERP implementation at Indian SMEs.
- *Quality Improvement Measures:* It is neccessory that data accuracy, consistency, frequency of use, redundancy, data relevancy, data cleansing, consolidation, transformation and validation related issues are handled and properly managed by the ERP consultants, ERP vendor and Indian SMEs for the successful ERP Implementaion at Indian SMEs.
- *Organization/Corporate Culture:* ERP consultants, ERP vendor and Indian SMEs should be ready to change or modify the culture by changing the way it works. The focus, decision making process, attitude to staff; stability etc should also be changed if needed for the successful fit with ERP implementation at Indian SMEs.
- *Implementation Cost:* The nature of ERP implementations at Indian SMEs are such that there are usually unforeseen and unexpected occurrences that may increase the overall costs for ERP implementation. Therefore, ERP consultants, ERP vendor and Indian SMEs should promote flexible budget policy for the successful ERP implementation at Indian SMEs.
- *Software Development, Testing, Trouble Shooting and Crises Management:* The need for troubleshooting skills will be an ongoing requirement for the successful ERP implementation at Indian SMEs. If possible ERP consultants, ERP vendor and Indian SMEs team should consider the inclusion of testing exercises as well as simulation exercises during all the phases of ERP implementation at Indian SMEs on the basis of major or minor scenarios.
- *IT Infrastructure:* ERP implementation at Indian SMEs involves a complex transition from legacy systems business processes to an integrated IT infra-structure and common business process throughout the life cycle of Indian SMEs.
- *Selection of ERP Package:* The choice of the right ERP package for Indian SMEs involves important decisions regarding budgets, timeframes, goals, and deliverables that will shape the entire ERP implementation process along with the future of ERP implementation at Indian SMEs.

Right ERP package may help to ensure minimal modification and successful use of ERP implementation at Indian SMEs.

- *Data Conversion and Integrity:* It means data loaded from existing legacy systems or documents must be of high quality for successful ERP Implementation at Indian SMEs. Timely and accurate data in a single consistent format is throughout fundamental requirement for the effectiveness of ERP implementation at Indian SMEs.
- *Legacy System Considerations:* The current business process and old systems determine the IT and change related requirements for the successful ERP implementaion at Indian SMEs. After evaluating the existing legacy system, ERP consultants, ERP vendor and Indian SMEs may be able to define the nature and problems that might be likely to meet during the ERP implementation at Indian SMEs.
- *Vanilla ERP:* It can be used with a minimum customization and for an uncomplicated implementation strategic changes in the business process of Indian SMEs to fit the ERP package best into the business processes with minium complexity and risk.
- *System Documentation:* Well-designed and well-built documentation related to ERP implementation at Indian SMEs and its use can save time and money on support costs after the ERP Implementation is in place for both the ERP consultants as well as for Indian SMEs.
- *Project Team:* A successful ERP implementation at Indian SMEs involves all of the functional departments and demands the effort, cooperation of technical and business experts as well as end users.
- *Implementation Strategy and Time Frame:* The advantages and disadvantages of different ERP implementation strategy for the Indian SMEs along with the projected time period should be measured, especially at a functionality level of Indian SMEs. the logic of an ERP implementation could conflict with the logic of the business process of Indian SMEs, in that case either the implementation will fail by wasting large sums of money and causing a great deal of disruption, or Indian SMEs will give important sources of competitive advantage to others.
- *Consultant Selection:* It is important for successful ERP implementation at Indian SMEs to have right quality and quantity of ERP consultants. These experts and consultants are normally from ERP vendors and ERP consulting companies. They are experienced and important during all the process and even after the implementation for the successful ERP implementation at Indian SMEs.
- *Vendor/Customer Relationship:* Implementation of successful ERP project at Indian SMEs is a group phenomenon driven by both ERP vendors/

consultants and adopting Indian SMEs (customer). ERP systems could not be able to provide a solution to Indian SMEs if problems were not understood from both the sides (customer as well as vendor).it is important that they should have cordial relationship with each other for the successful ERP systems at Indian SMEs.

- *Project Management:* It is necessary for the successful ERP implementation at Indian SMEs that a detailed project plan related to ERP project goals and objectives must be defined to the all involve parties like ERP consultants, ERP vendor and Indian SMEs etc.
- *Client Consultation:* Continuous consultation with the Indian SMEs (client)for the successful ERP implementation should occur early in the process; otherwise the chance of subsequent acceptance for ERP system from the client side (Indian SMEs) maybe low.
- *User Involvement:* If the employees(ERP user) of an Indian SMEs those who are not in the ERP implementation project team or are excluded from the entire ERP implementation process may resist or fear the new ERP system so user involvement should be as high as possible for the successful ERP at Indian SMEs.
- *User Education and Training:* Sufficient and timely training regarding the fundamental of ERP systems, education related to use and technical training in the area of the ERP project may help in successful ERP implementaion at Indian SMEs.
- *Personnel/Staff:* Full consideration should be given for the skills development needed by employees of an Indian SMEs. Sufficient training and education to current employees or hiring of outside consulting may help in successful ERP implementaion at Indian SMEs. with the help of ERP consultants/vendors, HR department of Indian SMEs should identify this need correclty and timely.
- *Employee Attitute and Morale:* It is important that the team leader and the other members those who are the part of ERP implementation at Indian SMEs should creates a stimulating work environment and recognizes the work of the employee to boost their morale, as it may also helps in creating positive attitude towards successful ERP implementation at Indian SMEs and in high level of staff retention.
- *Empowered Decision Making:* There is a need to empowered the ERP team to make necessary decisions in due time, so as to allow for effective timing with respect to the successful ERP implementation at Indian SMEs.
- *Poor Consultant Effectiveness:* ERP Consultants should not communicate ineffectively during the ERP implementation at Indian SMEs. Due to

language barriers and copied ERP configuration directly without proper analysis of ERP implementation systems at Indian SMEs may get fail. Lack of ERP consultant's effectiveness without applying professional skills to conduct BPR, to bridge the gap between ERP systems and Indian SMEs business processes may leads to the failure of ERP implementation.

- *Poor Quality of BPR:* Unclear vision of why or how to conduct BPR for Indian SMEs, and unprofessional advice for conducting BPR may be the one of the factor that results in the failure of ERP implementation at Indian SMEs.
- *Poor Project Management Effectiveness:* Top management and project managers need to ensure sufficient knowledge, skills, resource, planning and expertise for the successful ERP implementation at Indian SMEs before the start of real ERP implementation, as poorly managed ERP projects may results in failure of ERP implementation at Indian SMEs.
- *ERP Software Misfits:* Project teams relied on heavy customization by changing the ERP system program, or writing many management reports, or conducting data transfer as workarounds to solve problems while implementation ERP systems for an Indian SMEs may leads to the complexity and makes ERP package misfit for an Indian SMEs.
- *High Turnover Rate of Project Team Member:* This may happen due to the insufficient ERP knowledge and skill transfer among project team members during the ERP implementation at Indian SMEs.
- *Over Reliance on Heavy Customizations:* ERP software mismatch may leads to heavy customization in the areas of program and report customization while implementing ERP for Indian SMEs. Heavy customization could cause project delays, overspent budget and an unreliable system so it should be avoided for successful ERP implementation at Indian SMEs.
- *Poor IT Infrastructure:* Due to the insufficient financial resource provided by top management of Indian SMEs for the ERP implementation budget, a low performance IT infrastructure hardware may proposed by the ERP consultants and project manager so as to reduce the costs
- *Poor Knowledge Transfer:* Training materials and user documentation should not be in too brief and unhelpful for the ERP users of an Indian SMEs. Project team members should do proper knowledge transfer process to avoid ineffective training. Sufficient knowledge or skills to use, maintain and support the ERP implementation at Indian SMEs is must.

- Unclear concept of the nature and use of the ERP system at Indian SMEs from the user perspective may leads to the failure of ERP implementation at Indian SMEs.
- An unrealistic expectation from the top management of an Indian SMEs concerning the ERP implementation may makes ERP implementation success doubtful.
- *Too Tight Project Schedule:* Top management and the project manager should not reduce the budget of the ERP implementation at Indian SMEs unnecessarily, as it may results in too tight project schedule and rush in ERP implementation in order to meet the project deadline for an Indian SMEs.
- *User's Resistance to Change:* Limited knowledge of formalized business processes of Indian SMEs and the use of ERP systems may create resistance to change among the employees of an Indian SMEs.
- *Poor Top Management Support:* Top management of an Indian SMEs is expected to provide continuous support and commitment in the areas of ERP implementation at Indian SMEs, sufficient financial, human resource support and the resolution of political problems is necessary needed, otherwise it may gives failure to the ERP implementation at Indian SMEs.
- *Poor Quality of Testing:* Over-tight project schedule and insufficient knowledge in testing of an ERP implementation at Indian SMEs may results in a rush and low quality ERP implementation for an Indian SMEs.
- *Lack of Formal Communications:* All the involve parties of the ERP implementation at an Indian SMEs should be provided with a detailed implementation plan including targets and business objectives. They (ERP consultants, ERP vendor and Indian SMEs) should be kept informed about the ERP implementation progress on a regular basis.
- *Software Modifications:* ERP consultants, ERP vendors and Indian SMEs should chose to implement ERP package that suits to business process in order to avoid the failures in the business processes that were considered either strategic or reliable before the ERP implementation at Indian SMEs.
- *Informal Strategy:* Informal nature and the lack of planning should be avoided for the successful ERP implementation at Indian SMEs. Non formalized business strategy or communication may leads to the failure of ERP implementation at Indian SMEs

- *Part Time Dedications:* It is important for the successful ERP implementation at Indian SMEs that full time dedicate employees of the Indian SMEs should involve in ERP implementation rather than involving employees on overtime, part time and weekend's basis.
- *Functionality Problem with the Systems:* Successful ERP implementation should provide proper functionality to an Indian SMEs as accepted, to meet its regular business requirements.
- *Cost Over Runs:* The Management of an Indian SMEs and staff may not be happy if the benefits of the ERP implementation at Indian SMEs are less from the ERP implementation cost. Cost over runs should be avoided for the successful ERP implementation at Indian SMEs.

MANAGEMENT (MANAGERIAL) IMPLICATION

There are number of important implications for management (ERP consultants, ERP vendor and Indian SMEs) that arise from this study. There are multiple ways that ERP implementation can be achieved to add value to Indian SMEs. The options are varied and range from in house activity to interactions with external parties. Indian SMEs may gain competitive advantage from ERP but they must embark on a process of continuous improvement and learning in order to achieve successful ERP implementation. ERP consultants, ERP vendor and Indian SMEs should realize that implementing ERP is a form of what refer to as training and change.

This occurs when decisions taken are based on challenging existing knowledge and rethinking existing competencies and methods related to ERP implementation at Indian SMEs. ERP consultants, ERP vendor and Indian SMEs should reflect and inquire into issues related to strategic technology adoption and previous episodes of ERP implementation success or failure to learn. ERP consultants, ERP vendor and Indian SMEs should try to discover that facilitated or inhibited ERP implementation, invent and produce new strategies for ERP implementation, and evaluate and generalize whatever they have produced. It is important for ERP consultants, ERP vendor and Indian SMEs to take a long-term view. They should not consider an ERP implementation complete when they go live as there is bedding-in period for the Indian SMEs. A temporary dip in performance post going live can be attributed to the scope of the change involved for the Indian SMEs. Going live should be regarded as a milestone on a journey towards achieving the full benefits for Indian SMEs. Moreover, the full benefits will not be visible or fully experienced by everyone but overtime when the system become stable and ERP users have had time to adjust to the new working practices the benefits will become more visible to all, like to ERP consultants as well as to Indian SMEs. ERP consultants, ERP vendor and Indian SMEs will need to develop a core cross functional team of mangers to drive the process and senior management will need to provide effective support for the successful ERP implementation at Indian SMEs, it should be undergo specialist training themselves to understand the technical nature of the ERP project at Indian SMEs.

ERP consultants, ERP vendor and Indian SMEs will have to find ways to continuously energies their staff to accept the idea that ERP implementation is a process and not an episode or act. However, the process may change the career prospects and aspirations for both employees as well as managers of the Indian SMEs. Training and retraining will be necessary to get people to accept change and to do business in a totally different way for Indian SMEs. ERP consultants, ERP vendor and Indian SMEs who do not take this route may be caught by 'competitive convergence' and eventually overtaken by their competitors. ERP consultants, ERP vendor and Indian SMEs have yet to determine their precise requirements and whether they will drive the process or be driven by their business partners. Different ERP consultants and Indian SMEs may respond and embrace ERP in different ways and with different timescales. ERP consultants, ERP vendor and Indian SMEs readiness state will driven by key players implementing systems thereby, creating a standard solution within the industry. ERP is not simply a matter of adding a new application at Indian SMEs. ERP consultants, ERP vendor and Indian SMEs embarking on this route should consider the challenges. Business processes at Indian SMEs whether internal or external, must be examined and redesigned as necessary to take advantage of the ERP technology. An effective change management and communications programme must be run. The lessons learned from the other ERP implementation should be revisited and ensure that mistakes made then are avoided while implementation ERP at Indian SMEs. ERP consultants, ERP vendor and Indian SMEs should hold a series of workshops with a cross section of the users of the system and members of the implementation team.

These workshops will identify the causes of the current difficulties people have with the system and suggest possible solutions for Indian SMEs. A strong business case needs to be developed, with clear objectives for successful ERP implementation at Indian SMEs. Data revealed ERP implementation problems stemmed from the insufficient service of software vendors and applying consultancy services used with success in large organizations directly in SMEs with little or no adaptations or modifications to fit the SMEs smaller scale and internal environment that should not be done for successful ERP implementation at Indian SMEs.

There is a need to recognize the consulting requirement of Indian SMEs in ERP implementation. It confirms the roles and functions of ERP consultants in Indian SMEs and, based on the findings, several ideas for ERP practitioners are suggested. Since Indian SMEs are often unfamiliar with the process of ERP consulting, this may leads to anxiety. Most of the Indian SMEs are owner-managers who founded the business. It is difficult for these entrepreneurs to accept the need for outside expertise. Therefore, ERP consultants must be sure they establish a relationship based on confidence and expertise with the Indian SME owner from the start. Without this rapport, there is little hope of a successful ERP implementation at Indian SMEs. While cost may not be necessarily an order winner for ERP consultants working with any Indian SME client, a lower fee for the initial phase of the ERP project is an effective promotional strategy and could improve the ERP consultant's initial success at Indian SMEs. The ability to handle office politics is even more important for ERP consultants and Indian SMEs. The changing power structure in Indian SMEs may influence the level of resistance and trust from internal managers. Because Indian SMEs may have preconceived views and skepticism about ERP consultancy quality, In hat case practical solutions and effective execution are important for ERP consultants, particularly during the early stages of the ERP project where building client trust is critical for successful ERP implementation at Indian SMEs. The roles of ERP consultants in Indian SMEs may differ from the consulting roles in large companies. The effect of 'cut-and-paste' projects, copied from large organizations and directly applied within Indian SMEs may effect on the growth and profitability of the Indian SMEs. ERP consultants, ERP vendor and Indian SMEs have to understand the business improvement opportunities and engage knowledgeable people to ensure strategic fit. The studies show that the integration has to meet the business needs and custom-built systems have to be created for the business processes for the successful ERP implementation at Indian SMEs. This would involve both leadership and significant investment from both the side ERP consultants as well as Indian SMEs.

ERP consultants, ERP vendor and Indian SMEs have to prepare for working in new structures with different flavours, incentives and controls. The older employees are likely to be affected since such changes displace earlier skills and mindsets. As the analysis suggests, it has become necessary to strive for not only operational effectiveness but also differentiation and therefore, uniqueness has to be delivered by the ERP system for successful ERP implementation at Indian SMEs. The idea is not to imitate market but to tailor applications to the Indian SMEs overall strategy so as to extend competitive advantages and achieve sustainability. The technological strength of any ERP implementation may lies in enhancing service, responsiveness and leveraging existing strengths for Indian SMEs. The principles of team-work may decrease the risk for misunderstandings that may occur, between those who gather the requirements and those who develop ERP system for

Indian SMEs. A process that is further improves by the end-users and customer organization involvement may helps in ERP success at Indian SMEs. Focused on goals such as lowering total-cost-of-ownership through non-installation packages based on 'best practice' and a flexible innovation process with releases of building blocks rather than seldom releases of a new entire suite that is well known for its costly implementation may helps in successful ERP implementation at Indian SMEs. If possible ERP consultants, ERP vendor and Indian SMEs should also try to focus on on-demand-solutions (solutions offered via the internet) also known as software-as-a-service (SaaS), while this has only briefly been mentioned in the literature covered in this research yet. In short software-as-a-service is software delivered as a hosted application from a vendor or distributor that the Indian SMEs may access via a browser. The SaaS-model may enables the Indian SMEs to decrease the cost of implementation, maintenance and the overall administration of the application that furthermore is independent of existing IT-infrastructure, scalable and flexible.

In that sense the ERP consultants, ERP vendor and Indian SMEs may focus on its core business without worrying about technicalities that will be handled by the distributor. Improving understanding of the implementation stage of ERP through identification of key factors to the process may help in successful ERP implementation at Indian SMEs. This may help ERP consultants, ERP vendor and Indian SMEs to study their conditions against a set of identified CSFs and CFFs, which is expected to improve their chances of eliminating or reducing the risk of failure or improving the chances of success of their ERP projects at Indian SMEs. testing of a new combination of CSFs and CFFs to ERP implementation at Indian SMEs may shed light on the complex interaction and effect of these variables on the performance outcome, providing a better understanding of whether CSFs and CFFs roles are limited in contributing the outcome of ERP implementation phases at Indian SMEs or it goes beyond in contributing the performance of the Indian SMEs as well, helping ERP consultants, ERP vendor and Indian SMEs to understand the needs of potential ERP systems, and thus formulate their structure and development activities to increase their success chance. It may helps in laying the foundation of a new theoretical framework of 'successful ERP implementation ' at Indian SMEs to carry out process improvement and technology studies that focus on Indian SMEs, as they perform a significant role in Indian economies. In addition, the use of survey had provided valuable detail and insight into such a complex area for ERP consultants, ERP vendor and Indian SMEs. For ERP consultants, ERP vendor and Indian SMEs this study indicates that implementing ERP at Indian SMEs may provide significant benefits if some critical practices are in place. Such factors should aid to prioritize implementation efforts, resources, and maximize the chances of successful ERP implementation at Indian SMEs. Moreover, the implication is that the ERP consultants, ERP vendor and Indian SMEs have to look beyond ERP solution in order to build sustainable competitive advantage. These studies also express the lack of post implementation vision that may lead to difficulties in providing unique value proposition, up gradation and prioritization for the successful ERP implementation at Indian SMEs. Competitive advantage may comes from the way ERP consultants, ERP vendor and Indian SMEs implements the system and exploits the resulting data. The competitors may have ERP but it is useless if it is not integrated with the Indian SMEs business processes as every business is unique and like any tool it is essential to know how to utilize it for it to be an asset. ERP consultants, ERP vendor, Indian SMEs and IS managers should pay attention not only to improve the quality of ERP products, but also to improve user knowledge and involvement and to select suitable ERP package. Finally, all three customized survey instruments (questionnaires) can be utilized as a diagnostic tool. ERP consultants, ERP vendor and Indian SMEs can use the instrument to assess and analyze what aspects of their ERP systems are most problematical. ERP consultants, ERP vendor and Indian SMEs can compare satisfaction levels of their ERP systems with the expected levels to understand relative goodness or badness and to take necessary corrective actions to improve them. Another implication is that ERP systems for any Indian SMEs must be designed in such a way that they become easy to use, simple to learn, and flexible to interact with. ERP system that is easy to use is less threatening to the user. That is, perceived ease of use may have a positive influence on users' acceptance for the successful ERP implementation at Indian SMEs.

LIMITATIONS

- Sample size in case of CFFs was 50 which was comparatively small and that might affect the overall reliability.
- Although a sample size of 500 in case of CSFs was statistically sufficient for the analysis, a larger sample size might produce better insights and that might affect the overall reliability.
- The factor analysis was only exploratory and not confirmative.
- The study was limited to India and that to Indian SMEs context only due to its geographical focus in Indian context, the utility of findings in the cross-border and cross-cultural ERP projects context would be limited, as it cannot be generalized.
- The study was based on the opinion of respondents (questionnaires) and there may be bias.
- The questionnaire might have excluded some important factors.

- Only Cronbach's Alpha reliability test was used to test the reliability of the scale
- The validity of a measure cannot be truly established on the basis of a single study. Validation of measure requires the assessment of measurement properties over a variety of samples in similar and different context.
- The analysis and interpretation might not be exhaustive. The use of convenience samples may have limited insights in the process. There is inconsistency between definitions of SMEs size in various studies.
- Limited choices of implementation phases were examined.
- The information contained in this research work was intended only to provide a general summary. It does not suppose to be a complete description of the research issues.
- It may possible that the sample of this study might have suffered from selection bias as well as different ERP systems have different strengths. Further, some ERP consultants, ERP vendor and Indian SMEs may choose to implement ERP within a narrow scope rather than enterprise wide. Hence, the motivation for ERP system selection and its impact on outcomes could differ across ERP package.
- The concept of CSFs and CFFs were found to be quite complex and consist of a wider scope than the researcher had planned and hope for identified a total of 50 survey items. A more comprehensive study, more items should be included in the survey to assess the critical issues for the successful ERP implementation at Indian SMEs.
- Although a common practice in the literature was highly subjective and lacks the credibility of hard data. More quantifiable measures such as actual versus projected implementation time, actual versus projected cost of implementation, operational efficiencies such as cycle time reduction, return on investment on the ERP project, and increased market revenue would have provided a better understanding of ERP implementation success for Indian SMEs.
- ERP consultants, ERP vendor and Indian SMEs that may not have successfully implemented ERP may have been successful at a later point in time with appropriate modifications in their respective implementation strategies. Hence, it is necessary that longitudinal studies (over a longer period of time) at each of the stage of ERP implementation should be undertaken for Indian SMEs.
- The study provides a snap shot understanding of the implementation phases, and thus do not takes into account the dynamic nature of

changes in effect of CSFs and CFFs to improvements in performance and process for successful ERP implementation at Indian SMEs.

- The research study does not take into account the cross-border and cross-country issues for all the phases of successful ERP implementation at Indian SMEs, which could be critical in ERP context as several Indian SMEs may implement ERP on global basis.
- The study limits its focus on identification and examination of the CSFs and CFFs for all the phases of the ERP implementation at Indian SMEs. Further research would be required to identify and examine the CSFs and CFFs for each phase of the ERP implementation at Indian SMEs.While this research project was limited in scope, it became apparent through analyzing the literature that critical factors contributing to the success or failure of ERP implementation at Indian SMEs were complex and do not occur alone. They were actually intertwined with one another, and at many times, are hard to separate or isolate.

FUTURE RESEARCH/FUTURE WORK

The author identifies several research directions for the area of ERP research that this project concerned. With respect to future research, a number of different approaches could be considered. Single company case studies could be used to uncover some of the critical success and failure factors other than the covered thirty CSFs and twenty CFFs for the ERP implementation at Indian SMEs. Within sector case studies could be used to highlight the critical success and failure factors faced by particular sector. Cross-sector case studies could be used to validate these conclusions as well as to elucidate differences among sectors. Separate critical success and failure factors can be identified for each phase of the ERP implementation at Indian SMEs. A questionnaire-based survey could be used to validate the results of this research with the help of different theoretical framework and the large sample size for each phase of the ERP implementation at Indian SMEs. Finally, another aspect of ERP success and failure that is success and failure in adoption of ERP systems by the Indian SMEs can also be measured as an extension and validation of these works. Specific industries or organizational sizes might have different organizational characteristics and business requirements for ERP systems and this create a robust research framework and model which may be useful for understanding the critical success and failure factors for the successful ERP implementation and adoption at Indian SMEs. Further, the limitations of this work, which were highlighted above provide a basis for guiding such future efforts. Future researchers can use confirmatory factor analysis to validate the ERP implementation related models for Indian SMEs that were proposed in this research. By building upon effort in this way, deeper understanding of the nature of the dimensions of ERP implementation success and failure at Indian SMEs may be systematically increased.

More, research is needed to establish the distinction between ex *post* (experienced-based) and *ex ante* (expectation-based) dimensions of ERP implementation success and failure at Indian SMEs in any future ERP implementation measure framework. Future studies should consider investigating the impacts of other contingencies and stakeholders in the internal and external environment that were not included in this study (e.g., supplier/partner influence, government and competitors influence, etc.) for the successful ERP implementation at Indian SMEs. Future studies could consider separately the impact of industry (Indian SMEs) stability and competition on ERP implementation success and failure while adopting and implementing ERP package and each could be represented by appropriate indicators of Indian SMEs. ERP is also about people and not just technical matters, hence future research could even more try to attain the different stakeholders' opinion for ERP implementation and up gradation. A more in-depth study with multiple cases for consideration could be adopted in order to check whether the CSFs and CFFs that were identified in this study actually are consistent with what is actually occurring in other country's SMEs environment or not.

The CSFs and CFFs could also be linked to a more tangible function matrix where the individual CSF could be linked to a function and thus a better controlled mechanism can be devolved for successful ERP implementation at Indian SMEs. Following this, an international comparison between CSFs and CFFs for the ERP implementation at the Indian SMEs could be compared with overseas SMEs. This sort of research could be plausible and relevant due to a number of reasons. Firstly, the ERP research field is moving in a direction that focuses on country specific ERP implementations and secondly, the ERP research community has also focussed on differences between ERP implementation efforts in one country compared to another. The extent of research into ERP implementations at Indian SMEs environment is still extremely low compared to how much finance is invested in these implementations and how frequently the ERP implementations occur.

These projects are long term strategic IT/IS investments that may shape the Indian SMEs for quite a number of years and thus have the potential for great research sites for future investigation. A focus on ERP implementations at Indian SMEs and overseas SMEs would also be beneficial to the ERP vendors who could learn lessons for future implementations and maintenances efforts in different cultures and country around the world. Another connection linked to future research is the actual benefits of implementing an ERP system at Indian SMEs environment. The measurements of the return of the investment (ROI) have been a keen topic for research in the ERP literature and the author sees a future into ROI studies that focuses on the Indian SMEs environment. A contentious issue for debate could also be whether an ERP system works in Indian SMEs environment or not. This is naturally a question that should be addressed because of the number of costly ERP failures identified and the impact an ERP system has on the Indian SMEs that implements it and its users. The SaaS-model is therefore of interesting when researching in the future of ERP systems for Indian SMEs, however there does not seem to be much academic research published within this area yet. When looking at the SaaS-model it seems to challenges the distributors business in the ERP-implementation at Indian SMEs since the vendor can deliver solutions directly to the end-customer and thereby bypass the distributor. It could be seen as a further enhancement of the 'best practice' approach that undermines the competitive advantage of the distributors. In that sense the SaaS-model can be seen as a solution that favours the 'best practice' approach for Indian SMEs. It could be interesting to examine how ERP systems delivered SaaS meet the Indian SMEs IT needs and what the implications are for the ERP implementation at Indian SMEs, if the paradigm switches from perpetual licenses to SaaS offerings. Both the resource based perspective as well as the perspective of core competencies could offer interesting approaches when looking at the future ERP implementation at Indian SMEs.

It would be more value achieved to combine the results of qualitative and quantitative researches in future. In order to reduce the ERP implementation failure rate, it is useful to establish a robust framework of critical success and failure factors analysis for Indian SMEs. The interrelationship between the factors should receive more attention in future research. Prior research has indicated that critical success and failure factors can affect each other in a reinforcing manner. It would be beneficial in future research on critical factors to consider how certain factors affect each other in a reinforcing manner. Multiple case studies with various industries (e.g., service, trading and manufacturing) and various organizational sizes (e.g., small, medium and large) can be conducted to identify the reasons for ERP implementation success and failure. Though it has been stated previously that some CFSs and CFFs were more significant than others a proper analytical study of interrelationships of CSFs and CFFs dependency is yet to be made. In addition, it can be seen that factors such as top management support and project management for ERP implementation at Indian SMEs are not substantially different from factors that are critical to the success of most IT projects and to organizational change of other kinds. Furthermore, most of the identified CSFs and CFFs are non-industry specific and there is a confusion about whether the identified CFSs and CFFs vary across industry sectors. More research need to be focused in more industry specify CSFs and CFFs.

Therefore more effort in these areas should be a focus for future research. Awareness of the cultural assumptions embedded in ERP and introduction of mechanisms to mitigate any cultural mismatch may improve the likelihood of the successful ERP process and outcome at Indian SMEs. Future studies are needed to fully explicate the research framework and identify its theoretical and managerial implications for Indian SMEs. ERP across organizational boundaries has the potential to create similar problems in all participating Indian SMEs. These issues will be more difficult to manage as each organization can only deal with the problems within its four walls.

Further study in this area could help anticipate the kinds of problems that may arise and propose measures those Indian SMEs could take to avoid them.ERP is not a culturally-neutral phenomenon. Rather, it is loaded with cultural values of the vendors, developers, and implementation consultants. Its transferability to other cultures that do not necessarily share those embedded cultural values will continue to be challenging while implementation ERP systems for Indian SMEs. Therefore, understanding how ERP consultants, ERP vendor and SMEs (including those in developing countries) in different cultures accommodate and/or resist the cultural assumptions embedded in ERP implementation will contribute knowledge to the application of ERP in the global context. In addition, future research is needed to develop standard norms for evaluating specific ERP modules, to investigate the relative importance of the determinants of ERP key-user satisfaction, and to realize the relationship between ERP implementation stage and user satisfaction for successful ERP implementation at Indian SMEs.ERP vendors will continue to extend their systems to include web-based procurement applications, to support the online outsourcing and maintenance processes of ERP systems for Indian SMEs,. Other major efforts relating to the continuous future research and development of ERP systems at Indian SMEs are dedicated to embedding more internet-based features that may provide Indian SMEs for global reach to their suppliers and customers. This research has presented a survey of research relating to some major ERP implementation issues for Indian SMEs, Much research is still needed to better understand the ERP phenomenon from a balanced perspective for Indian SMEs. Several themes have been discussed in this work, and future work will continue to survey the other areas described in the framework. It is expected that the current and future work will collectively provide ERP researchers and practitioners with a good reference to research and practice in this emerging field for successful ERP implementation at SMEs.

In terms of future research, due to the limited number of existing methodologies for ERP selection and implementation, more research is still needed to investigate the correlation between the ERP selection process and the failure or success of the ERP implementation for any SMEs in general. Also, the generalization of the methodology described in this work to other industries, other SMEs, larger organizations, and technology driven ERP investments should be investigated in detail.

CONCLUSION

The objective of this research work was to identify and rank the critical success and failure factors that contribute in the ERP implementation at Indian SMEs. For this purpose, the author has analyzed Indian ERP consultant's opinions and their ranking for CSFs as a parameter. After the analysis, the following conclusions were drawn: The top most critical success factor for the successful ERP implementation at Indian SMEs was clear business plan and vision followed by top management commitment and support. Exploratory hypotheses (statements) were accepted with some new dimensions. It shows that enterprise, vendor, technology and end-user related critical success factors of the large enterprise also have contribution in the successful ERP implementation at Indian SMEs .ERP system implementation at Indian SMEs are more than a new information technology. They are more business-process-oriented than technology-oriented. (Davenport, 2000) says an ERP is not a project; it is a way of life. The research framework issues raised in this work were intended for ERP researchers and professionals who are interested in looking at the CSFs and KCSFs for the successful ERP implementation at Indian SMEs. ERP systems have become the most common IT strategy for most large companies included SMEs. Indian SMEs are also moving towards ERP systems. They need to adopt a proactive approach towards ERP implementation and consider it as a business solution rather than a mere IT solution.

This research argues that ERP implementation at Indian SMEs should extend its scope beyond the configuration to the strategic, managerial, technical and organizational issues by considering these thirty critical success factors and twenty critical failure factors for the successful ERP implementation at Indian SMEs that may put Indian SMEs on the competitive position. It can be concluded from the study that thirty critical success factors and twenty critical failure factors of the LEs also contribute in the ERP implementation at Indian SMEs with different priorities during all the phases of ERP implementation. The top most critical failure factor for the failure of ERP implementation at Indian SMEs was poor quality of testing followed by poor top management commitment and support, unrealistic expectation of top management from ERP systems and so on. ERP market is becoming quickly saturated. As a result, ERP consultants and ERP vendor are also tapping into the Indian SMEs market. Recognizing the concerns of Indian SMEs about the time and cost of ERP implementation, these ERP vendors may add value to their relationship with their potential clients by addressing the business case, cutting costs and implementation time by providing them with rapid implementation tools. Implementing an enterprise resource planning requires a wide range of knowledge. The research framework issues raised in this work were intended for ERP researchers and professionals who are interested in looking at the CFFs and KCFFs for the failure of ERP implementation in Indian SMEs. Indian SMEs are the backbone of the economy and are today faced with global competition due to LPG (Liberalization, Globalization and Privatizations). Therefore it becomes imperative to look for means of responding to the dynamic markets of growth. This research work argues that ERP consultants, ERP vendor and Indian SMEs often fail in recognizing the technical, financial, strategic, managerial and organizational impacts related to the ERP implementation as a consequence, the evaluation of ERP system for Indian SMEs, instead of choosing a system supporting specific business functions, it is a strategic decision that, mostly within Indian SMEs, should be supported by in-depth evaluation.

Proper knowledge about the ERP products, proper budget planning and appropriate training to the staffs is needed to avoid the failure of ERP implementation at Indian SMEs.All success is rooted in either luck or failure. If it begins with luck, there is nothing to learn but arrogance. However, if it begins with failure and learns to evaluate, it also leads to success. Failure becomes knowledge. Out of knowledge it gain wisdom, and it is with wisdom that can make true success. There is a need to learn from previous ERP failure. It is found from the study that all the critical failure factors have different priority in terms of their mean ranks in the failure of ERP implementation at Indian SMEs. It is hoped that this research will help to bridge the current literature gap and provide practical advice for both ERP academicians and practitioners. More studies will be conducted in future in order to further examine the black box of ERP implementation at Indian SMEs in order to avoid the failure of ERP implementation at Indian SMEs. In conclusion, it might be better to know the organizational structure of the Indian SMEs in detail in terms of the features that it has. Then, before the ERP implementation starts or during the decision period, before the implementation of the system, the disadvantages can be eliminated in order to get the level of success desired for Indian SMEs. Most of the ERP consultants suggested that minimal customization of their software is the best way to gain full benefits of ERP systems at Indian SMEs and insisting on changing the Indian SMEs business processes if needed for the successful ERP implementation at Indian SMEs. However, most of the time Indian SMEs may want to keep their business processes with minimal changes and ask the ERP consultants to customize software. This might necessitate a balance point between customization of software and changing business processes. The current trend of ERP implementation at Indian SMEs approach is using a best-of-breed option in which separate software packages were selected for each process or function. The key however is to develop competitive advantage for Indian SMEs through strategic ERP resources by absorbing the system in a unique manner without eroding the vital lead. This study contributes that the poor ERP consultant effectiveness and poor project management effectiveness may be the causes of low quality BPR, which in turn may contributes to users' resistance to change at Indian SMEs. In the 21st century, the business environment is changing with Indian SMEs are facing new extreme competition, new markets, changing technologies, demanding customers, loss of traditional leadership styles, uncertainty and unprecedented threats from global markets. There is tremendous pressure on Indian SMEs to provide better service to customers, greater variety, reliable delivery dates, short throughput time, efficient global coordination and lower total costs in the complete supply chain. ERP systems have been a major information technology used by businesses today in hopes of gaining competitive advantage for Indian SMEs too. The study shows that the ERP places demands on management for rewarding competence, empowering employees, training, etc., the choice of vendor, technology, mindset of people about work, organization, strategy, and user friendliness, all play an important role in building sustainable advantage for successful ERP implementation at Indian SMEs.

Many Indian SMEs are becoming global and the multi-site ERP implementations offer specific challenges particularly with respect to teamwork, communications, decentralized units, commitment of site management, and so on. Customizing of applications remains difficult but that difficulty of task itself could contribute to sustainability of competitive advantage for Indian SMEs. This requires lot of efforts, allocation of resources, hiring consultants and substantial costs for successful ERP implementation at Indian SMEs. So, for the present time, this research has voiced both operational effectiveness and strategic positioning together for the successful ERP implementation at Indian SMEs, as it become vital strategic tools in today's competitive business environment. This research attempts to investigate the critical success and failure factors in implementing ERP systems at Indian SMEs. Change management is essential to the success of ERP implementations at Indian SMEs. The move from operational silos to a single integrated system can create many problems for Indian SMEs if not managed correctly. Getting ready for the implementation is a very important step in ERP implementations for Indian SMEs. Being aware of the disadvantages and getting rid of them can help Indian SMEs get on the way to a successful ERP implementation. For example, having strong project teams is an important issue for the ERP implementation at Indian SMEs. As found in the literature, there is a lack of strong project teams in and without this knowledge of the relationship between teams and implementation success; Indian SMEs and ERP consultants would not take any precautions. Yet, ERP implementation at Indian SMEs is a very big and complex project that can affect all procedures, employees, and the technology within the organization this project requires every resource that the Indian SMEs has. When it is known that technological interchange has a strong contribution in the implementation success at Indian SMEs, which is one of the results of this study, Indian SMEs may take action before the ERP implementation to make technology available for all aspects of this project. Again, awareness of potential problems may affect the ERP implementation success at Indian SMEs. ERP consultants, ERP vendor and Indian SMEs that managed these issues effectively may have higher probability of ERP implementation success. In-depth study with Indian SMEs personnel may provide insightful details to the factors that contribute in the ERP project success. Such detailed insights extend to distinctive factors may help in future as well. While implementation an ERP package for Indian SMEs, ERP consultants, ERP vendor and Indian SMEs should not modify the software unnecessary. However, the study detailed the problems involved in this modification, i.e. that software integration and testing became a challenge due to the lack of technical expertise on the part of the staff and the lack of business expertise on the part of the external consultant for the successful ERP implementation at Indian SMEs. Thus, the findings point to the need for implementations to ensure that both technical and business expertise is integrated during software testing while implementation ERP for Indian SMEs.

Furthermore, findings including the success and failure of ERP implementation at Indian SMEs with part-time dedication of staff, lack of formal communication, emphasis on software (rather than process) modification, and the lack of formal strategy processes appeared to be somehow counter-intuitive.These findings provide additional insight into the issues involved in managing ERP implementations at Indian SMEs. It seems that some of the finding from this research work appeared to concur with the literature, but others appeared to be either innovative or counter to existing knowledge. However, as noted earlier, this research does enhance the understanding of the nature of ERP implementation at Indian SMEs. It provides some insights into the complex nature of ERP implementations at Indian SMEs that earlier surveys perhaps could not have. Many Indian SMEs do not achieve success in their ERP implementation projects. The aim of this research was to explore the possible CSFs and CFFs for ERP implementation at Indian SMEs. Previous research on the subject matter was thoroughly explored to form a solid basis for the study. Shanks et al (2000) synthesized ERP project lifecycle phases was selected as a part of ERP implementation framework for Indian SMEs .These findings could assist in implementing ERP system at Indian SMEs. There is no set formula for successful ERP implementation at Indian SMEs and the failure or success does not depend on a single factor. Each step of the ERP implementation at Indian SMEs has to be carefully monitored so that all the business processes are properly mapped to the ERP package. The top management should also ensure the apprehensions and thereby the end user's resistance to change is taken care of by showing them the bigger picture for ERP implementation at Indian SMEs. This can be done by studying the potential causes of resistance and using proven and effective strategies for the successful ERP implementation at Indian SMEs. The key here is to keep abreast of the entire change management process. Top management should not lose track of the progress at any point in the entire ERP implementation process at Indian SMEs.

This is important because ERP implementations at Indian SMEs are very prone to mishaps if not monitored by competent resources. Enterprise Resource Planning applications are known to be tough to tame and there are numerous ways in which things can go wrong leading to total failure of the entire ERP implementation at Indian SMEs. If the ERP package is implemented properly, then the Indian SMEs stands to benefit in the long run. These benefits could be in the form of operations efficiency, enhanced delivery and effective business intelligence. But the entire process of ERP implementation is resource intensive, process oriented and this is the reason why many ERP implementations fail at Indian SMEs and the success rate is low. Implementing ERP can become a thought altering experience for those involved. Following a proven and effective methodology may greatly increase an Indian SMEs likelihood of success the first time itself. Successful implementation of an ERP software solution at Indian SMEs is to apply people, process and product initiatives within a structured methodology framework. The difficult task in an ERP implementation at Indian SMEs is to bring all the above together and align them toward the goals of an organization. When people, processes and the product are aligned towards the organizational goals then the ERP implementations at Indian SMEs are bound to be a success thereby may be reaping benefits and rapid return on investments. This research work examines and discusses thirty critical success and twenty critical failure factors contributing to ERP implementation at Indian SMEs. The results of this research suggest that the role performed by ERP consultants is important for filling the "knowledge gap" within the different phases of ERP implementation at Indian SMEs. Project champion should exercise effective control and monitoring of the ERP project and ERP consultant effectiveness.

BPR should also receive attention for all ERP implementation phases at Indian SMEs, as this factor is important for matching business processes to ERP system functions for Indian SMEs. The implementation projects of ERP systems are big, strategic and complex projects which involve lots of risks, what is reflected on time, scope and costs of ERP project implementation at Indian SMEs.

Because of that, ERP consultants, ERP vendor and Indian SMEs have to create conditions, in which they can implement chosen solution in expected time, scope and evaluated costs. This means, that ERP consultants, ERP vendor and Indian SMEs should be aware of what are the most important critical factors for successful ERP implementations at Indian SMEs. ERP systems put in place a disciplined way of working and provide better visibility to the working of the Indian SMEs. Indian SMEs should not be consider as one homogenous group, but should be acknowledged the differences between these two groups of companies i.e. LEs and SMEs. Increase in the interdependence between different operations and difficulties in pinpointing the problem areas were considered as reasonable challenges for the successful ERP implementation at Indian SMEs.ERP systems may affect nearly every aspect of Indian SMEs performance, functioning, and measures of ERP system success must reflect this fact. The process of ERP implementation at Indian SMEs demands the preparation of business processes (i.e. business fit), preparation of people (i.e. corporate culture) and preparation of technical systems (i.e. legacy systems), change management competencies, and project management (i.e. planning and competencies etc). Implementation of ERP needs a great attention and that ERP implementation is of high complexity at Indian SMEs. It is, therefore, of interest to investigate factors related to selection of ERP implementation approach for Indian SMEs. The impact of cultural differences at Indian SMEs plays an important role in successful ERP systems. Harmonization of business processes and Indian SMEs structures in multi-cultural country like India is challenging due to the language differences, differences in legacy systems, differences in business practices from one culture to the other etc.

Cultural conflicts, prestige, and differences in organization/corporate culture with regard to management authority, openness, formality, and control mechanisms all should be taken into care for the successful ERP implementation at Indian SMEs. Cultural factors do matter with the implementation and the success of ERP systems at Indian SMEs. Successful enterprise resource planning implementation at Indian SMEs also influences by effective project management principles. ERP consultants, ERP vendor and Indian SMEs implementing or considering implementing an ERP system that attempts to integrate internal functions with planning and execution activities of both customers and vendors are at risk if they do not understand basic project management fundamentals of ERP projects. Top management support is very invaluable in ensuring that ERP projects come to fruition at Indian SMEs. This support might include providing strategic direction by being actively involved in various high-level cross-functional ERP implementation teams. Implementation of an ERP system is not a matter of changing the hardware or software systems, instead it entails transforming the Indian SMEs to a higher level of performance through a streamlined business process. When carefully conceived and successfully executed, ERP systems can changed the way Indian SMEs conduct their business for the better advancement. Identification of these critical factors permits ERP consultants, ERP vendor and Indian SMEs to obtain a better understanding of issues surrounding for ERP implementation at Indian SMEs. ERP consultants, ERP vendor and Indian SMEs can use the factors identified and validated in this study to better prepare themselves for a successful implementation of ERP systems at Indian SMEs. This study provides insights to ERP consultants and Indian SMEs who are either embarking on ERP implementation or considering implementing ERP systems. Successful implementation of ERP at Indian SMEs mandates continuous monitoring and self diagnosis throughout the implementation process. ERP implementation should not be viewed as just an IT solution but as a system that would transform the Indian SMEs into a more efficient and effective organization. Successful implementation of ERP at Indian SMEs is intricately tied to top management setting the strategic direction of the implementation process. This is accomplished by a continuous support and monitoring of the ERP implementation process at the Indian SMEs.

A mere lip service or lukewarm support from top management may be the "kiss of death" for any ERP implementation at Indian SMEs. Sound and thorough understanding of project management principles and its application is critically linked to the successful ERP implementation at Indian SMEs. This may be accomplished by establishing the scope of the project, establishing the project team and their responsibilities with clear statement of work, and defining the performance objectives. Because ERP implementation are about integrating different business functions, interdepartmental communication and collaboration within the project team found to be the core process for the successful ERP project progress at Indian SMEs. Presence and attitudes of the surrounding stakeholders, i.e. top management, project management, project champion and software vendor, were identified as the root factors driving success of this core process of ERP implementation at Indian SMEs. Consideration of similar ERP implementations may be incentives to encourage employee involvement, and experience of working with similar software, selecting ERP software and vendor for successful ERP implementation at

Indian SMEs. Regarding the link between factors and ERP implementation phases, majority of the respondents were identified that all factors should start from the early stages to the end of the ERP project at Indian SMEs. Most of the respondents felt that the CFFs were adversely affecting the ERP implementation at Indian SMEs. ERP consultants, ERP vendor and Indian SMEs wishing to extend their processes will have to develop more trusting and collaborative relationships with their business partners. While extended ERP allows information quicker and reduces the period of uncertainty it still needs to be managed.

Despite the wealth of ERP related academic and industry literature that concludes that implementing ERP does lead to process improvement and better ways of doing business, there is a lack of research on how Indian SMEs are extending the capabilities of their ERP systems outside the bounds of the enterprise. Many factors have been put forward in the literature to explain the successful performance of LEs, however it may not generalize that finding and prescriptions about Indian SMEs performance are equally applicable to LEs and other SMEs as they may confront with different set of challenges when implementing ERP. This work attempts to address literature gap related to Indian SMEs only. The future looks bright as the technology and business maturity has reached a greater critical mass for ERP implementation. Indian SMEs will also have access to affordable ERP solutions that offer enterprise-level performance. Indian SMEs will have the ability to compete with larger firms. However, selecting the right system can be a challenging task. Indian SMEs should do a thorough analysis of its business needs prior to researching ERP vendors. Each product is different and can provide varying levels of customization. Once there is a clear understanding of the services needed, it will be easier to determine which ERP product is best suited for the Indian SMEs business. Choosing the appropriate ERP product is a CSF in the success of the ERP implementation at Indian SMEs, as well as may be in the ongoing operational effectiveness of the Indian SMEs. All in all, ERP may translate into a smart way for Indian SMEs to construct a path for future growth and strategic advantages. While a large number of empirical and non-empirical studies have made valuable contributions in identifying several CSFs to implementation stage of ERP systems for LEs and assessing ERP success neither these studies have been able to deliver a generally agreeable and conclusive set of CSFs and CFFs for the ERP implementation at Indian SMEs, nor the implementation difficulties of ERP projects have subsided. In essence, this study thus takes a step forward in proposing a new systematic direction to research on CSFs and CFFs for ERP implementation in particular at Indian SMEs. By adopting a structured and integrated approach, the study attempts to plug the shortcomings of traditional studies. This research work contend that as generally most of the larger enterprise implement an ERP of their own and the implementation discipline associated, Same way an Indian SMEs can go beyond aligning on mediocrity to cultivate leadership(championship) in real time.

It is a combination of art and science skills twinned with an attitude of ERP consultants, ERP vendor and Indian SMEs that may excellence in ERP implementation at Indian SMEs. The main features of the proposed ERP theoretical framework have been described in terms of the underlying concept, a step-by-step process model and associated guidelines for successful ERP implementation at Indian SMEs. The framework specifically addresses the gaps identified in the review of critical success and failure factors for all the phases of ERP implementation as such it contributes to advancing the knowledge on the ERP implementation process at Indian SMEs, it also providing specific advice to ERP consultants, ERP vendor and Indian SMEs in an ERP selection process. An important characteristic of the framework is its emphasis on the evaluation process as an iterative process of continuous ERP implementation, change and alignment for the successful ERP implementation at Indian SMEs. The important output for the Indian SMEs is a choice of ERP system and vendor that is appropriately aligned with clearly defined business and IT strategies and IT processes infrastructure of Indian SMEs.

In summary, this theoretical framework has the following advantages:

- The theoretical framework is fairly intuitive, simple and cost-effective, and requires specialist skills to plan and carry out the process from ERP preparation to ERP selection for successful ERP implementation at Indian SMEs.
- The theoretical framework addresses the evaluation and selection of ERP consultants, ERP vendor and Indian SMEs as an integrated part of the process, and thereby helps the Indian SMEs to avoid the risk of choosing an ERP system that does not have the required vendor support.
- The fact that the theoretical framework aims to incorporate the dynamic complexity of the decision problem through its iterative and flexible nature. The theoretical framework provides a more holistic perspective on the ERP implementation process at Indian SMEs. By continuously focusing on capturing the interrelationship of how the different factors of the strategic ERP model contribute in all the phases of ERP implementation at Indian SMEs, the ERP model is able to capture the dynamics of the entire Indian SMEs system thus may helps in achieving the required strategic fit and functional integration for the successful ERP implementation at Indian SMEs.

- The ERP model and guidelines are generic enough and have a dynamic and flexible nature, which make them useful for a wide range of Indian SMEs of practically all sizes, while also being applicable to both business and technology driven ERP investments. The proposed theoretical framework represents a useful tool for ERP consultants, ERP vendor and Indian SMEs with regards to the evaluation and selection of ERP systems and vendors. The theoretical framework can be successfully applied for the successful ERP implementation at Indian SMEs.

This research work has explored the factors for the success and failure of the ERP implementation at Indian SMEs and has proposed a framework of critical success and failure factors that are deemed crucial for ERP implementation at Indian SMEs. This work was complimented by the analysis of Indian ERP consultant's opinion. The 'one-size-fits-all' packaged consultancy services may confuse Indian SMEs owner-managers and create a negative image of using ERP services. In addition, ERP implementation at Indian SMEs require comprehensive services, which most traditional software package lack and these services can only be effectively executed when a long-term partnership exists between the ERP consultants, ERP vendor and Indian SMEs. Because the relationship between client and consultant begins prior to work activities, it becomes a critical issue for ERP consultants, ERP vendor and, especially at Indian SMEs.

Establishing credibility with internal managers, transferring power from Indian SME owner-managers, and identifying consultants distinct roles with ERP systems and their changing roles during the different implementation phases are all essential and useful techniques for successful ERP implementation at Indian SMEs. Customization of an ERP may be a complex and often, a costly activity with potentially critical implications for the overall performance of an Indian SMEs. The evidence from this exploratory study substantiates this notion and elicits many different factors that may contribute in the ERP customization outcomes for the successful ERP implementation at Indian SMEs. The resulting models of ERP implementation reveal an intricate network of interrelated factors, providing a framework for explaining ERP activities and the potential gap between desirable and actual ERP implementation at Indian SMEs. Given the complexity of managing ERP project suggested by ERP model, this research work further argue that it is imperative that customizations are managed mindfully. Ignoring simplistic solutions, for an ERP project's specific context, may likely not result in an effective ERP solution at Indian SMEs.

The Strategic ERP model for successful ERP implementation at Indian SMEs may provide guidance for developing and implementing such a mindful

ERP implementation strategy. The main purpose of this research was to develop the ERP implementation success and failure model and to identify the factors associated with the ERP implementation at Indian SMEs. Most of the ERP related research in the past was from the large enterprises context that developed surveys or proposed research models are without ERP theories because this type of research approach is still relatively new in ERP field. In most of the ERP implementation related field researchers were using social science approaches, but solid theories were used in formulating these ERP implementation related research models. Most of the ERP related research in the other sectors has tried to identify the factors and formulate models without using the theoretically validated models. This research was the first study attempting to identify the 50 factors for the ERP implementation at Indian SMEs with strong background theories of ERP and IT/IS implementation related research. Therefore, the academic contribution of this study can be found in a deliberate attempt to formulate the ERP implementation success and failure model for the Indian SMEs where generally businesses are operated like small-small projects. Therefore, the proposed ERP implementation success and failure model will be helpful for the Indian SMEs, ERP consultants and decision makers to have a better understanding in regard to the success of ERP implementation. By using the proposed approach and the ERP implementation models presented in this work ERP consultants, ERP vendor and Indian SMEs may develop their own ERP implementation success and failure model that extract the factors specific to their enterprise, that may be used as a reference and a guideline. This study is among the first to discuss the 30 CSFs and 20 CFFs with the dimensions in the framework for assessing or understanding ERP implementation success and failure at Indian SMEs. Finally, the proposed framework is valuable in explaining the origins of the problem of misfits and how to solve or exaggerate this problem. Due to the fact that research on ERP implementation at Indian SMEs is conspicuously limited, this work has been an attempt to contribute to a better understanding of the same. A theoretical framework based on all ERP implementation phases and the CFs has been presented and an exploratory survey has been carried out to investigate the CFs for the ERP implementation at Indian SMEs. Study shows that the results of the survey support most of the factors that have been identified from literature review of the LEs. This research project was intended to provide both theoretical and practical insights into the implementation of an ERP system at Indian SMEs environment. An ERP implementation is a large information system implementation project with a vast impact on a number of different areas regarding the Indian SMEs that implements it and its stakeholders.

Identifying only one key critical success and failure factor is impossible and ambiguous due to the complexity of an ERP implementation project, but this research found several factors, specifically focused on an Indian SMEs environment, that can all contribute to the successful ERP implementation project for Indian SMEs. It is hoped that the theory and research findings presented in this book can aid the development of the ERP and the IS research field specific to Indian SMEs. It is also hoped that this study will serve as a guideline for ERP researchers and professionals wishing to investigate success and failure factors or issues associated with the ERP implementation at Indian SMEs.

Bibliography

- Achanga, P., Shehab, E., Roy, R. and Nelder, G. (2006), "Critical Success Factors for Lean Implementation Within SMEs", *Journal of Manufacturing Technology Management,* Vol. 17 No. 4, pp. 460-71.
- Adam, F. and O'Doherty, P. (2000), "Lessons from Enterprise Resource Planning Implementations in Ireland – Towards Smaller and Shorter ERP Projects", *Journal of Information Technology,* Vol. 15 No. 4, pp. 305-16.
- Agrawal, M. and Pak, M. (2001), "Getting Smart About Supply Chain Management", *The McKinsey Quarterly,* Vol. 2, pp. 22-27.
- Akkermans, H. and van Helden, K. (2002), "Vicious and Virtuous Cycles in ERP Implementation: A Case Study of Interrelations Between Critical Success Factors", *European Journal of Information Systems,* Vol. 11 No. 1, pp. 35-46.
- Aladwani, A. M. (2001) 'Change Management Strategies for Successful ERP Implementation', *Business Process Management Journal,* Vol. 7, pp.266-275.
- Allen, D. and Kern, T. (2001), 'Enterprise Resource Planning Implementation: Stories of Power, Politics and Resistance', in Proceedings of the IFIP Working Group 8.2 Conference on Realigning Research and Practice in Information Systems Development, *The Social and Organizational Perspective,* Boise, Idaho, USA, pp. 149-162.
- Al-Mashari M (2001), "Process Orientation Through Enterprise Resource Planning (ERP): A Review of Critical Issues", *Knowledge and Process Management,* Vol.8, No.3.
- Al-Mashari, M. (2002), 'Enterprise Resource Planning (ERP) Systems: A Research Agenda', *Industrial Management and Data Systems,* Vol. 102, pp.165-170.
- Al-Mashari, M. and Zairi, M. (1999).BPR Implementation Process: An Analysis of Key Success and Failure Factors. *Business Process Management Journal,* Vol. 5, No. 1, 87 –112.
- Al-Mashari, M. and Zairi, M. (2000). The Effective Application of SAP R/3: A Proposed Model of Best Practice. *Logistics Information Management* Vol.13, No.3, pp. 156-166.
- Al-Mashari, M., Al-Mudimigh, A. and Zairi, M. (2003), "Enterprise Resource Planning: A Taxonomy of Critical Factors", *European Journal of Operational*

Research, Vol. 146 No. 2, pp. 352-64.

- Argyrols, C. and Scho¨n, D. (1978), Organizational Learning: A Theory of Action Perspective, Addison-Wesley, and Reading, MA.
- Ash, C. G. and Burn, J.M. (2003), "A Strategic Framework for the Management of ERP Enabled e-Business Change", *European Journal of Operational Research*, Vol. 146 No. 2, pp. 374-87.
- Bancroft, N. H., Seip, H. and Sprengel, A. (1998), Implementing Sap R/3: How to Introduce a Large System into a Large Organization, Hanning, pp. 307.
- Barker, T., and Frolick, M. N. (2003), "ERP Implementation Failure: A Case Study" *Information Systems Management*, Auerbach, pp.43-49.
- Baskerville, R., Pawlowski, S. and Mclean, E. (2000), 'Enterprise Resource Planning and Organizational knowledge: Patterns of Convergence and Divergence', in *Proceedings of the 21st International Conference on Information Systems*, Brisbane, Australia, pp. 396-406.
- Beekhuyzen, J. (2001), 'Organizational Culture and Enterprise Resource Planning (ERP) Systems Implementation', *School of Computing and Information Technology Honors Book*, Brisbane, Australia, Griffith University, p. 135.
- Bell, S. and Orzen, M. (2007), "Small, Yet Mighty", APICS Magazine, Vol. 17 No. 6, pp. 40-43.
- Bendoly, E. and Jacobs, F.R. (2004), "ERP Architectural/Operational Alignment for Order Processing Performance", *International Journal of Operations and Production Management*, Vol. 24 No. 1, pp. 99-117.
- Bernroider, E. and Koch, S. (2001), "ERP Selection Process in Midsized and Large Organizations", *Business Process Management Journal*, Vol. 7 No. 3, pp. 251-7.33
- Berryman, K. and Heck, S. (2001), "Is the Third Time the Charm for B2B?", *The McKinsey Quarterly*, Vol. 2, pp. 18-23.
- Bingi, P.; Sharma, M.K. and Godla, J. (1999), "Critical Issues Affecting an ERP Implementation", *Information Systems Management*, Vol. 16 No. 3, pp. 7-14.
- Boykin R. F., (2001) "Enterprise Resource Planning Software: A Solution to the Return Material Authorization Problem", *Computers in Industry* Vol. 45, pp. 99-109.
- Brown, C. V. and Vessey *et al.* (2000), "The ERP Purchase Decision: Influential Business and IT Factors".
- Brown, C. V. and Vessey, I. (1999), 'ERP Implementation Approaches: Toward a Contingency Framework', in *Proceedings of the 20th International Conference on Information Systems*, Charlotte, North Carolina, pp. 441-416
- Brown, C. V. and Vessey, I. (2003) Managing the Next Wave of Enterprise Systems: Leveraging Lessons from ERP. *MIS Quarterly Executive* 2(1), pp 65-77.
- Buckhout, S., Frey, E. and J., N. J. (1999), 'Making ERP Succeed: Turning Fear Into Promise', *Strategy and Business*, Vol. Second, pp. 60-72.

- Bulkeley, W.M. (1996) A Cautionary Network Tale: Fox-Meyer's High-tech Gamble. *Wall Street Journal Interactive Edition.*
- Buonanno, G., Faverio, P., Pigni, F., Ravarini, A., Sciuto, D. and Tagliavini, M. (2005), "Factors affecting ERP System Adoption: A Comparative Analysis Between SMEs and Large Companies", *Journal of Enterprise Information Management,* Vol. 18 No. 4, pp. 384-426.
- Burt, D.N., Dobler, D.W. and Starling, S.L. (2003), World Class Supply Management: The Key to Supply Chain Management, McGraw-Hill, New York, *Business Process Management Journal,* Vol. 10 (4), pp 359-86.
- Caldas, M. and Wood, T., (1998), "How Consultants Can Help Organizations to Survive by ERP"
- Chang, S., Gable, G., Smythe, E., and Timbrell, G. (2000) A Delphi Examination of Public Sector ERP Implementation issues. In *Proceedings of International Conference of Information Systems,* pp 494-500.
- Chatfield, C. (2000), 'Organizational Influences on the Successful Implementation of an ERP System', *Faculty of Engineering and Information Technology,* Honors' Book, Brisbane, Australia, Griffith University, pp. 113.
- Chen, R., Sun, C., Helms, M.M. and Jih, W. (2008), "Role Negotiation and Interaction: An Exploratory Case Study of the Impact of Management Consultants on ERP System Implementation in SMEs in Taiwan", *Information Systems Management,* Vol. 25 No. 2, pp. 159-73.
- Chien, S.; Hu, C.; Reimers, K. and Lin, J. (2007), "The Influence of Centrifugal and Centripetal Forces on ERP Project Success in Small and Medium-sized Enterprises in China and Taiwan", *International Journal of Production Economics,* Vol. 107 No. 2, pp. 380-96.
- Chung, S. H. and Snyder, C. A. (2000), 'ERP Adoption: A Technological Evolution Approach', *International Journal of Agile Management Systems,* vol. 2, pp. 24-32.
- Collins, R.S. and Schmenner, R.W. (1993), "Achieving Rigid Flexibility: Factory Focus for the 1990s", *European Management Journal,* Vol.11 No.4, pp. 443-7.
- Collins, R.S., Cordon, C. and Julien, D. (1998), "An Empirical Test of the Rigid Flexibility Model", *Journal of Operations Management,* Vol.16 No.3, pp. 133-46.
- Cotteleer, M.J. (2002) ERP: Payoffs and Pitfalls. Harvard Business School Working Knowledge
- Crowley, A. (1999), "Training Treadmill: A Rigorous Plan of End-User Education is Critical to Whipping ERP Systems into Shape." PC Week, Ziff Davis Media, NY.
- Davenport, H.T. (2000), Mission Critical: Realizing the Promise of Enterprise Systems, Harvard Business School Press.
- Davenport, T.H. (1998), "Putting the Enterprise into the Enterprise System", *Harvard Business Review,* Vol. 76 No. 4, pp. 121-31.
- Davenport, T.H. and Brooks, J.D. (2004), "Enterprise Systems and the Supply Chain", *Journal of Enterprise Information Management,* Vol. 17, No. 1, pp.

8-19.

- David Ray Anderson, Dennis J. Sweeney, Thomas Arthur Williams (2005), *Statistics for Business and Economics,* South-Western Pub, 4th Edition.
- Deep, A., Guttridge, P., Dani, S. and Burns, N. (2008), "Investigating Factors Affecting ERP Selection in Made-to-order SME Sector", *Journal of Manufacturing Technology Management,* Vol. 19 No. 4, pp. 430-46.
- Deloitte Consulting (1999), Leveraging the e-Business Marketplace – Business-to-Business e-Procurement Trends: Opportunities and Challenges, Deloitte Consulting, London.
- Deutsch, C. (1998) Software That Can Make a Grown Company Cry. *The New York Times* CXLVIII (51), 1, pp 13.
- Diederich, T. (1998) Bankrupt Firm Blames SAP for Failure. Computer World
- Donovan, M., (1998), "There is No Magic in ERP Software: It's in Preparation of the Process and People", Midrange ERP, September, p.8.
- Donovan, M., (2001), "Successful ERP Implementation the First Time"
- Edwards, P., Peters, M. and Sharman, G. (2001), "The Effectiveness of Information Systems in Supporting the Extended Supply Chain", *Journal of Business Logistics,* Vol. 22 No. 1, pp. 1-27.
- Eisenhardt, K.M. (1989), "Building Theories from Case Study Research", *Academy of Management Review,* Vol. 14 No. 4, pp. 532-50.
- Elarbi, N (2001)"ERP and Business Continuity", Sungard, Philadelphia.
- Eshelman, R.G., Juras, P.E. and Taylor, T.C. (2001), "When Small Companies implement...Big Systems", *Strategic Finance,* Vol. 82 No. 8, pp. 28-33.
- Esteves, J. and Pastor, J. (2001), 'Enterprise Resource Planning Systems Research: An Annotated Bibliography', Communications of the Association for Information Systems, Vol. 7, pp. 1-52.
- Esteves-Souza, J. and Pastor-Collado, J. (2000), "Towards the Unification of Critical Success Factors for ERP Implementations", *Proceedings of the 10th Annual Business Information Technology Conference, Manchester,* p.9
- Eurostat (2007), "European Business , Chapter 1: Business Economy Overview"
- Fan, M.; Stallaert, J. and Whinston, A. (2000), "The Adoption and Design Methodologies of Component-based Enterprise Systems", *European Journal of Information Systems,* Vol. 9 No. 1, pp. 25-35.
- Ferratt, T. W., Ahire, S., and De, P. (2006), "Achieving Success in Large Projects: Implications from a Study of ERP Implementations" *Interfaces,* pp.458-469.
- Finney, S. and Corbett, M. (2007), "ERP Implementation: A Compilation and Analysis of Critical Success Factors", *Business Process Management Journal,* Vol. 13 No. 3, pp. 329-47.
- Gable G, Rosemann M and Sedera W (2001) 'Critical Success Factors of Process Modelling For Enterprise Systems', pp. 1128-1130.

- Gable, G. (2003) Consultants and Knowledge Management. *Journal of Global Information Management* 11(3) pp 1-4.
- Gable, G., Sedera, D. and Chan, T. (2003) Enterprise Systems Success: A Measurement Model. *Proceedings of the Twenty Fourth Annual International Conference on Information Systems,* Washington, December, pp.576-591.
- Gable, Guy, and Glenn, Stewart (1999), "SAP R/3 Implementation Issues for Small to Medium Enterprises", 5th Americas Conference on Information Systems
- Garg Venkitakrishnan, (2006). "ERP Concepts and Practice", Prentice Hall India.
- Gargeya, V B and Brady C (2005) "Success and Failure Factors of Adopting SAP in ERP System Implementation", *Business Process Management Journal,* Emerald Group Publishing, pp.501-516.
- Gattiker, T.F. (2002), "Anatomy of an ERP Implementation Gone Awry", *Production and Inventory Management Journal,* Vol. 43 No. 3/4, pp. 96-105.
- Gattiker, T.F. and Goodhue, D.L. (2002), "Software Driven Changes to Business Processes: An Empirical Study of Impacts of Enterprise Resource Planning (ERP) Systems at the Local Level", *International Journal of Production Research,* Vol. 40 No. 18, pp. 4799-814.
- Gattiker, T.F. and Goodhue, D.L. (2005), "What Happens After ERP Implementation: Understanding the Impact of Interdependence and Differentiation on Plant-level Outcomes", *MIS Quarterly,* Vol. 29 No. 3, pp. 559-85.
- Ghobadian, A. and Gallear, D.N. (1996), "Total Quality Management in SMEs", *Omega,* Vol. 24 No. 1, pp. 83-106.
- Goulielmos, M. (2003),"Outlining Organizational Failure in Information Systems Development", *Disaster Prevention and Management,* Vol 12, No.4, pp. 319-327
- Graham, G. and Hardier, G. (2000), "Supply Chain Management Across the Internet", *International Journal of Physical Distribution and Logistics Management,* Vol. 30 No.4, pp. 286-95.
- Gunasekaran, A.; Okko, P.; Martikainen, T. and Yli-Olli, P. (1996), "Improving Productivity and Quality in Small and Medium Enterprises: Cases and Analysis", *International Small Business Journal,* Vol. 15 No. 1, pp. 59-72.
- Gupta A., (2000), "Enterprise Resource Planning: The Emerging Organizational Value Systems", *Industrial Management and Data Systems,* Vol. 100, No.3, pp. 114-18.
- Haberman, F. and Scheer, A. W. (2000), 'Making ERP a Success', *Communications of the ACM,* Vol. 43, pp. 56-61.
- Hallows J (1998) *Information Systems Project Management,* Tokyo, p. 283.
- Hamilton, S., and Chervany, N. L. (1981), "Evaluating Information System

Effectiveness Part I. Comparing Evaluation Approaches", *MIS Quarterly*, Society for Management Information Systems, pp.55-69.

- Herzog, T. (1996), Research Methods in the Social Sciences, Prentice-Hall, Upper Saddle River, NJ.
- Hillebrand, B.; Kok, R.A.K. and Biemans, W.G. (2001), "Theory-testing Using Case Studies: A Comment on Johnston, Leach, and Liu", *Industrial Marketing Management*, Vol. 30 No. 8, pp. 651-57.
- Hirt, S. G. and Swanson, B. E. (2001), 'Emergent Maintenance of ERP: New Roles and Relationships', *Journal of Software Maintenance and Evolution: Research and Practice*, Vol. 13, pp. 373-397.
- Hitt, L.M.; Wu, D.J. and Zhou, X. (2002), "Investment in Enterprise Fesource Planning: Business Impact and Productivity Measures", *Journal of Management Information Systems*, Vol. 19 No. 1, pp. 71-98.
- Hong, K.-K. and Kim, Y.-G. (2002), "The Critical Success Factors for ERP Implementation: An Organizational Fit Perspective", *Information and Management*, Vol. 40 No. 1, pp. 25-40.
- Huin, S.F. (2004), "Managing Deployment of ERP Systems in SMEs Using Multi-agents", *International Journal of Project Management*, Vol. 22 No. 6, pp. 511-17.
- Huin, S.F.; Luong, L.H.S. and Abhary, K. (2003), "Knowledge-based Tool for Planning of Enterprise Resources in ASEAN SMEs", *Robotics and Computer-Integrated Manufacturing*, Vol. 19 No. 5, pp. 409-14.
- Ifinedo, P. 2006*a*, Enterprise Systems Success Measurement Model: A Preliminary Study, *Journal of Information Technology Management*, Vol.17, No. (1), pp.14-33.
- Industry Canada (2006), "Key Small Business Statistics "
- Intermec (1999), "Aligning Your Data Collection and ERP Implementation Decisions" Intermec Technologies Corporation
- Jacobs, F.R. and Bendoly, E. (2003), "Enterprise Resource Planning: Developments and Directions for Operations Management Research", *European Journal of Operational Research*, Vol. 146 No. 2, pp. 233-40.
- Jacobs, F.R. and Weston Jr., F.C. (2007), "Enterprise Resource Planning (ERP) – A Brief History", *Journal of Operations Management*, Vol. 25 No. 2, pp. 357-63.
- James, D. and Wolf, M.L. (2000), "A Second Wind for ERP", *The McKinsey Quarterly*, No. 1, pp. 100-8.
- Januschkowetz, A. (2001), "Use of Enterprise Resource Planning Systems for Life Cycle Assessment and Product Stewardship," Carnegie Mellon University, Pittsburgh, Pennsylvania.
- Jenson, R. I. and Johnson, R. (1999), 'The Enterprise Resource Planning System as a Strategic Solution', *Information Strategy: The Executives Journal*, Vol. 17, pp. 28-34.
- Jones, M.C. and Young, R. (2006), "ERP Usage in Practice: An Empirical

Investigation', *Information Resources Management Journal*, Vol. 19 No. 1, pp. 23-42.

- Kale P. T., Banwait S. S., Laroiya S. C., (2007), "Review of Key Performance Indicators of Evaluation of Enterprise Resource Planning System in Small and Medium Enterprises", *XI Annual International Conference of Society of Operation Management*, India.
- Karahanna, E., Straub, D. W., and Chervany, N. L. (1999), "Information Technology Adoption across Time: A Cross-Sectional Comparison of Pre-Adoption and Post-Adoption Beliefs" *MIS Quarterly, Society for Management Information Systems*, pp.183-213.
- Kehoe, D. and Boughton, N. (2001), "Internet-based Supply Chain Management – A Classification of Approaches to Manufacturing, Planning and Control", *International Journal of Operations and Production Management*, Vol. 21 No. 4, pp. 516-24.
- Keller, E. (1994), "ERP Selection Process: Methodology and Vendor Comparison."
- Keller, G. and Teufel, T. (1998). SAP R/3 Process—oriented Implementation: Iterative Process Prototyping, Reading, MA: Addison-Wesley.
- Kennerley, S. and Neely, B. (2001), "Enterprise Resource Planning: Analyzing the Impact", *Integrated Manufacturing Systems*, Vol. 12 No. 2, pp. 103-13.
- Kinni, B.T. (1995), "Process Improvement, Part 2", *Industry Week*, Vol. 244 No. 4, pp. 45-50.
- Koch, C. (2001), "BRP and ERP: Realizing a Vision of Process with IT", *Business Process Management Journal*, Vol. 7 No. 3, pp. 285-96.
- Koch, C. (2002), "ABC: An Introduction to ERP, Getting Started with Enterprise Resource Planning (ERP)."
- Kothari, C.R. (1991). Research Methodology: Method and Techniques Second Edition, New Age Publications (Academic), India.
- Kumar, V.; Maheshwari, B. and Kumar, U. (2002), "Enterprise Resource Planning Systems Adoption Process: A Survey of Canadian Organizations", *International Journal of Production Research*, Vol. 40 No. 3, pp. 509-23.
- Langenwalter, G. (2000) Enterprise Resources Planning and Beyond: Integrating Your Entire Organization. St. Lucie Press, Boca Raton, FL.
- Laukkanen, S., Sarpola, S. and Hallikainen, P. (2007), "Enterprise Size Matters: Objectives and Constraints of ERP Adoption", *Journal of Enterprise Information* Management, Vol. 20 No. 3, pp. 319-34.
- Lawrence, F.B., Jennings, D.J. and Reynolds, B.E. (2005), ERP in Distribution, Thomson South Western.
- Lee, G.L. and Oakes, I. (1995), "The 'Pros' and 'Cons' of Total Quality Management for Smaller Firms in Manufacturing: Some Experiences Down the Supply Chain", *Total Quality Management*, Vol. 6 No. 4, pp. 413-26.
- Lee, H.L., Padmanabhan, V. and Whang, S. (1997), "Information Distortion in

a Supply Chain: The Bullwhip Effect", *Management Science,* Vol. 43 No. 4, pp. 546-58.

- Lee, S., Arif, A. U., and Jang, H. (2004), "Quantified Benefit of Implementing Enterprise Resource Planning through Process Simulation" *Canadian Journal of Civil Engineering*. NRC Canada, pp.263-271
- Leon A., (1999), "Enterprise Resource Planning", Tata McGraw-Hill.
- Levy Margi, Powell Philip, (2006), "Strategies for Growth in SMEs: The Role of Information and Information Systems", *Information Processing and Management: an International Journal*. Vol 42.
- Light, B. (2000), 'Enterprise Resource Planning Systems: Impacts and Future Directions', in Systems Engineering for Business Process Change: *Collected Papers from the EPSRC Research Programme,* ed. Henderson, P., London, pp. 117-126.
- Loh, T.C. and Koh, S.C.L. (2004), "Critical Elements for a Successful Enterprise Resource Planning Implementation in Small-and Medium-sized Enterprises", *International Journal of Production Research,* Vol. 42 No. 17, pp. 3433-55.
- Lu, C.-C. (2006), "Growth Strategies and Merger Patterns Among Small and Medium-sized Enterprises: An Empirical Study", *International Journal of Management,* Vol. 23 No. 3, pp. 529-47.
- Lucas, H. C. J. (1981), Implementation, the Key to Successful Information Systems, Columbia University Press, New York, p. 208.
- Lyytinen, K. (1988) Expectation Failure Concept and System Analysts' View of Information System Failures: Results of an Exploratory Study. *Information and Management,* Vol. 14, pp 45-56.
- Mabert, V.A.; Soni, A. and Venkataramanan, M.A. (2000), "Enterprise Resource Planning Survey of U.S. Manufacturing Firms", *Production and Inventory Management Journal,* Vol. 41 No. 2, pp. 52-8.
- Mabert, V.A.; Soni, A. and Venkataramanan, M.A. (2003a), "The Impact of Organization Size on Enterprise Resource Planning (ERP) Implementations in the US Manufacturing Sector", Omega, Vol. 31 No. 3, pp. 235-46.
- Mabert, V.A.; Soni, A. and Venkataramanan, M.A. (2003b), "Enterprise Resource Planning: Managing the Implementation Process", *European Journal of Operational Research,* Vol. 146 No. 2, pp. 302-14.
- Mabert, V.M., Soni, A. and Venkataramanan, M.A. (2001), "Enterprise Resource Planning: Measuring Value", *Production and Inventory Management,* Vol. 42 No.4, pp. 46-51.
- Mahrer, H. (1999), 'SAP R/3 Implementation at the ETH Zurich: A Higher Education Management Success Story', in *Proceedings of the 5th Americas Conference on Information Systems,* Milwaukee, WI, USA, pp. 788-790.
- Majed, A. (2000) Enterprise-wide Information Systems: The Case of SAP R/3 Application. In *Proceedings of the Second International Conference on Enterprise Information Systems,* pp 3-8.
- Majed, A., Abullah, A. and Mohamed, Z. (2003) Enterprise Resource Planning:

A Taxonomy of Critical Factors. *European Journal of Operational Research,* Vol.146, pp 352-364.

- Mandal, P. (2001), 'Implementing SAP in Project Management Environment: A Case', in *Proceedings of the 2nd Annual GITM World Conference,* Texas, USA, pp. 1-13.
- Mandal, P. and Gunasekaran, A. (2003), "Issues in Implementing ERP: A Case Study", *European Journal of Operational Research,* Vol. 146 No. 2, pp. 274-83.
- Markus, M.L.; Axline, S.; Petrie, D. and Tanis, C. (2000a), "Learning from Adopters' Experiences with ERP: Problems Encountered and Success Achieved", *Journal of Information Technology,* Vol. 15 No. 4, pp. 245-65.
- Markus, M.L.; Tanis, C. and Van Fenema, P.C. (2000b), "Multisite ERP Implementations", *Communications of the ACM* , Vol. 43 No. 4, pp. 42-6.
- Martinsons M G (2004),"ERP in China: One Package, Two Profiles" *Communications of the ACM,* Vol.47, No.7, pp. 65-68.
- McAdam, R. (2000), "Quality Models in an SME Context: A Critical Perspective Using a Grounded Approach", *International Journal of Quality and Reliability Management,* Vol. 17 No. 3, pp. 305-23.
- McAdam, R. (2002), "Large Scale Innovation—Reengineering Methodology in SMEs: Positivistic and Phenomenological Approaches", *International Small Business Journal,* Vol. 20 No. 1, pp. 33-50.
- McAfee, A. (2002), "The Impact of Enterprise Technology Adoption on Operational Performance: An Empirical Investigation", *Production and Operations Management,* Vol. 11 No. 1, pp. 33- 53.
- McCartan-Quinn, D. and Carson, D. (2003), "Issues Which Impact Upon Marketing in the Small Firm", *Small Business Economics,* Vol. 21 No. 2, pp. 201-13.
- McKie, S. (2001), "The Great Leap Forward"
- Mentzer, J.T., DeWitt, W., Keebler, J.S., Min, S., Nix, N.W., Smith, C.D. and Zacharia, Z.G. (2001), "Defining Supply Chain Management", *Journal of Business Logistics,* Vol. 22 No. 1, pp. 1-25.
- Meredith, J. (1998), "Building Operations Management Theory Through Case and Field Research", *Journal of Operations Management,* Vol. 16 No. 4, pp. 441-54.
- Miles, M.B. and Huberman, A.M. (1994), Qualitative Data Analysis: An Expanded Sourcebook, Sage, London.
- Mintzberg, H., (2004), Managers not MBAs: A Hard Look at the Soft Practice of Managing and Management Development, Prentice Hall.
- Mintzberg, M.; Lampel, J.; Quinn, J.B. and Ghosal, S. (2003), The Strategy Process: Concepts Contexts Cases, Upper Saddle River, NJ: Prentice Hall.
- Monk, Ellen; Wagner, Bret (2009). Concepts in Enterprise Resource Planning, 3rd edition.
- Morris, M.W.; Leung, K.; Ames, D. and Lickel, B. (1999). "Views from Inside

and Outside: Integrating Emic and Etic Insights About Culture and Justice Judgment", *Academy of Management Review*, Vol. 24 No. 4, pp. 781-96.

- Motwani J D Mirchandani *et al.* (2002), "Successful Implementation of ERP Projects: Evidence from Two Case Studies", *International Journal of Production Economics*, Vol. 75, No, 2, pp 83.
- Munjal Shefali, (2006), "Small is Beautiful: ERP for SMEs'
- Murphy, K. E., and Simon, S. J. (2002), "Intangible Benefits Valuation in ERP Projects", *Information Systems Journal*, Blackwell Science Ltd., pp.301-320.
- Muscatello, J.R.; Small, M.H. and Chen, I.C. (2003), "Implementing Enterprise Resource Planning (ERP) Systems in Small and Midsize Manufacturing Firms", *International Journal of Operations and Production Management*, Vol. 23 No. 8, pp. 850-71.
- Nah, F.F.-H. and Delgado, S. (2006), "Critical Success Factors for Enterprise Resource Planning Implementation and Upgrade", *Journal of Computer* Information Systems, Vol. 46 No. 5, pp. 99-113.
- Nah, F.F.-H.; Zuckweiler, K.M. and Lau, J.L.-S. (2003), "ERP Implementation: Chief Information Officers' Perceptions of Critical Success Factors", *International Journal of Human-Computer Interaction*, Vol. 16 No. 1, pp. 5-22.
- Nelson R J and I Millet (2001), "A Foundation Course in ERP and Business Process: Rational, Design, and Educational Outcomes", *Seventh Americas Conference on Information Systems.*
- Nelson, E. and Ramstad, E. (1999) Hershey's Biggest Dud Has Turned Out to be New Computer System. *The Wall Street Journal CIV*, Vol.85, pp A1-A6.
- Nelson, R. R., and Cheney, P. H. (1987), "Training End Users: An Exploratory Study" *MIS Quarterly*, Society for Management Information Systems, pp.547-559.
- Neuman, L. W. (1997), Social Research Methods: Qualitative and Quantitative Approaches, Allyn and Backer, Needlam Heights, MA, USA, p. 550.
- Newman, M. and Zhao, Y. (2008), "The Process of Enterprise Resource Planning Implementation and Business Process Re-engineering: Tales from Two Chinese Small and Medium-sized Enterprises", *Information Systems Journal*, Vol. 18 No. 4, pp. 405-26.
- Nielsen, J. L. (2002), 'Implementation of an Enterprise Resource Planning System and Its Effects on the Knowledge Perspective (Tacit and Explicit focus)'
- Norris, G., Hurley, J.R., Hartley, K.M. and Dunleavy, J.R. (2001), e-Business and ERP: Transforming the Enterprise, John Wiley, London.
- O'Leary, S. (2000), Enterprise Resource Planning Systems: Systems, Life Cycle, Electronic Commerce and Risk, Cambridge University Press, Cambridge.
- Olhager, J. and Selldin, E. (2003), "Enterprise Resource Planning Survey of Swedish Manufacturing Firms", *European Journal of Operational Research*, Vol. 146 No. 2, pp. 365- 73.
- Oliver, D. and Romm, C. (2000), 'ERP Systems: The Route to Adoption', in

Proceedings of the 6th Americas Conference on Information Systems, Long Beach, California, USA, pp. 1039-1044.

- Ould (1995), Modelling and Analysis for Re-engineering and Improvement: Wiley, Chichester and New York.
- Pandian T. K., (2006), "Big Issues in ERP for Small Units", *Business Line.*
- Pareek, Uadai (2003),"*Training Instruments in HRD and OD", Second Editions,* Tata McGraw-Hill Publishing Company Limited, New Delhi, India.
- Parr, A. and Shanks', G. (2000) A Model of ERP Project Implementation. *Journal of Information Technology,* Vol. 15, No.2, pp 289-303.
- Patton, M.Q. (1987), *How to Use Qualitative Methods in Evaluation,* Sage, Beverly Hills, CA.
- Pawar, S. and Driva, B. (2000), "Electronic Trading in the Supply Chain: A Holistic Implementation Framework", *Logistics Information Management,* Vol. 13 No. 1, pp. 21-32.
- Pender, S. (2001), "The Basic Links of SCM"
- Perry, W. E. (1992), "Quality Concerns in Software Development: The Challenge Is Consistency" *Information Systems Management,* Auerbach, pp.48-52.
- Pettigrew, A.M. (1990), "Longitudinal Field Research on Change: Theory and Practice", *Organization Science,* Vol. 1 No. 3, pp. 267-92.
- Pinto, J. K. and Slevin, D. (1987), 'Balancing Strategy and Tactics in Project Implementation', *Sloan Management Review,* Vol. 29, pp. 33-41.
- Poba-Nzaou, P., Raymond, L. and Fabi, B. (2008), "Adoption and Risk of ERP Systems in Manufacturing SMEs: A Positivist Case Study", *Business Process Management Journal,* Vol. 14 No. 4, pp. 530-50.
- Porter, M. (2001), "Strategy and the Internet", *Harvard Business Review,* March, pp. 63-78.
- Ptak, C. (2000) *ERP: Tools, Techniques, and Applications for Integrating the Supply Chain.* St. Lucie Press, Boca Raton, FL.
- Quattrone, P. and T. Hopper (2001), "What Does Organizational Change Mean, Speculations on a Taken for Granted Category", *Management Accounting Research,* pp.403-435.
- Quiescenti, M., Bruccoleri, M., La Commare, U., Noto La Diega, S. and Perrone, G. (2006), "Business Process-oriented Design of Enterprise Resource Planning (ERP) Systems for Small and Medium Enterprises", *International Journal of Production Research,* Vol. 44 No. 19, pp. 3797-811.
- R. Nandagopal,K. Arul Rajan, N. Vivek(2007),"*Research Methods in Business",* First Edition, Excel Books, New Delhi, India
- Ragowsky, A.; Stern, M. and Adams, D.A. (2000), "Relating Benefits from Using IS to an Organization's Operating Characteristics: Interpreting Results from Two Countries", *Journal of Management Information Systems,* Vol. 16 No. 4, pp. 175-94.
- Rajagopal P., (2002), "An Innovation-Diffusion View of Implementation of

Enterprise Resource Planning (ERP) Systems and Development of a Research Model", *Information and Management*, Vol. 40, pp. 87-114.

- Ranganathan C and I Samarah (2001), "Enterprise Resource Planning Systems and Firm Value: An Event Study Analysis", Twenty-Second International Conference on Information Systems.
- Ranganathan C. and Kannabiran J., (2004), "Effective Management of Information Systems Function: An Exploratory Study of Indian Organizations", *International Journal of Information Management*, Vol. 25, pp.247–266.
- Rao, S.S. (2000), "Enterprise Resource Planning: Business Needs and Technologies", *Industrial Management and Data Systems*, Vol. 100, No. 2, pp. 81-88.
- Raymond, L. and Uwizeyemungu, S. (2007), " A Profile of ERP Adoption in manufacturing SMEs", *Journal of Enterprise Information Management*, Vol. 20 No. 4, pp. 487-502.
- Raymond, L.; Bergeron, F. and Rivard, S. (1998), "Determinants of Business Process Reengineering Success in Small and Large Enterprises: An Empirical Study in the Canadian Context", *Journal of Small Business Management*, Vol. 36, No. 1, pp. 72-85.
- Robey, D.; Ross, J.W. and Boudreau, M.-C. (2002), "Learning to Implement Enterprise Systems: An Exploratory Study of the Dialectics of Change", *Journal of Management Information Systems*, Vol. 19, No. 1, 17-46.
- Robinson, P. (2000), *"ERP (Enterprise Resource Planning) Survival Guide"*.
- Rosemann, M. and Wiese, J. (1999), 'Measuring the Performance of ERP Software – A Balanced Scoreboard Approach', in *Proceedings of the 10th Australasian Conference on Information Systems*, Wellington, New Zealand, pp. 773 - 784.
- Ross, J. (1998) The ERP Revolution: Surviving versus thriving. *MIT White Paper*, Cambridge, MA.
- Ross, J. W. and Vitale, M., (2000). "The ERP Revolution: Surviving versus thriving", *Information Systems Frontiers*, Vol. 2, No. 2, pp. 233-41.
- Ross, J., Vitale, M. and Willcocks, L. (2003), The continuing ERP Revolution: Sustainable Lessons, New Modes of Delivery, in Second-wave Enterprise Resource Planning Systems. Graeme Shanks, Peter Seddon, and Leslie Willcocks (Eds.) Cambridge University Press, Cambridge.
- Sankar, C. S. and Rau, K. (2006) Implementation Strategies for SAP R/3 in a Multinational Organization: Lessons from a Real-World Case Study, Cybertech Publishing, Hershey.
- SAP (1999), "SAP AG: R/3® System: The Three-tier Client/Server Architecture at the Heart of the R/3 System." SAP AG, Walldorf, Germany.
- Sapsford, R. and Jupp, V. (1996), Data Collection and Analysis, Sage, London.

- Sarkis, J. and Sundarraj, R.P. (2000), "Factors for Strategic Evaluation of Enterprise Information Technologies", *International Journal of Physical Distribution and Logistics Management,* Vol. 30 No.4, pp. 196-220.
- Scalet, S.D. (2001), "The Cost of Secrecy"
- Schmid, B.F. (1993), "Electronic markets", *Wirtschaftsinformatik,* Vol. 35 No. 5, pp. 465-80.
- Schniederjans, M.J. and Kim, G.C. (2003), "Implementing Enterprise Resource Planning Systems with Total Quality Control and Business Process Reengineering: Survey Results", *International Journal of Operations and Production Management,* Vol. 23 No. 4, pp. 418-29.
- Scott, J. E. and Vessey, I. (2000), 'Implementing Enterprise Resource Planning Systems: The Role of Learning from Failure', Information Systems Frontiers; *Special Issue of On The Future of Enterprise Resource Planning Systems,* Vol. 2, pp.213-232.
- Serafeimidis, V. and Smithson, S. (1999), "Rethinking the Approaches to Information Systems Investment Evaluation", *Logistics Information Management,* Vol. 12, No. 2, pp. 94-107.
- Shang, S. and Seddon, P.B. (2000), "A Comprehensive Framework for Classifying the Benefits of ERP Systems", *Proceedings of the Sixth Americas Conference on Information Systems,* Long Beach, pp. 1005-14.
- Shanks, G.; Parr, A.; Hu, B.; Corbitt, B.; Thanasankit, T. and Seddon, P. (2000), "Differences in Critical Success Factors in ERP Systems Implementation in Australia and China: A Cultural Analysis", *Proceedings of the Eighth European Conference on Information Systems,* Vienna, pp. 537-44.
- Shehab E. M., Sharp M. W., Supramaniam L., Spedding T. A., (2004) "ERP: An Integrative Review",
- Sheu, C.; Chae, B. and Yang, C.-L. (2004), "National Differences and ERP Implementation: Issues and Challenges", *Omega,* Vol. 32 No. 5, pp. 361-71.
- Shin, I. (2006), "Adoption of Enterprise Application Software and Firm Performance", *Small Business Economics,* Vol. 26 No. 3, pp. 241-56.
- Silverman M (1987), The Art of Managing Technical Projects, Prentice-Hall, Englewood Cliffs, N J, pp 346.
- Siriginidi S. R., (2000), "Enterprise Resource Planning in re-engineering business" Business Process Management Journal, Vol. 6, pp. 376-91.
- Siriginidi S. R., (2000),"Enterprise Resource Planning in Re-engineering Business", *Business Process Management Journal,* Vol. 6 (5), pp. 376-91.
- Soh, C.; Kien, S.S. and Tay-Yap, J. (2000), "Cultural Fits and Misfits: Is ERP a Universal Solution?", *Communications of the ACM,* Vol. 43 No. 4, pp. 47-51.
- Soja, P. (2006), "Success Factors in ERP Systems Implementations: Lessons from Practice", *Journal of Enterprise Information Management,* Vol. 19 No. 4, pp. 418-33.

- Somers, T.M. and Nelson, K. (2001), "The Impact of Critical Success Factors Across the Stages of Enterprise Resource Planning Implementations", *Proceedings of the 34th Hawaii International Conference on Systems Sciences,* Maui, p.10
- Stanworth, J. and Curran, J. (1981), "Size of Workplace and Attitudes to Industrial Relations", *British Journal of Industrial Relations,* Vol. 1 No. 1, pp. 14-25.
- Stefanou, C.J. (2001), "A Framework for the Ex-ante Evaluation of ERP Software", *European Journal of Information Systems,* Vol. 10 No. 4, pp. 204-15.
- Stein, T. (1998), "Dell Takes 'Best-of-Breed' Approach In ERP Strategy."
- Stensrud E., (2001), "Alternative Approaches to Effort Prediction of ERP Packages", *Information and Software Technology,* Vol. 43, pp 413-423.
- Stratman, J.K. and Roth, A.V. (2002), "Enterprise Resource Planning (ERP) Competence Constructs: Two-stage Multi-item Scale Development and validation", *Decision Sciences,* Vol. 33 No. 4, pp. 601-28.
- Strauss, A. and Corbin, J. (1990), *Basics of Qualitative Research: Grounded Theory Procedures and Techniques,* Sage, Newbury Park, CA.
- Stuart, I.; McCutcheon, D.; Handfield, R.; McLachlin, R. and Samson, D. (2002), "Effective Case Research in Operations Management: a Process Perspective", *Journal of Operations Management,* Vol. 20 No. 5, pp. 419-33.
- Sumner, M. (2000), 'Risk Factors in Enterprise Wide Information Management System Projects', Research Work Presented to Special Interest Group on Computer Personnel Research Annual Conference, *Proceedings of the ACM SIGCPR Conference on Computer Personnel Research,* Chicago, Illinois, United States.
- Sun, A.Y.T.; Yazdani, A. and Overend, J.D. (2005), "Achievement Assessment for Enterprise Resource Planning (ERP) System Implementations based on Critical Success Factors (CSFs)", *International Journal of Production Economics,* Vol. 98 No. 2, pp. 189-203.
- Teo, H. H., Wei, K. K., and Benbasat, I. (2003), "Predicting Intention to Adopt Interorganizational Linkages: An Institutional Perspective" *MIS Quarterly,* Society for Management Information Systems, pp.19-49.
- Themistocleous, M., Irani, Z., O'Keefe, R., and Paul, R. (2001) ERP Problems and Application Integration Issues: An Empirical Survey. In *Proceedings of the 34th Hawaii International Conference on System Sciences,* pp 9045-9054.
- Trauth, E. M. (2000), 'The Choice of Qualitative Methods in IS Research', in *Qualitative Research in IS: Issues and Trends,* ed. Trauth, E. M., Idea Group, Hersey, USA, pp. 308.
- Uervirojnangkoorn, M. (2001), 'The Impact of Enterprise Resource Planning (ERP) Systems on Management—A Case Study in University', School of Computing and Information Technology, Masters Book, Brisbane, Griffith University, p. 91.

- Umble, E. J. and Umble, M(2002) "Avoiding ERP Implementation Failure", Industrial Management Society, pp.25-33.
- Umble, E.J.; Haft, R.R. and Umble, M.M. (2003), "Enterprise Resource Planning: Implementation Procedures and Critical Success Factors", *European Journal of Operational Research*, Vol. 146 No. 2, pp. 241-57.
- US Census Bureau (2004), "Statistics about Business Size (including small business) from the U.S. Census Bureau"
- Van Everdingen, Y.; Van Hillegersberg, J. and Waarts, E. (2000), "ERP Adoption by European Midsize Companies", *Communications of the ACM*, Vol. 43 No. 4, pp. 27-31.
- Van Hoek, S. (2001), "e-Supply Chains – Virtually Non-existing", *Supply Chain Management: An International Journal*, Vol. 6 No. 1, pp. 21-28.
- Venkatesh, V, and Davis, F. D. (2000), "A Theoretical Extension of the Technology Acceptance Model: Four Longitudinal Field Studies" *Management Science*, pp.186-204.
- Venkatraman, N. and Henderson, J.C. (1998), "Real Strategies for Virtual Organizing", *Sloan Management Review*, fall, pp. 33-47.
- Visala, S. (1992), 'Ethical Dilemmas in Information Systems Research and Development', in *Proceedings of the ACM, SIGGPR Conference on Computer Personnel Research*, Cincinnati, Ohio, USA, pp. 21-220.
- Voss, C., Blackmon, K., Hanson, P. and Oak, B. (1995), "The Competitiveness of European Manufacturing – A Four-country Study", *Business Strategy Review*, Vol. 6 No. 1, pp. 1-25.
- Walden, E. A. and Browne, G. J. 2002, Information Cascades in the Adoption of New Technology, *Twenty-third International Conference on Information Systems.*
- Weber, R.P. (1990), *Basic Content Analysis*, Sage, Newbury Park, CA.
- Weider, B.; Booth, P.; Matolcsy, Z.P. and Ossimitz, M.-L. (2006), "The Impact of ERP Systems on Firm and Business Performance", *Journal of Enterprise Information Management*, Vol. 19 No. 1, pp. 13-29.
- Wieder, B. (1999), 'ERP-Software Integration at Australian Universities – Recent Developments in Integrated Business Education', *in Proceedings of the CTI Accounting Finance and Management Conference*, Brighton, p. 17.
- Wilk, R J (1993), "The Use of Monetary Incentives to Increase Survey Response" pp.33-34.
- Willis, T.H.; Willis-Brown, A.H. and McMillan, A. (2001), "Cost Containment Strategies for ERP System Implementations", *Production and Inventory Management Journal*, Vol. 42 No. 2, pp. 36-42.
- Windsor, B. (2001), "Best-of-breed *vs* ERP. A Debate Running Out of Steam?"
- Wong, A., Patrick.Y.K.C, Scarbrough and Davison (2005),"Critical Failure Factors in ERP Implementation"
- Yen D. C., Chou D. C., Chang J., (2002),"A Synergic Analysis for Web-based

Enterprise Resource Planning Systems", *Computer Standards and Interfuces*, Vol. 24 ,pp 337-46.

- Yin, R.K. (1994), Case Study Research: Design and Methods, *1st Ed. Thousand Oaks*, CA: Sage Publications.
- Yin, R.K. (2003), Case Study Research: Design and Methods, *3rd Ed. Thousand Oaks*, CA: Sage Publications.
- Zefer, S, (2001) "Esupply Chain Management Creating Sustainable Competitive Advantage".
- Zeng, M., Q. Yin, *et al.* (2002). "Study on Enterprise Resource Planning in the Process Industry." *Control and Instruments in Chemical Industry,* Vol.29, No.1, pp. 8-12.
- Zeng, Y., R. H. L. Chiang, *et al.* (2003). "Enterprise Integration with Advanced Information Technologies: ERP and Data Warehousing." *Information Management and Computer Security,* Vol.11, No.3.
- Zhang, L.; Lee, M.K.O.; Zhang, Z. and Banerjee, P. (2003), "Critical Success Factors of Enterprise Resource Planning Systems Implementation Success in China", *Proceedings of 36th Hawaii International Conference on System Sciences,* Big Island.
- Zhao, J. L. and E. A. Stohr (2000). "Building Workflow Engines for Commerce Logic Automation."
- Zheng, S. Yen, *et al.* (2000). "The New Spectrum of the Cross Enterprise Solution: The Integration of Supply Change Management and Enterprise Resource Planning Systems" *Computer Information Systems,* Vol. 41,No.1,pp. 84.
- Zhu, K., K. L. Kraemer, *et al.* (2002). A Cross Country Study of Electronic Business Adoption Using the Techno Organization-Environment Framework. *Twenty-Third International Conferences on Information Systems.*
- Zimmermann, H.-D. (2000). "Understanding the Digital Economy: Challenges for New Business Models."
- Zoryk-Schalla, A. J., J. C. Fransoo, *et al.* (2003). "Modelling the Planning Process in Advanced Planning Systems." *Information and Management journal*

Web Link

www.acm.org
www.amrresearchcorp.com
www.articlesbase.com
www.bitpipe.com
www.brighthub.com
www.business.technology.com
www.businessdictionary.com
www.census.gov
www.cfo.com

www.chiefexcutive.net
www.cio.com
www.computer.org
www.computerworld.com
www.coolquotes.com
www.dcmsme.gov.in
www.dmreview.com
www.domainb.com
www.en.wikipedia.org
www.epicor.com
www.epp.eurostat.ec.europa.eu
www.erp.ittoolbox.com
www.erp-jobs.com
www.erp-lol.com
www.erppandit.com
www.erpsoftware-news.com
www.erpwire.com
www.flipkart.com
www.gartner.com
www.geac.com
www.gleez.com
www.google.com
www.gv.br
www.hbswk.hbs.edu
www.ieee.org
www.infor.com
www.intelligententerprise.com
www.intuitivemfg.com
www.invensys.com
www.iw.com
www.juran.com
www.lawson.com
www.leon-leon.com
www.mbtmag.com
www.microsoft.com
www.networkmagazineindia.com

www.oracle.com
www.pcmag.com
www.portal.acm.org
www.qad.com
www.sage.com
www.sagesoftware.co.in
www.sap.com/
www.scmagazine.com
www.sda-asia.com
www.searchwinit.techtarget.com
www.seradex.com
www.softwareceo.com
www.softwaremag.com
www.sooperarticles.com
www.spss.com
www.ssaglobal.com
www.strategis.ic.gc.ca
www.techtarget.com
www.thinkexist.com
www.vnunet.com
www.wikipedia.org
www.yahoo.com
www.yourdictionary.com

Index

S